$5–

TAMING
GLOBAL
FINANCE

Other books by Robert A. Blecker

U.S. Trade Policy and Global Growth (editor)

*Fundamentals of U.S. Foreign Trade Policy
(with S.D. Cohen and J.R. Paul)*

Beyond the Twin Deficits

Other books from the Economic Policy Institute

The State of Working America 1998-99

Getting Prices Right

Risky Business: Private Management of Public Schools

Reclaiming Prosperity

School Choice: Examining the Evidence

The New American Workplace

Beware the U.S. Model

Unions and Economic Competitiveness

TAMING GLOBAL FINANCE

◆

A Better Architecture for Growth and Equity

Robert A. Blecker

ECONOMIC POLICY INSTITUTE

To my children,

Matthew and Emily

Table of contents

Acknowledgments

First, I wish to acknowledge the Economic Policy Institute and especially its president, Jeff Faux, for having the vision to commission a survey of the literature on reform of the global financial system at a time (summer of 1997) when the Asian crisis had barely begun and almost no one anticipated how serious it would become or how far it would spread. I am also humbled by the confidence that EPI expressed in me by asking me to undertake this task. As my work progressed, I faced the challenge of trying to synthesize an enormous range of existing studies while new information and new proposals were forthcoming almost daily. Thus, what began as a short report mushroomed into a book that took somewhat longer than intended to complete. I must therefore also thank EPI for its patience and support in the process of completing this endeavor.

Along the way, I benefited enormously from the assistance and comments of many friends and colleagues. Eileen Appelbaum and Rob Scott of EPI provided tremendous moral and managerial support, as well as invaluable editorial advice. Jane D'Arista, Jeff Faux, Catherine Mann, and Tom Palley provided exceptionally detailed and useful suggestions on earlier drafts of the manuscript. I also received helpful comments and constructive criticisms from Dean Baker, John Grieve Smith, Peter Morici, Bill Schweke, Lance Taylor, Peter Uimonen, and John Williamson. I learned much about the issues addressed in this book from my participation in a parallel project on international capital markets at the Center for Economic Policy Analysis, New School for Social Research, spearheaded by John Eatwell and Lance Taylor, as well as in a "brainstorming" meeting held at the Political Economy Research Institute, University of Massachusetts at Amherst, led by Jerry Epstein and Bob Pollin (with co-sponsorship from EPI). I also wish to acknowledge helpful discussions with various colleagues in the American University Department of Economics, especially Colin Bradford, Robin Hahnel, Alan Isaac, and Howard Wachtel.

I benefited from research assistance by Yonatan Alemu, Kalamogo Coulibaly, Ryan Helwig, and Matthew Shearer, as well as library assistance from Terrel Hale and Violetta Loyesvsky. Monica Hernandez helped in preparing the table of contents and in the photocopying and mailing of drafts for review. I am especially thankful for EPI's senior editor, Patrick Watson, who not only did an outstanding job in copyediting the manuscript, but also guided me through the entire editorial process with unfailing good humor and patience. Kim Weinstein produced and designed the book with her usual efficiency, style, and grace. Nan Gibson, Brian Lustig, David Misra, and Linda Ellis all helped with publicity and sales.

Finally, I am grateful to the Ford Foundation for its support of EPI's work on global finance, including this publication.

—ROBERT A. BLECKER

Preface

In April 1997, a World Bank report on developing nations assured its readers that "as markets become more discerning, contagion effects of the kind seen after the Mexican crisis are not likely to be long-lasting." Three months later the sudden devaluation of the Thai baht sparked a currency crisis that rippled throughout the world, shattering financial markets and leaving massive unemployment and political unrest in its wake. Today, there is little confidence that the financial virus has been contained, or, if it has, that the world will soon recover from its devastating effects.

The World Bank was hardly alone in its misplaced faith in the post-Cold War deregulated economic world order. The global financial crisis sent a seismic intellectual shock through the ranks of economic policy makers, economists who advise them, and journalists who interpret their policies for the public. The shock has touched off a new and somewhat chaotic debate over the governance of the global economy. First World political leaders who had helped destroy constraints on global hot money are now calling for a new regulatory architecture. Economists who sang the praises of Asia's market economies now denounce them for "crony capitalism." Financial gurus who had promoted opportunities to get rich quick in exotic emerging markets now lecture their customers on the risks of investing in the unknown.

Long before the collapse of the East Asian financial markets, the Economic Policy Institute was a forum for concern about the stability of unregulated global capital flows and their effects on the real economy of production and employment. About the same time that the World Bank issued its optimistic report, EPI, with the help of the Ford Foundation, launched a program of research and public education into the nature of global financial markets.

As part of this program, we asked Professor Robert A. Blecker of American University, a well-known international economist, to analyze three related issues:

- To what degree does the expert literature support the model of unregulated finance that the major international institutions (e.g., the U.S. Treasury, the International Monetary Fund, the World Bank) have been pursuing? The answer to this question helps us determine whether recurring financial crises are the products of idiosyncratic behavior or more systemic flaws.

- How much do global financial markets constrain nations attempting to pursue policies of full employment and social equity? The answer to this question indicates the extent to which the governance of the global economy should be responsible for job growth and income distribution as well as the health of financial markets.

- What are the merits of the major proposals that have been put forward to reform global financial markets?

Professor Blecker's analysis, contained in these pages, is a major contribution to our understanding of the global financial crisis and what to do about it. His evaluation of the current array of proposals and his examination of the economics of economic sovereignty are an invaluable guide to the reader trying to understand the fundamental issues at stake. And his report that even mainstream economics itself has for some time challenged the conventional wisdom that "discerning" investors will ensure the stability of financial laissez-faire reminds us how important it is to question policy makers when they confidently assert that their actions are based on "sound economics."

Jeff Faux
President, EPI

Executive summary

Encouraged by the United States and the International Monetary Fund (IMF), many developing countries launched a great experiment in opening their capital markets to free flows of short-term foreign investment in the early 1990s. For a few years, bank lending and portfolio investment in these "emerging markets" skyrocketed, but before long, beginning with the Mexican peso crisis of December 1994, the emerging market boom collapsed. By 1997, the financial panic broke out in Thailand, and it soon spread like a contagion to other countries in Asia, followed by Russia and Brazil. In each case, the financial crisis unleashed a general economic collapse, causing massive unemployment and cutting living standards. Although the U.S. economy has continued to grow, it has already felt the effects of the Asian crisis through a widening trade deficit and lost manufacturing jobs.

The IMF, closely following the dictates of the U.S. Treasury Department, tried to alleviate the financial distress by applying the traditional cures of currency devaluation, budget cutting, and high interest rates—while insisting that the countries maintain open capital markets. Essentially, the IMF and U.S. government continue to promote what have become known as "Washington Consensus" policies. Yet in the financial crises of the 1990s, this policy package has often only deepened the financial panic and failed to prevent the contagion from spreading to other countries. IMF bailouts have succeeded in shielding large multinational banks from the full consequences of their own risky lending practices, but they have failed to restore economic growth and to protect average citizens in the debtor countries.

As a result of these developments, the Washington Consensus has begun to break down. More and more economists are questioning the policies of fiscal austerity, monetary contraction, and financial liberalization that formerly commanded nearly universal support among leaders in the profession. At the same time, a wide-ranging debate has opened up about how to design a "new architecture" for the global financial system. This debate includes numerous proposals for regulating domestic financial markets, containing volatile capital flows, constructing new international institutions, stabilizing international currency values, and coordinating national macroeconomic policies.

This book surveys the emerging debate about the global financial system and evaluates the policy options for reforming it. The analysis consists of three parts: an assessment of the costs and benefits of capital market liberalization; a critical review of the theoretical models underlying the Washington Consensus on macroeconomic policies; and an examination of alternative policy proposals for constructing a new financial architecture. The analysis in this book is intended to inform a broad audience of policy makers, political activists, media professionals, college students, and concerned citizens about the state of the expert debate on global financial policy—and to enable them to participate more knowledgeably in that debate.

Proponents of liberalizing capital markets promised that it would bring three benefits: a more efficient allocation of global savings, thus stimulating growth; enhanced financial opportunities for international investors, especially the ability to diversify risks across countries; and greater discipline on national governments, forcing them to adopt sound economic policies. Critics, on the other hand, have charged that financial liberalization causes four types of costs: international investment based on inadequate information tends to be speculative and fails to enhance efficiency; capital mobility constrains governments from adopting autonomous monetary policies; the threat of capital flight leads to contractionary or deflationary macroeconomic policies; and the volatility of capital flows increases real economic instability.

On the whole, the costs of capital market liberalization have generally outweighed the benefits. Although more research is clearly needed, there are no empirical studies to date that demonstrate significant gains in either efficiency or growth from liberalized financial flows, while at least one study shows that capital market liberalization fosters higher real interest rates that can discourage productive investment. There is, moreover, overwhelming evidence that liberalized capital flows tend to be extremely volatile and have contributed to the spread of financial crises around the world. Although these crises have been most severe in countries with weak regulation and supervision of their domestic financial markets, a recent opening to external capital flows is a common feature in all the countries that have experienced financial crises in the 1990s.

Instead of delivering more sustainable, long-term economic growth, capital market liberalization has worsened economic instability in countries where booms were fueled by speculative capital inflows and then cut short by panic-stricken outflows. Rather than investing where the long-term prospects are greatest, investors seem to move their funds into and out of countries in herd-like fashion, causing self-fulfilling bubbles and panics based on limited information and fickle expectations. The end result is a global economy that is less stable without being more efficient.

The evidence reviewed here also shows that liberalized financial markets constrain national policy makers, but the constraints vary in their nature and severity in different countries at different times. The ways in which capital flows constrain macroeconomic policies depend on a country's size and openness to trade, its exchange rate system (fixed or flexible), the magnitude and composition of its international debts, and its susceptibility to inflation. Generally, larger and more closed economies with flexible exchange rates, small foreign currency debts, and low inflation are less constrained than smaller and more open countries with fixed exchange rates, large foreign currency liabilities (especially with short maturities), and high inflation.

While international investors do indeed reward countries that prioritize low inflation in their macroeconomic policies, they do not always support policies that result in slow growth and high unemployment. On some occasions, international investment flows have actually pressured policy makers to lower their interest rates, such as in the United Kingdom in 1992 and the United States in 1998. Moreover, even when countries use high interest rates and fixed exchange rates to attract foreign investors, the resulting large capital inflows often lead to speculative bubbles in financial markets and exaggerated boom-bust cycles in productive activity. Far from disciplining policy makers, then, speculative capital flows can temporarily suspend ordinary limits on growth, only to cause a subsequent crash when investors suddenly perceive higher risks and head for the exits.

The fact that Washington Consensus policies have neither prevented nor cured financial crises suggests the need to reconsider the intellectual foundations of this approach. This book reviews the major strands in international financial modeling and shows how the theories have evolved away from the early models that implied easy cures for balance-of-payments crises, either through automatic market adjustments or simple policy correctives such as currency devaluation, fiscal austerity, and monetary contraction. These policies are much less effective and more costly in practice than they appeared to be in theory, and yet they still underlie the policy prescriptions of the IMF and the U.S. government. In many recent cases, these policies have failed to restore investors' confidence and have instead worsened financial panics.

Much contemporary policy analysis rests on models which assume that flexible exchange rates respond in predictable ways to changes in macroeconomic "fundamentals," such as interest rates and fiscal policies. Yet empirical studies of the post-1973 period of floating exchange rates show that these models have a poor ability to predict short- and medium-run fluctuations. As a result, the traditional policy prescriptions that rely on such predictions are no longer credible. New theoretical models reveal that movements in exchange rates can become delinked from the underlying fundamentals, and instead follow various types of "self-fulfilling expectations," such as speculative bubbles and panics. Fixed exchange rates can suffer speculative attacks, not only when the pegged rate is unsustainable but even if the peg might be sustainable in the absence of such an attack. When a crisis breaks out, self-fulfilling panics can force adjustments that are far in excess of what would be required to restore equilibrium (e.g., eliminate a balance-of-payments deficit) in the absence of the panic. These newer models are beginning to identify the causes and consequences of financial market instability, but as yet have had little influence on policy debates.

U.S. and IMF officials have recently shifted to promoting more "orderly" liberalization efforts in developing countries—thus tacitly admitting that capital market liberalization has been pushed too far in the past. The official U.S. and IMF proposals for a new financial architecture emphasize policies designed to make financial markets work more efficiently. These proposals stress the need for greater transparency on the part of banks, firms, and governments, as well as for improved regulation and supervision of banks and other financial institutions. Such proposals place most of the burden of reform on the debtor countries, requiring them to make fundamental changes in their domestic institutions in order to be better prepared to handle massive inflows of foreign funds.

Essentially, the official new architecture proposals seek to make the world a safer place for international investors. But no amount of transparency and supervision can eliminate the inherent information problems in international capital markets or prevent global financial flows from destabilizing domestic economies. In order to make international capital flows serve the broader public interest in a more stable, equitable, and prosperous global economy, further policy reforms are needed in four interrelated areas:

1.   *Regulating capital movements.* A variety of measures such as capital controls, exchange controls, and transactions taxes (including a "Tobin tax" on foreign exchange transactions) can help to discourage short-term speculative capital flows, restore greater national policy autonomy, and encourage more stable, long-term investment. Different types and degrees of controls may be needed in different countries, depending on their specific situations and structures. Chilean-style reserve requirements on capital inflows may be adequate in some countries; Malaysian-style controls on foreign exchange may be needed elsewhere. The U.S. and other industrial countries should increase prudential regulations on capital outflows and reduce the incentives to be used as "safe havens" for capital fleeing other countries.

2.   *Reforming international institutions.* The international financial system has become integrated to a point where the need for global regulation cannot be avoided. Simply abolishing the IMF and allowing markets to discipline errant countries would be a mistake because it would invite greater instability and harsher adjustments. While in the future it may be desirable to create new global institutions, such as a world central bank or international supervisory agency, most such proposals are politically unrealistic at present—although regional institutions such as an Asian Monetary Fund are more feasible in the short term. Today, the most immediate priority is to fundamentally reorient the governance and policies of the IMF by replacing its top leadership; instituting more democratic control and accountability; broadening its mission to emphasize

global prosperity and distributional equity; tailoring its crisis intervention policies to better meet the needs of specific debtor countries; and shifting more of the adjustment burden in crisis situations onto creditors.

3. *Managing exchange rates.* Neither extreme of perfectly flexible or rigidly fixed exchange rates is generally desirable. The best way to reduce exchange rate volatility is to establish a compromise system of "target zones" among the major currencies (especially the dollar, euro, and yen), with wide enough "crawling bands" around the targets to allow moderate exchange rate fluctuations—and with regular, small adjustments in the targets and bands to keep them credible. To discourage speculative attacks, massive and automatic intervention should be conducted by central banks or a new international stabilization fund whenever rates threaten to go outside the bands. Other countries should be free to experiment with alternative exchange rate arrangements or to join the target zone system—and would benefit from greater stability among the major currencies anyway.

4. *Coordinating macroeconomic policy.* Supporting the exchange rate targets and promoting more rapid global growth with more balanced trade and full employment will require economic coordination among the G-7 countries. International coordination of monetary policy would permit reductions in interest rates without creating incentives for speculative capital flight. Countries that agree to coordinate their interest rates need to retain other policy levers for domestic adjustment, however, especially by using fiscal policy more flexibly for countercyclical purposes and by using prudential restrictions (e.g., reserve requirements) more actively for monetary control.

Even if full-fledged macroeconomic policy coordination at the global level is difficult to achieve, major countries like the United States and the members of the European Union are far from paralyzed. Such large countries or blocs have plenty of room for maneuver to embark on new policies that could help to restore global prosperity and avert the possibility of a global crash. With or without a formal coordination agreement, it is vital for the Europeans and the Japanese to pursue domestic expansionary policies and to reduce their trade surpluses in order to boost global demand. It is also vital that the U.S. lower its interest rates further in order to stop attracting so much capital out of other countries and allow the dollar to move to a lower level that is more consistent with balanced international trade.

Introduction

Since the late 1970s, virtually all industrialized countries and a large number of developing countries and ex-socialist economies have opened up their capital markets to largely unregulated international transactions. Around the globe, nations have lifted restrictions on foreign investment, removed controls on currency exchanges, and eliminated restrictions on foreign ownership of assets. While some restrictions remain and a few major countries have not gotten on the bandwagon (China and India, for example), capital markets in most countries have become wide open, and portfolio funds are far more mobile internationally than ever before.[1] These policies of reducing or eliminating barriers to capital movements have been promoted by powerful actors in the international arena, especially the International Monetary Fund (IMF) and the U.S. government, which have promised that liberalizing capital markets would boost economic growth and development by allocating global capital to its most efficient uses.

Contrary to these promises, the liberalization of international capital markets has instead led to a series of severe financial crises in the 1990s. Starting in Mexico in 1994, then spreading to Thailand and other East Asian countries in 1997, and now enveloping Russia, Brazil, and other countries, volatile flows of speculative "hot money" have fueled currency crises, stock market collapses, and financial panics. By the latter half of 1998, the financial contagion had spread to Japan, whose currency was falling while its banking system struggled with a mountain of bad loans, and to the United States, where the near-failure of a secretive and unregulated "hedge fund" (Long-Term Capital Management) induced a multi-billion dollar private bailout orchestrated by the Federal Reserve. In this environment, numerous economic analysts and political leaders began to warn of parallels to the stock market crash of 1929 and the Great Depression that followed. Calling the current situation "the biggest financial challenge facing the world in a half-century," U.S. President Bill Clinton issued a call on September 14, 1998, for designing major reforms of the "architecture" of the international financial system (Clinton 1998).

Less dramatic than these major crises, but of equal importance, is the fact that international capital flows have come to dominate ordinary trade in goods and services in terms of their impact on the balance of payments and exchange

1

rates.[2] For example, by April 1998, global foreign exchange transactions had reached an estimated $1.5 trillion *per day* (Bank for International Settlements 1998b), enough to finance all of the merchandise imports in the world for *three entire months*.[3] As a result of this enormous amount of currency trading, global financial pressures frequently cause perverse changes in exchange rates that destabilize the global trading system and undermine domestic economic production. For example, in both the early 1980s and again in the late 1990s, net capital inflows into the United States have been large enough to push up the value of the dollar in spite of rising trade deficits (which, according to traditional theories, should cause the value of a currency to fall). The result has been ever-widening trade deficits that have depressed employment and wages in U.S. manufacturing industries and transformed the United States into the world's largest debtor nation.[4]

Critics of financial liberalization have long argued that the increasing mobility of financial capital since the 1970s is an important cause of problems such as slower growth, rising inequality, high unemployment, and heightened economic insecurity.[5] Two German authors summarize the broad case against free capital mobility as follows:

> The more dependent countries become on the goodwill of investors, the more ruthless must governments be in favouring the already privileged minority who have sizeable financial assets. Their interests are always the same: low inflation, stable external value of the currency, and minimum taxation of their investment income....The financial short-circuit between different countries forces them into a competition to lower taxes, to reduce public expenditure, and to renounce the aim of social equality—a competition which brings nothing other than a global redistribution from those at the bottom to those at the top. Rewards go to whoever creates the best conditions for big capital, while sanctions loom for any government that obstructs this law of the jungle. (Martin and Schumann 1997, 61)

Another critic writes,

> it appears that the integration of global trade and finance has tightened the constraints on expansionary policy throughout the world. Balance-of-payments problems are likely to emerge more quickly, and the channels have enlarged through which import and speculative leakages can flow. Moreover, even the sovereignty of advanced countries is diminished due to the veto power of global capital markets over any policy that threatens inflation and thereby the value of nominally fixed assets. (Pollin 1998, 435)

While not necessarily endorsing this whole critique, a growing number of economists who are otherwise known as strong supporters of free trade in goods and services have concluded that the costs of free mobility of capital now outweigh the benefits, at least in the developing world, where domestic financial regulations tend to be inadequate. For example, Jagdish Bhagwati (1998, 7) argues that global financial policies are being dictated by a "Wall Street–Treasury complex," which promulgates an ideology of capital market liberalization that represents the interests of wealthy American investors and the financial services industry. Jeffrey Sachs (1998a, 24) argues that the IMF has "worked mightily, and wrongheadedly, to make the world safe for...short-term money managers." Paul Krugman (1998a) asserts that the "global capital market" is the "proximate cause" of the Asian crisis and that the only solution for insulating these countries from such shocks is the temporary restoration of capital controls (see also Krugman 1998b). Referring to U.S. and IMF efforts to reassure international lenders as a "confidence game," Krugman writes:

> During the past four years, seven countries—Mexico, Argentina, Thailand, South Korea, Indonesia, Malaysia, and Hong Kong—have experienced severe economic recessions, worse than anything the United States has seen since the '30s, essentially because playing the confidence game forced them into macroeconomic policies that exacerbated slumps instead of relieving them....This is a truly dismal, even tragic record. Isn't there a better way?
>
> Well, as long as countries are wide open to massive movements of hot money—to huge inflows when the markets like them, then to equally large outflows when confidence is shaken for some reason—the answer is no. As long as capital flows freely, nations will be vulnerable to self-fulfilling speculative attacks, and policymakers will be forced to play the confidence game....
>
> Maybe such a system can survive, but I doubt it. If allowing free capital movement means that economic policy must play by the rules of the confidence game, sooner or later the world is going to decide that it is a game not worth playing. (Krugman 1998a)

So far, most policy makers in the U.S. government and the IMF have resisted these calls for a fundamental rethinking of the merits of global financial liberalization. Instead, official proposals for a "new architecture" for the international financial system have been exceptionally timid, focusing mainly on calls for greater "transparency"—more complete and more widely available data on countries' financial positions—and improved "surveillance"—monitoring of the risks in the liability structures of individual nations and financial institutions. But on the fundamental point of the wisdom of the drive to liberalize capital markets, the world's financial policy makers are unwavering. IMF Managing Director Michel Camdessus (1998) asserts that, while greater transparency and better surveillance are needed, "Orderly capital account liberalization should also remain on the reform agenda." U.S. Treasury Secretary Robert Rubin (1998) puts most of the blame for the Asian crisis on "badly flawed financial sectors in a few developing countries" along with "unsound policies" by their governments; while he admits that there was also "inadequate risk assessment by international creditors and investors," he pointedly refuses to support most types of limits on international capital movements as a means of avoiding the overlending syndrome. In other words, the U.S. government and the IMF continue to blame the victims while insisting that they accept more of the same types of policies that have led to their current predicament.

John Maynard Keynes once wrote that

> Practical men, who believe themselves to be quite exempt from any intellectual influences, are usually the slaves of some defunct economist. Madmen in authority, who hear voices in the air, are distilling their frenzy from some academic scribbler of a few years back. (Keynes 1936, 383)

This is nowhere more true than in the case of the policy makers who continue to promote capital market liberalization even as they struggle to prevent the mess that it has created from deflating the entire global economy. In fact, the academic theories that supported unfettered capital flows are now defunct, since those theories have been supplanted by newer ones that recognize the potentially destabilizing properties of unregulated capital markets.

The critique of capital market liberalization does not imply that all capital flows should be blocked; on the contrary, there is a desperate need for channeling more stable and productive long-term investments into the less-developed regions of the world economy. The issue, rather, is whether unregulated flows of short-term portfolio capital are helping or hindering the type of capital movements that would provide for more equitable and sustainable growth in developing and industrialized countries alike. While the answer to this question may vary for different types of countries with different internal conditions, it seems increasingly clear that one cannot presume that the benefits of unregulated capital flows outweigh the costs. As we shall show at length in what follows, many serious scholars of international finance have been warning for years that deregulating capital markets across the board was an invitation to chronic instability—especially in countries whose domestic financial systems were not adequately developed and supervised, and possibly in countries with more developed financial systems as well. But to date, too many policy makers remain "slaves of some defunct economist."

The doctrine that currently enslaves financial policy makers has a name: it is called the "Washington Consensus." [6] As World Bank Chief Economist Joseph Stiglitz explains,

> The Washington consensus held that good economic performance required liberalized trade, macroeconomic stability, and getting prices right....Once the government dealt with these issues—essentially, once the government "got out of the way"—private markets would allocate resources efficiently and generate robust growth. (Stiglitz 1998)

Stiglitz, a leading scholar of economic development and one of the few dissenters among major policy makers, observes that the Washington Consensus was formed in response to the Latin American debt crisis in the 1980s. In that case, most of the affected countries had large budget deficits and high inflation. As a result, the consensus view was that governments should emphasize fiscal austerity and tight monetary policies to keep inflation under control, while relying on domestic deregulation and free international trade to stimulate growth. In retrospect, Stiglitz observes,

> The focus on inflation—the central macroeconomic malady of the Latin American countries, which provided the backdrop for the Washington consensus—has led to macroeconomic policies that may not be the most conducive for long-term economic growth, and it has detracted attention from other major sources of macro-instability, namely, weak financial sectors. In the case of financial markets the focus on freeing up markets may have had the perverse effect of contributing to macroeconomic instability by weakening the financial sector. (Stiglitz 1998)

All the evidence from the Asian crisis suggests that the maintenance of Washington Consensus policies at best was not sufficient to ward off financial crisis and contagion effects, and at worst contributed to causing them. Yet most U.S. and IMF officials continue to insist that countries should follow these same types of policies with renewed vigor as a means of restoring investor confidence and reviving economic growth.

This book is devoted to exploring the debate over international financial market liberalization and the policy options for putting the global economy back on a more sound footing. In order to understand this multi-faceted debate, it is necessary to investigate two different but related areas. First, it is essential to review the fundamental arguments for and against capital market liberalization. Advocates of free capital mobility claim that it will promote economic efficiency and growth, that it provides valuable financial services for investors, and that it disciplines governments to adopt sound macroeconomic policies.

Critics respond that liberalized capital markets suffer from endemic problems of incomplete information that prevent them from achieving their intended efficiency goals, while fostering greater instability in both financial markets and productive activity. In addition, critics contend that capital market liberalization leads to a loss of monetary policy autonomy and produces a bias toward contractionary or deflationary macroeconomic policies. These arguments are evaluated in Chapter 1.

The debate over capital market liberalization raises a series of related questions about macroeconomic policy in a world of mobile capital. How much does capital mobility really discipline or constrain national policy makers, and, to the extent that it does, are the induced policy changes benign or detrimental? Are the Washington Consensus policies pushed by the IMF and the U.S. government appropriate for managing national economies in a world of liberalized capital flows? Do such policies help to prevent financial crises, or can they actually stimulate them or make them worse? What kinds of new policies are required to lessen financial turmoil, if traditional policy prescriptions are failing to do the job? These questions lead into our second topic, which is a review of the economic models of international finance that are used to analyze the impact of capital mobility. These theories are discussed in Chapter 2, which surveys the major theories of the balance of payments and exchange rates from the oldest to the most recent and also briefly discusses the empirical evidence pertaining to each theoretical approach. This chapter shows that Washington Consensus macroeconomic policies are based on outmoded models of international finance that ignore the central role of capital mobility and the instability that it creates. Policy makers at the IMF and in the U.S. government are indeed listening to "academic scribblers of years back," while ignoring a significant body of newer research that reveals the pitfalls of capital market liberalization and conventional economic policy prescriptions. Both Chapters 1 and 2 also identify important areas in which more research is needed into the effects of global capital flows on economic policy and performance.

Based on the analysis in the first two chapters, Chapter 3 then presents a range of options for reforming the international financial system. Most of the conventional proposals for a "new architecture" currently under discussion at the U.S. Treasury and among the G-7 countries are limited to improved regulations for the financial sector itself, focusing particularly on greater transparency and surveillance of financial institutions. This approach essentially amounts to making the world a safer place for liberalized capital flows, assuming that the latter are both inevitable and desirable. We argue that the conventional new architecture proposals are not sufficient to stabilize the global economy and are especially inadequate if the objective is to make financial markets serve broader social interests such as more equitable and sustainable growth, rather than the narrow interests of wealthy investors. In order to achieve these larger goals, new policies are needed in four interrelated areas: reinstituting capital controls, reforming international organizations like the IMF, managing exchange rates, and coordinating national macroeconomic policies. Within each of these four areas, we identify key proposals that have been made in recent years and evaluate their usefulness for controlling the gyrations in international financial markets. We argue that no single policy initiative offers a panacea; only concerted and mutually supportive efforts in all four areas can be effective. Moreover, the types of policies that will be most effective vary according to different countries' economic structures, levels of development, and domestic policy orientations. Our objective in this discussion is to widen the currently constricted debate with a broader menu of policy alternatives designed to promote more broadly shared and stable growth in the global economy of the 21st century.

Chapter 1

Alternative Views of Financial Liberalization

This chapter considers the arguments for and against the free mobility of financial capital between countries. All of the arguments discussed here concern international transactions in financial assets—currencies, stocks, bonds, bank deposits, bank loans, "derivative" instruments such as stock options, and "pooled" funds such as mutual funds and hedge funds—rather than direct foreign investment by multinational corporations. Although these two types of investment are related to some extent,[1] a discussion of the controversies about direct foreign investment would take us too far afield.[2] The liberalization of financial capital raises a distinct set of issues from those that arise in regard to direct investment, and the former can be discussed independently of the latter.[3]

Few would question the importance of financial markets and institutions in the development of capitalism or the need for financial intermediation to lubricate the wheels of economic growth. As two leading critics of the current global financial system acknowledge, "a sophisticated financial sector is *necessary* for the organization of production and distribution. An international financial system is necessary to sustain world trade and investment" (Eatwell and Taylor 1998a, 1, emphasis in original). At the same time, most economists accept the need for some governmental monitoring and prudential regulation of major financial institutions, especially banks—which have special responsibilities because of their ability to create the deposit liabilities that constitute most of a country's money supply. Where reasonable people disagree is about the extent to which financial markets and institutions should be controlled, regulated, or supervised by governmental authorities within countries, as well as the degree to which international capital flows and currency transactions should be managed, taxed, or otherwise restricted.[4]

It is often claimed that technological innovations in communications and computers have made financial liberalization inevitable (see, e.g., Obstfeld 1998). Certainly, the revolutions in electronic communications and data processing have greatly facilitated financial transactions and tremendously reduced the costs of shifting funds around the globe. But technology is not destiny, at least not when it comes to economic policy. The new technologies could also make it easier to monitor and regulate capital flows, if governments had the will to use them to that effect. Capital market deregulation is a political decision that has to be justified on economic grounds—i.e., whether its benefits exceed its costs—and on ethical grounds—i.e., whether it creates widely shared benefits or special advantages for the few.

Indeed, the trend toward the liberalization of international capital movements has been driven in no small measure by interest group pressures, most notably from the financial services industry itself (large banks, brokerage houses, mutual funds, insurance companies, and other financial institutions), as well as from nonfinancial corporations with international investments, both of which seek maximum freedom to move funds around the world without restrictions. Likewise, opposition to free capital mobility has come from those concerned about the practical effects of such mobility in the real world, especially the consequences for ordinary workers and local communities in both developing countries and industrialized countries. Thus, the scholarly debate over capital movements, like all policy debates, has not occurred in a vacuum. Still, it is important to review this debate on its own terms in order to have an intellectual framework for assessing the impact of capital market liberalization policies.

The case for capital market liberalization

The three main arguments in favor of open capital markets are that they increase allocative efficiency, enhance financial services, and impose discipline on government policy (see Fischer and Reisen 1992; Mussa and Goldstein 1993; Eichengreen and Mussa 1998; U.S. Council of Economic Advisers 1999). We will discuss each of these arguments in turn.

Increasing allocative efficiency

The allocative efficiency argument rests on the notion of "financial intermediation": financial markets and financial institutions function as intermediaries between ultimate savers and borrowers in society—those with excess funds to lend out, and those with a need to borrow funds to finance their investment or consumption expenditures. If all savers had to find borrowers to whom to lend their excess funds, savings might not find their way to the borrowers with the greatest needs, and there would be high costs for making loans. Financial markets (such as bond and stock markets) and financial institutions (such as banks, pension funds, and insurance companies) develop in order to facilitate this process. There is a presumption in standard analyses of financial intermediation that this process increases overall economic efficiency by channeling funds to those activities that offer the highest social returns, while at the same time increasing the total amount of saving and investment undertaken. Thus, the development of financial intermediaries and the liberalization of financial services are often seen as crucial ingredients in the overall growth and development of capitalist market economies (Gurley and Shaw 1967; McKinnon 1973).

The allocative efficiency argument for the liberalization of international capital movements follows simply and directly from these classical arguments in favor of financial liberalization in general. If the excess savings of some countries can freely flow to borrowers in other nations, then total world savings should find their most beneficial uses, and the entire world economy should be more productive as a result. Suppose, for example, that there are investment projects in, say, China, that offer high rates of return but cannot be adequately financed by Chinese savings, while there are excess savings in another country (say, Japan) that will have to flow into investments offering lower returns if they are kept at home. In this case, global economic efficiency can be increased if the excess Japanese savings can be invested in the Chinese investment projects: the world gets more productive investments (in China), while the savings get higher returns (in Japan). As one scholar puts it,

> The main justification for international capital movement is that it shifts savings from locations where they are abundant and cheap relative to investment opportunities to places where they are scarce and expensive....Where capital is more productive in one country than another, it should be moved from the country where it is less to the country where it is more productive. (Kindleberger 1967, quoted in Dufey and Giddy 1978, 193)

The efficiency case for free international mobility of capital also has a parallel in the classical case for free trade in goods and services. Free trade in goods and services is supposed to maximize the efficiency of global production at any point in time by enabling producers in each country to specialize in the commodities they can produce with the relatively lowest costs (i.e., the goods and services in which they have a "comparative advantage").[5] International capital movements can be viewed analogously as involving the exchange of consumption by different countries over time: net lender countries are trading off current consumption for future returns, while net borrower countries are able to increase their present consumption (or investment) in exchange for future obligations to repay. Theoretically, this results in a more efficient "intertemporal" allocation of resources: "Where savers in one country have lesser preference for current consumption than those in another, total welfare is increased by shifting the consumption of one into the future and the other into the present" (Kindleberger 1967, quoted in Dufey and Giddy 1978, 193).

The analogy to free trade in goods and services should alert us to two important qualifications to the case for free capital mobility. Even assuming the idealized conditions under which free trade brings aggregate benefits, the gains from trade generally come at the expense of two types of social costs: redistributional effects and adjustment costs. Redistributional effects occur when some classes of productive factors (e.g., less-skilled workers in the U.S. economy) lose out as a result of competition with imported goods made by foreign producers using cheaper inputs of the same factor (e.g., Chinese or Mexican labor). Adjustment costs are felt when those who lose jobs or sales to imports cannot easily shift into other occupations or industries, and hence end up unemployed or with idle capacity as a result. While there is much debate over the magnitude of these problems, all serious economists acknowledge that they exist.

The same sorts of distributional and adjustment problems that arise from international trade can also result from international investment. Redistributional effects occur when, for example, investment is shifted from a less profitable outlet in one country to a more profitable outlet abroad. While the investors (and those employed by the foreign investment) thus gain, those in the home country who would have benefited from the domestic investment (especially domestic workers) are worse off than they would have been if the investment had been made at home, holding other factors constant. Adjustment costs can be felt, for example, if capital market liberalization leaves some domestic players unable to compete (e.g., domestic financial intermediaries may be displaced by large foreign financial services companies). Also, businesses that used to obtain preferential credit through a favored domestic channel may find that their credit is rationed or available only at higher interest rates from a "reformed" (and possibly foreign-owned) financial institution.

Although there is a theoretical presumption that these types of losses are outweighed by efficiency gains, there is little hard evidence to prove it. In fact, there has been remarkably little effort to empirically measure the theoretically expected gains from financial market liberalization. The few studies that exist have found that such gains are at best elusive, and may even be negative (i.e., there may be gains from maintaining capital controls). Grilli and Milesi-Ferretti (1995) conclude that capital controls are associated with higher average inflation rates but lower real interest rates, suggesting that liberalization of capital flows can actually discourage productive investment at least through interest rate effects. Grilli and Milesi-Ferretti also find a positive but statistically weak effect of capital account controls on growth rates and a negative and also statistically weak effect of current account controls on growth rates.[6] Rodrik (1998) finds that capital controls have no statistically significant effect on economic growth either positively or negatively, when other determinants of growth are accounted for.[7]

Also, it should be noted that the allocative efficiency gains from capital mobility can be offset by public welfare losses due to "negative externalities," such as increased pollution or environmental degradation. Negative externalities are social costs that are not charged through market prices to those who create the costs. In the language of economic theory, externalities create "distortions" in resource allocation. According to the so-called "theory of the second-best," the liberalization of some economic restrictions (such as those on capital flows) can possibly be welfare-reducing in the presence of other distortions (see Bhagwati and Srinivasan 1983). For example, foreign capital may flow into projects that require excessive deforestation or that cause severe soil erosion, because the private returns to such projects are large while the social costs are not borne by those who profit from the investment.[8]

More research is clearly needed to estimate the costs and benefits of capital market liberalization as well as the distribution of the gains and losses among different types of economic agents (e.g., corporations and their workers, small savers versus large investors), which none of these studies has yet addressed. At this point, all we can say is that the case for substantial efficiency gains from capital market liberalization has not yet been proven, and certainly cannot be assumed as a basis for policy.

Enhancing financial services

Liberalization of international capital markets also provides a range of potentially important financial services to international businesses, commercial interests, and portfolio investors. For example, importers may need to obtain hard currencies (e.g., U.S. dollars) in order to purchase goods from foreign countries that will not accept payment in local currency. Thus, open currency markets can provide liquidity by enabling international traders to obtain foreign exchange more easily (or at lower cost) than in controlled currency markets. Another example is the hedging of risk. If a business has obligations due in a foreign currency, it is exposed to "exchange risk": the risk that the home currency will depreciate during the intervening period. By using vehicles such as forward exchange contracts, a risk-averse business firm can cover its position and avoid the exchange risk by locking in the currently prevailing forward exchange rate.[9]

A third example is the ability of banks (and other financial intermediaries) to "transform maturities" by borrowing short (e.g., by taking in deposits) and lending long. This is a useful service since individual bank depositors are usually uncertain about the timing of their future withdrawals and thus value liquidity, while banks normally face much less uncertainty about depositors as a group because individual depositors usually withdraw their funds at different times (except in the case of a bank panic). The transformation of maturities can be extended on an international scale if banks take in funds in one country and lend them out in another country. However, this practice can sometimes get banks into trouble, as in the case of banks in many Asian countries (e.g., Korea) that borrowed abroad in foreign currencies at short maturities (from large, multinational banks in other countries, especially Japan) and then lent domestically for longer maturities—often in enterprises that were not really creditworthy. Many of these banks could not repay their short-term foreign currency debts during the panic of 1997-98.

Yet another type of financial service is specific to international investment and is especially relevant to the financial crises of the late 1990s. Financial liberalization allows investors to diversify their portfolios across assets from different countries (as emphasized by Eichengreen and Mussa 1998). If the risks of investing in different nations are uncorrelated with each other (i.e., economic performance varies randomly across countries), then such diversification allows investors to achieve a more optimal balancing of risk and return in their portfolios. Investors can lend money to a variety of countries that offer high returns with high risks, expecting that losses in any particular country will be more than outweighed by gains elsewhere. This strategy falls apart, however, if the risks become correlated across countries, as occurred due to the "Asian contagion" effects in 1997-98, when financial markets began collapsing across the globe. Moreover, this strategy potentially sows the seeds of its own failure if it leads to large infusions of funds into a lot of countries at the same time, based on scanty information about their true conditions and prospects—a point to which we shall return below.

These are just a few examples of financial services that open international capital markets and foreign exchange markets can provide and that would not be available (or would have higher costs) if such markets were more closed. However, even aside from the possibility of correlated risks, there are several other caveats to this argument. First, the demand for these types of services is greatly increased by financial liberalization itself as well as by the adoption of floating exchange rates (which requires more hedging instruments to deal with increased exchange risk). Second, the instruments created to provide such services can actually end up increasing the amount of risk in the global financial system by increasing the volume of funds moving in and out of various financial markets at the same time (Eatwell 1996b). In these respects, the financial services argument for capital market liberalization is somewhat circular: the more that such markets are liberalized, the more demand there is for their services. Also, if liberalization of financial markets leads to a more concentrated global financial services industry, small customers may find themselves receiving inferior service from large institutions (quite likely foreign owned) that are more responsive to the needs of larger clients.

Finally, it is worth noting that the provision of new financial services can sometimes undermine the efficiency gains from liberalized capital flows. As Kregel (1998a) argues, the shift toward more use of derivative instruments has led to a refocusing of international banking activity, away from making traditional loans that required continuous monitoring of risk to serving as intermediaries in off-balance sheet transactions,[10] in which the risks are shifted to the ultimate purchasers (who generally lack the knowledge required to evaluate the true risks in the positions they are taking). In part, this shift has been driven by a desire to evade the new Basle capital adequacy standards with innovative financial instruments that are not subject to those standards. When banks thus become more concerned with earning fees and commissions instead of guaranteeing a steady stream of interest payments, it becomes less likely that capital will flow to ultimate uses that offer optimal combinations of risk and return. As Kregel concludes,

> it is the role of most derivative packages to mask the actual risk involved in an investment, and to increase the difficulty in assessing the final return on funds provided. As a result, certain types of derivative[s] may increase the difficulties faced by private capital markets in effectuating the efficient allocation of resources. (Kregel 1998a, 679)

Imposing policy discipline

It is often argued that international capital mobility imposes a salutary form of discipline on national policy makers by ensuring that they maintain "sound fundamentals" in their macroeconomic and monetary policies. According to this view, national policy makers who might otherwise be prone to run excessive budget deficits or to permit inflationary increases in the money supply will be reined in by international investors, who might charge default premiums for higher country risk, force depreciation of overvalued currencies, or threaten to cut off credit to errant debtors. Two prominent supporters of this view maintain that, "While the discipline exercised by capital markets over governments is neither infallible nor always applied smoothly and consistently, we find that markets have on the whole encouraged adjustments in policies that go in the right direction" (Mussa and Goldstein 1993, 258).

The policy discipline argument implies that national policy makers have considerably less autonomy when capital markets are liberalized than they would have otherwise. In the pro-liberalization view, this loss of autonomy is beneficial, since it prevents governments from adopting policies that are not sustainable in the long run anyway. The policies that capital mobility is supposed to enforce generally coincide with those believed to be the correct policies under the Washington Consensus view: conservative fiscal policies (low budget deficits or budget surpluses), tight monetary policies (high interest rates and slow monetary growth), deregulated domestic markets, free trade, and so on. Thus, this argument for capital market liberalization actually rests on a set of beliefs about what are the "right" domestic macroeconomic policies—and a belief that these coincide with the policies that attract international investment.

In the policy discipline view, capital mobility merely enforces constraints that are already inherent in a country's economy—such as limits on how fast the country can grow or how much employment it can create without causing excessive inflation. Investors' reactions simply help to maintain a preordained (and socially optimal) equilibrium by preventing governments from adopting policies that would thwart the operation of the free market system. In effect, this view holds that the type of policies favored by financial interests—basically, policies that stress price stability and sound money—are the only sustainable policies in the long run anyway. There is thus a convenient marriage of theory and self-interest, in which those who stand to gain the most from financial market liberalization can claim that whatever serves their interests naturally serves the broader social interest. As a result, the policy discipline argument easily slides into an ideological belief that "what's good for Wall Street is good for America" (or even the world). If the policies favored by financial interests and the Washington Consensus are neither necessary nor beneficial, however, then whatever discipline is imposed by financial markets (assuming it is effective) can be harmful instead of helpful.

Critical perspectives
on capital market liberalization

Criticisms of financial liberalization can be grouped into four categories: problems of information and uncertainty, reduced monetary policy autonomy, contractionary biases in macroeconomic policies, and destabilizing effects of capital flows that tend to amplify business cycles. These four criticisms overlap to some extent, but they represent conceptually distinct allegations about the problems caused by global financial integration, and they will be discussed separately in what follows.

Problems of information and uncertainty

The analogy between free capital mobility and free trade (discussed above) breaks down because international investment is plagued by severe informational problems that are not found in ordinary trade in goods and services. When one imports, say, bananas or bicycles, one usually has fairly solid information about the quality of the goods and their cost.[11] But this is not the case with international investments, which involve placing bets about an inherently uncertain future. One cannot know with certainty, for example, whether an asset will hold its value, whether borrowers will be able to service their debts, or whether a currency will depreciate. There are, of course, some types of international financial arbitrage that offer fairly certain returns (e.g., an investment in a safe foreign treasury bill with the proceeds converted back to domestic currency via a forward contract), but one can never know with certainty beforehand whether alternative, more risky investments would bring higher yields.

Decisions about international investment are therefore based on purely subjective evaluations of the probabilities of future events, or even on mere feelings of optimism or pessimism about a country's future prospects.

Keynes (1936) was the first to identify these types of information and uncertainty problems with regard to investment in general. He argued that, not only can the future not be predicted, but even the probabilities of possible future events occurring cannot be known with any certainty. Discussing this point in terms of modern economic theory, Stiglitz (1998, 18) writes that "Problems of incomplete information, incomplete markets, and incomplete contracts are all particularly severe in the financial sector." In the case of international investment, these informational problems are even more severe than for domestic investments, since foreign investors generally have less information about a country's assets and their true future prospects than do domestic investors.

As a result of the intrinsic information problems in financial markets, these markets are often driven by what is called "herd behavior" or self-fulfilling prophecies. If an individual investor believes that most other investors will buy or sell a certain asset (e.g., a stock or currency), then it is rational for that investor to do the same. But if a large number of investors all act on the same beliefs, they will make the asset rise or fall in value as expected—even if the asset price need not have changed if so many investors had not bought or sold the asset simultaneously. Thus, financial markets can be characterized by self-fulfilling expectations. As a result, asset prices can skyrocket in a bubble and subsequently collapse in a panic, without regard to the underlying fundamentals (e.g., expected future profits) that should theoretically determine the true value of an asset.

Information problems also give rise to the type of contagion effects seen in the financial crises in Latin America, Asia, and other developing regions in the 1990s. Suppose that investors have poured money into a country like Argentina or Indonesia based on a perception that these are good places to invest, but with little precise information about the countries' macroeconomic policies, financial conditions, and so on. Then a crisis breaks out in another country, say Mexico or Thailand. Suddenly, investors who were poorly informed about the true risks of investing in such countries can turn from being overly optimistic to being unduly pessimistic. Information that was previously available but unheeded—such as evidence of large trade deficits, overvalued currencies, or inadequate hard currency reserves—suddenly gets noticed and even exaggerated, fueling fears of an impending crisis. As investors rush for the exits—all believing (correctly) that they will lose less if they get out before the others—the fear of a crisis becomes a self-fulfilling prophecy. Such contagion effects can occur in countries whose economic fundamentals, while not unproblematic, were not serious enough to generate a crisis on their own.

One recent theoretical model of currency crises and speculative panics (Calvo and Mendoza 1996) analyzes why such information problems are likely to be especially severe when a large number of countries have liberalized their capital markets. This model is based on the fact that information is not a free good, and investors need incentives in order to be willing to pay the costs of obtaining it. Since individual investors can reduce the overall risk of their portfolios by diversifying their investments across countries (assuming that country risks are uncorrelated), they have less incentive to seek information about each individual country in which they invest when their portfolios are highly diversified internationally than they would have otherwise. Thus, international capital market integration makes herd behavior (and hence bubbles, panics, and contagion) much more likely to occur. And if contagion effects are strong enough to make the risks in different national markets positively correlated, they undermine the purported benefits from capital market liberalization that arise from the international diversification of risk.[12]

While these types of problems are generally recognized to exist in international financial markets today, the way in which they undermine the case for capital mobility is not always appreciated. Information problems do not merely create costs (e.g., greater volatility) that have to be weighed against the benefits of open capital markets; rather, they also undermine the presumption of large efficiency gains from free international mobility of capital. In order for investors to invest in the places with the highest expected returns to their capital, they must have full information about the likely returns to all available investment opportunities as well as the true risks involved. In the global economy, however, the simultaneous liberalization of capital markets in a large number of countries reduces the amount of information relied upon by diversified investors in making their decisions about any individual country's true prospects. If investors are not making fully informed decisions about countries' long-term prospects, there can be no presumption that capital is flowing toward those countries where it will be used most productively. To the extent that investors follow self-fulfilling expectations about short-term trends and move their money in and out of countries in herd-like fashion, then, the efficiency argument for free capital mobility ceases to apply.

Reduced monetary policy autonomy[13]

A second criticism is that global financial liberalization undermines the autonomy of central banks in setting national monetary policies. This view originated with concern over the growth of international banks and offshore currency markets (the so-called "Eurodollar" markets) in the 1970s, which appeared to make national monetary control more difficult (see Dufey and Giddy 1978; Moffitt 1983; Wachtel 1990; D'Arista 1998). One thing that seems agreed upon by most observers (including both supporters and opponents of capital market liberalization) is that the growth of these markets created pressures that encouraged the deregulation of domestic banking and financial services. Offshore currency markets originally arose out of efforts by large banks and depositors to avoid national regulations (such as interest rate ceilings and reserve requirements) and to evade capital controls in the 1960s and early 1970s. Once external (and unregulated or less-regulated) markets existed, domestic financial institutions lost deposit and loan business to offshore competitors, and this competition in turn placed pressure on domestic governments to relax or abolish credit allocation policies and interest rate restrictions.

Credit allocation policies. Governments have often used banking and financial regulations for what are called "credit allocation" purposes, i.e., to channel funds in socially desired directions, in which those funds might not flow if the decisions were left up to private markets. For example, restrictions on interstate banking and international capital flows can force banks to re-lend local savings within depressed regions domestically, instead of pumping the funds into booming areas elsewhere in the country or the world. Or, the creation of a set of legally restricted financial institutions that have to lend to particular activities can be used to channel financial flows toward sectors favored for public policy reasons (e.g., the U.S. savings and loans, which used to be confined to making residential mortgages, or development banks in developing countries, which had to lend in support of government-directed industrial plans).

The rise of offshore banking and the opening of international capital markets clearly undermines the effectiveness of such policies. As Dufey and Giddy explain,

> Domestic banks so constrained are therefore at a competitive disadvantage vis-à-vis Eurobanks that are subject to no credit allocation. Consequently, credit tends to be rerouted through the external markets whenever credit allocation reduces the relative competitiveness of domestic intermediation. Just as the increasing incidence of credit allocation contributes to the growth of the Eurocurrency markets, the existence of these markets tends to frustrate attempts at indirect credit allocation. Industrialized countries that seek to channel funds to favored sectors by means of domestic financial institutions are increasingly discovering that the funds to be reallocated largely disappear into the external market and that the additional costs are borne by those who do not have access to these markets. As a result, the customers that end up with the higher-cost loans and lower-yielding deposits tend to be smaller domestic businesses and less affluent investors. The primary beneficiaries are usually large business units from whose reach the funds are supposed to be allocated away. (Dufey and Giddy 1978, 192)

Of course, to supporters of capital market liberalization, the elimination of such credit allocation policies is a good thing, since it allows financial markets to allocate capital more efficiently and to provide better financial services. Critics, however, believe that credit allocation policies are necessary and desirable for two reasons. First, they enable governments to address significant social needs that private credit markets are unlikely to recognize, such as the need to finance low-income housing in the U.S. or infant industries in developing countries.[14] And second, these policies serve a prudential function in bank regulation, since they prevent banks from overlending and reassure depositors that their funds are secure (and thus help to prevent bank panics).

In addition, critics argue that the abandonment of credit allocation policies diminishes the range of tools that central banks can use to manage their monetary and credit policies. Historically, monetary authorities have relied upon credit allocation techniques such as quantitative credit controls, interest rate ceilings, and reserve requirements on bank deposits to help control the total amount of credit and the money supply. These techniques provide instruments that the central bank can adjust periodically in order to loosen or restrain the availability of credit as economic conditions dictate.[15] In this sense, the abandonment of credit controls and the weakening of prudential regulations make monetary policy making more difficult—and more reliant on a single tool, namely interest rate management via open market operations. As D'Arista (1998) explains,

> Increased capital mobility, the liberalization of domestic financial markets and shifts in credit flows to securities markets outside the direct influence of monetary policy have made implementing monetary policy more difficult in all countries (Federal Reserve Bank of Kansas City 1993). They have eroded the central banks' ability to control the supply of credit, forcing them to rely more on their ability to change interest rates through open market operations [in order] to influence the demand for credit. But, as early as the 1969 US credit crunch, it became apparent that efforts to control aggregate demand through open market operations require that "...interest rates generally have to become higher and more variable" (BIS 1995). In the process, they become powerful inducements for procyclical surges of foreign portfolio investment that undermine the policy objectives sought by the change in interest rates. Thus, the most damaging effect of the liberalization of global financial markets may be the loss of central banks' power to implement countercyclical policies.

Interest rate policy. This then raises the question of whether capital mobility further constrains monetary policy by limiting central banks' ability to control interest rates, which are the one remaining lever of monetary policy after credit allocation policies have been largely abandoned. When monetary policy can operate only on the demand for credit by adjusting its price (i.e., the interest rate), D'Arista and others argue, the result is both excessive volatility in interest rates and a higher average level of interest rates. Several critics have argued that capital mobility prevents individual countries from adjusting interest rates in response to domestic needs. For example, Moffitt (1983, 228) wrote that "The global integration of national financial markets has made it impossible even for powerhouses like West Germany to lower interest rates enough to stimulate their economy." Even in the United States, Moffitt claimed, "a prolonged campaign to bring down interest rates would simply lead to a flight from the dollar and a new dollar crisis." In a similar vein, Wachtel (1990, 266) wrote that as a result of the "reduced influence of domestic monetary policy...it is simply not feasible for the United States to lower its real interest rates without coordinating such moves with its two international partners [Germany and Japan]."

While it is true that capital mobility can constrain interest rate policy, these quotes exaggerate in claiming that capital mobility makes it impossible for national central banks to control their own countries' interest rates—especially in large countries like Germany and the United States. The degree of autonomy of the national monetary authorities to set interest rates depends on a variety of other conditions besides the openness of capital markets, including country size, openness to trade, international debts, inflationary pressures, and—above all—the exchange rate regime (fixed or flexible rates). All of these factors interact to determine how much leeway a nation's monetary authorities have in setting interest rates.[16]

A useful framework for understanding these issues is the idea of the policy "trilemma" (illustrated in **Figure 1.1**), which is the impossibility of a country simultaneously having the following three things: open capital markets, control over the exchange rate, and an independent monetary policy (see, e.g., Obstfeld 1998; Taylor 1998b). From this perspective, open capital markets do not completely eliminate monetary policy autonomy, but they do force a country to choose between controlling its exchange rate (the external price of its currency) and controlling its interest rates (the internal price of credit). A country with open capital markets can still control its interest rates if it is willing to let its exchange rate float freely—but if such a country wants to manage its exchange rate, it must then give up control over interest rates and set them at levels that are consistent with the exchange rate targets. We shall come back to discuss the reasons why a country might not want to accept a flexible exchange rate (and the risk of depreciation) below, but first we discuss the mechanics of why a fixed exchange rate eliminates interest rate autonomy while a flexible rate does not.

FIGURE 1.1 The international policy 'trilemma'

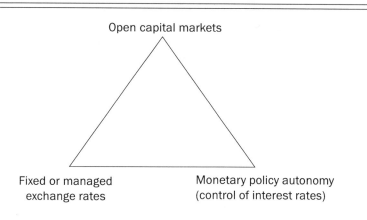

Note: The "trilemma" is the problem that countries can achieve only two of the three objectives simultaneously. See text for further discussion and sources.

Consider what happens in a small country with open capital markets when, for example, foreign interest rates rise.[17] The degree to which the country's central bank has to respond in kind depends heavily on the extent to which the country's exchange rate is fixed or flexible (see Epstein 1993). If the exchange rate is flexible and if the government is indifferent to whether the currency depreciates, then the central bank is not obligated to match the increase in foreign interest rates. Capital will leave the country in pursuit of higher interest rates abroad, and the capital outflow will cause the currency to depreciate until balance-of-payments equilibrium is restored (for example, through increased exports and decreased imports at the new exchange rate). If a country's exchange rate is fixed, however, and if the country's capital markets are wide open, the central bank has to match the foreign interest rate hike in order to prevent capital from fleeing the country and thus alleviating the pressure on the currency to depreciate.

A country with a fixed exchange rate can try to avoid adjusting its interest rates when foreign interest rates change through foreign exchange market intervention, i.e., the central bank can sell or buy foreign currencies as needed to maintain the currency "peg" (the target for the fixed exchange rate). For example, if foreign interest rates rise and capital outflows put pressure on the government to devalue the currency, the central bank can sell off some of its reserves of foreign exchange in exchange for domestic currency, which tends to bolster the value of the latter (essentially, the central bank is supplying more foreign exchange in order to satisfy the excess demand for foreign exchange at the prevailing exchange rate). But in so doing, the central bank risks sparking a speculative attack, since speculators will see the dwindling foreign exchange reserves as a sign that the central bank's ability to defend the exchange rate is weakening—and they will bet on an eventual devaluation by selling even more of the currency. Sooner or later, as those reserves become depleted (and they will be depleted sooner, if a speculative attack ensues), the central bank is forced to abandon its intervention and either devalue the currency or let it float.[18]

Thus, rising foreign interest rates offer a country with a fixed exchange rate and open capital markets a stark choice—either raise interest rates to defend the currency or else abandon the exchange rate peg and devalue (or float) the currency. Exchange market intervention to support the currency usually just postpones the day of reckoning; only closing the capital market can permit a country to maintain a lower interest rate without devaluing its currency. An example of this predicament occurred when Germany raised its interest rates in 1991-92 in response to the costs of reunification, thus forcing the other countries in the European Exchange Rate Mechanism (ERM) at the time to raise their interest rates if they wanted to maintain their pegs to the German mark.[19] The United Kingdom originally announced that it would defend the parity of the pound within the ERM by raising interest rates. However, after a speculative attack on the pound made it clear that this policy was untenable, the U.K. decided to leave the ERM so that it could lower its interest rates and let the pound depreciate. Thus, abandoning the fixed exchange rate increased Britain's monetary policy autonomy, and—once the pound was allowed to float—capital mobility did not prevent interest rates from falling.[20]

If a country's exchange rate is flexible, then, the central bank can lower domestic interest rates (or fail to raise them, when foreign interest rates rise) as long as it is willing to tolerate a currency depreciation. Epstein (1993) points out that there need not be a dramatic depreciation or currency crisis as long as lower interest rates do not unleash fears of sharply increased inflation. He also argues that the harmful effects of depreciation have been exaggerated, at least for the U.S. economy, where depreciation does not seem to lead to a significant increase in inflation.[21] Even if inflation increases, most research shows that the real economic costs of moderate inflation are negligible, and one recent study (Akerlof, Dickens, and Perry 1996) finds that low inflation may actually improve growth performance compared with zero inflation.[22] Moreover, in countries whose trade balances are responsive to changes in relative prices (which seems to be true in most of the major industrialized countries, as shown by Cline 1989 and Bosworth 1993), a depreciation can have beneficial effects in increasing net exports and stimulating national income.[23] Thus, monetary policy is significantly less constrained under a system of flexible exchange rates than in a system of fixed exchange rates, even if capital is highly mobile.

However, countries may not be indifferent to the level of their exchange rates and hence may not wish to let them float freely. Even if the exchange rate is not officially fixed, it can be influenced by central bank intervention in what is known as a "dirty" or "managed" float. There are potentially valid reasons, which depend on the structure of the country, for wanting to fix or manage exchange rates. For example, in small countries that are very open to trade (i.e., have high ratios of imports to gross domestic product (GDP)), allowing the currency to depreciate can lead to significantly increased inflation due to higher costs of imports. Correspondingly, a fixed exchange rate (or a slowly crawling peg) can be an important lever for containing inflationary pressures in countries where high inflation has been a chronic problem. For developing countries that have borrowed heavily in foreign currencies (e.g., Mexico in dollars or Korea in yen), depreciation is especially costly because it increases the burden in domestic currency terms of servicing a debt denominated in a foreign currency (i.e., it takes more pesos or won to meet a given obligation in dollars or yen). By the same token, however, a large country with a floating exchange rate that is not very dependent on imports or direct foreign investment, does not have high inflation, and does not have large debts denominated in foreign currency (such as the United States) is unlikely to suffer severe consequences from a moderate depreciation of its currency, and in this respect is less constrained in its ability to set interest rates below foreign levels (see Pollin 1998). Thus, capital mobility per se does not necessarily render interest rate policy ineffective in all countries, as some critics have implied.

Still, capital mobility does tighten the constraints facing many developing countries, as the current economic crisis in Brazil illustrates. In 1998, the Brazilian government tried to avoid the fate that earlier engulfed Mexico, Thailand, Indonesia, Russia, and other countries when speculative attacks forced them to devalue their currencies. Re-elected Brazilian President Fernando Henrique Cardoso[24] promised to raise interest rates and slash the budget deficit in order to preserve the fixed exchange rate for the nation's currency, the real. Brazil was rewarded for this policy stance by the IMF and the U.S. government, which backed up Brazil's austerity plan by arranging a $41.5 billion package of credits. Although interest rates were raised, the budget deficit remained high, and foreign investors lost confidence in the government's commitments and took billions of dollars out of the country. After losing several billion dollars of reserves trying to defend the exchange rate peg, the Brazilian government gave up in January 1999 and devalued the real—and after further losses of reserves, let the real float (whereupon it depreciated further).

What induced the Brazilian government to try to keep interest rates so high and to slash government spending was not the pressure from foreign investors alone, however, but also the government's commitment to a fixed exchange rate coupled with the country's enormous overhang of foreign currency debt and its long history of high inflation. If Brazil had been willing to let its currency depreciate, it could potentially have lowered its interest rates and avoided harsh fiscal cutbacks. But Brazil's desire to keep its exchange rate fixed was motivated by its long-term inflationary dynamic, which was only recently brought under control by the introduction of the new currency and other measures, and which was likely to be revived by the devaluation. Also, if Brazil did not have such a massive foreign debt, it would not be so dependent on continued capital inflows to roll over existing debts, and would not have to worry so much about pleasing foreign creditors. Ironically, the Brazilian government is still (as of early 1999) maintaining high interest rates (and promising fiscal austerity) in an effort to restore foreign investors' confidence and keep the real from falling further. Brazil's dependency on foreign capital clearly contributes to the constraints it faces, but these constraints are all the more binding because of the country's structural problems (debt and inflation) and its continued effort to manage its exchange rate.

To summarize, interest rate policy is certainly constrained by international capital mobility, but the tightness of the constraints varies depending on factors such as exchange rate regimes, country size, development levels, and foreign debts. Generally, the constraints on interest rate policy are tighter when exchange rates are fixed or managed, which is more likely to be the case in smaller and less-developed countries where depreciation is costly due to factors such as high import ratios, large foreign-currency-denominated debts, and strong inflationary pressures. By the same logic, larger countries—and smaller countries that do not have these problems (e.g., countries with low inflation that have not borrowed heavily in foreign currencies, or which have flexible exchange rates) have greater autonomy to set their own interest rates. Thus, the United States, the EMU, and even the United Kingdom have much more autonomy in this regard, simply because they are large players in global financial markets (and as long as they are willing to tolerate fluctuations in their exchange rates). This conclusion is buttressed by numerous econometric studies that demonstrate significant, real effects of Federal Reserve monetary policy on interest rates, bank credit, and other macroeconomic and financial variables in the U.S. economy since the 1980s when capital markets were liberalized, as well as similar findings for other countries.[25]

Contractionary macroeconomic policy bias

The third criticism of capital mobility is that it imposes a contractionary bias on macroeconomic and monetary policy. As one author puts it,

> Capital mobility allows financial capital to vote with its feet and veto policy it does not like. In general, financial interests prefer mildly deflationary policies as this preserves the value of financial assets. As a

result, rather than lowering global interest rates, capital mobility may have contributed to institutionalizing deflationary monetary policy. (Palley 1998b, 17)

This argument is premised on the fact that inflation redistributes income from creditors to debtors, and hence financial investors prefer to invest in countries that make price stability the highest priority. Thus, it is argued, portfolio capital tends to reward countries that maintain high interest rates and low budget deficits (or budget surpluses). And the more that financial markets and capital flows are liberalized, the easier it is for financial investors to pull their capital out of countries that adopt more expansionary monetary and fiscal policies.

This criticism is related to the argument about reduced autonomy for national monetary policy, but it is both more specific and more general: it is more specific because it claims that there is a particular direction in which policy is constrained, and it is more general because it expands the realm of policies that are constrained beyond monetary policy to include fiscal policies, tax systems, regulatory regimes, and any other policies that affect international financial interests. International financial flows are thought to reward countries that slash government spending, cut taxes on investment income, deregulate financial markets, privatize state enterprises, liberalize foreign trade, and generally adopt more conservative policy regimes (essentially, countries that follow the Washington Consensus policy package). The implication of this argument is that we should expect countries with open capital markets to be pushed in the direction of slower growth, higher unemployment, and more unequal distributions of income than they would have otherwise.

There is no question that economic policies around the world have generally shifted in a more conservative direction in the last two decades of the 20th century. Macroeconomic policies have become deflationary (or, more accurately, disinflationary) in the sense that reducing or controlling inflation has become the chief objective of monetary and fiscal policies. In the United States, for example, the Federal Reserve Board (the Fed) has made low inflation the overriding objective of its monetary policy, while the federal government has achieved a budget surplus after three decades of chronic deficits. In Europe, monetary policy is driven by a similar objective of low inflation with the added dimension of using high interest rates to make the new euro a strong currency, while fiscal deficits are constrained by agreement among the countries joining the European Monetary Union (EMU). The question, however, is whether this policy shift has been forced upon governments and central banks by capital market liberalization, or whether it is the result of a political and ideological sea change in which conservative policies that favor wealthy interests have gained ascendancy over liberal or social democratic policies more concerned with full employment, high wages, and rapid growth, which predominated in the industrial countries during the "golden age of capitalism" between the 1950s and the early 1970s. From the latter viewpoint, the drive to open up capital markets is just a part of this overall shift in the orientation of economic policy, rather than an independent cause of the conservative drift of monetary and fiscal policies.

The idea that governments must adopt conservative economic policies in order to placate international investors is often explained in terms of a need to maintain "credibility":

> The overwhelming scale of potential capital flows means that governments must today, as never before, attempt to maintain market "credibility"....A credible government is a government which pursues a policy that is "market friendly," that is, a policy that is in accordance with what the markets believe to be "sound" and "efficient." Particularly favoured are measures designed to meet a "prudent" pre-determined monetary target or imposing nominal anchors on monetary policy, and balancing the budget (preferably by cutting public expenditures rather than raising taxes). Governments that fail to pursue "sound" and "prudent" policies are forced to pay a premium on the interest costs of financing their programmes. Severe loss of credibility will lead to a financial crisis. (Eatwell 1996b, 35)

As discussed earlier, the idea that financial liberalization disciplines national governments to maintain "credible" policies is often cited as an argument in favor of capital market liberalization. To supporters of such liberalization, the type of policies favored by financial investors—basically, policies that stress price stability and sound money—are the only sustainable policies in the long run. In this view, international financial pressures simply help to maintain a preordained, "natural" market equilibrium. Those like Palley and Eatwell who believe that international capital mobility imposes an undue deflationary bias on policy (rather than merely enforcing "sound fundamentals") essentially stand the policy discipline argument on its head, asserting that the policies that governments are pressured to adopt by international capital flows are unnecessarily conservative and contractionary—and that they favor certain interests at the expense of others (essentially, financial interests over industrial, labor, and community interests). In this alternative view, a unique or natural economic equilibrium does not exist. Rather, there is a range of possible outcomes that differ in regard to the distribution of their costs and benefits, and capital mobility limits the range of choices to policies that prioritize low inflation over other economic objectives.[26]

In evaluating the argument of a bias toward contractionary policies, it is important to start from the premise that what international financiers care about above all else is making money. They do not care about economic policies per se, but only about how any given set of policies is likely to affect the returns on their investments. Those who make the policy bias argument are certainly right in emphasizing investors' fear of inflation, which reduces the real value of assets (such as bank loans or government bonds) and yields (such as interest payments) that are denominated in nominal terms. However, the link between policies and inflation is not a simple one. Expansionary monetary or fiscal policies that might be inflationary in some situations may not be in others.[27] If inflationary fears can be mitigated, governments may be able to pursue more expansionary policies without fear of unleashing massive capital flight (see Epstein 1993; Pollin 1998). Furthermore, speculators are motivated by the likelihood of the gains to be made from betting on particular policy shifts, such as a currency devaluation. They do not care whether the policy shift in question would be intrinsically expansionary or contractionary, but only whether the current policy regime is unsustainable for some reason that allows them to bet on its demise.

This perspective allows us to see why capital flows have enforced contractionary policies in some situations and not in others. In the late 1970s and early 1980s—the period that motivated the arguments of Moffitt and Wachtel, cited earlier—inflation rates were generally high in most regions of the global economy, including the United States, Latin America, and most of Western Europe. In large measure, this high inflation was due to cost-push pressures from energy prices (sparked by the oil price shocks of 1973-74 and 1978-79) and labor costs (due to the productivity slowdown and intensified labor-management conflict in the U.S. and other countries). In some cases, especially in Latin America and other developing regions, the monetization of large government budget deficits (i.e., increased money supplies created by central bank purchases of the government bonds issued to finance the budget deficits) also worsened inflationary pressures. In this environment, international investors were especially wary of expansionary fiscal and monetary policies that were seen as accommodating inflation or threatening to increase it further. Thus, the fact that expansionary efforts such as those of Jimmy Carter in the U.S. and Francois Mitterand in France (among others) were thwarted by capital flight and currency crises lends some validation to the policy bias argument.

But after inflationary pressures subsided in most countries in the late 1980s and 1990s, investors' fears of expansionary policies appear to have diminished as well, in several instances. Consider again the example of the United Kingdom in the early 1990s. After Germany raised its interest rates, the U.K. risked depressing its domestic economy if it followed suit in order to maintain the value of the pound relative to the mark. Speculators believed that higher interest rates would be politically unsustainable in the U.K. and therefore bet that the pound would have to depreciate. The ensuing speculative attack forced the British government to reverse course by leaving the ERM, cutting interest rates, and allowing the pound to depreciate. In this case, international speculators effectively compelled the British government to adopt a more expansionary policy stance. Moreover, the policy shift was relatively successful. Since 1992, the U.K. has enjoyed the most steady growth of any major European country (see Blecker 1998a), and its unemployment rate has fallen significantly and is now below the average European Union (EU) level (OECD 1998, 40). Of course, this outcome was predicated on confidence that the devaluation of the pound would not rekindle inflation, but the point is that speculative pressures pushed the U.K. to lower rather than to raise its interest rates in 1992-93.

Another example can be found in the American reaction to the Asian financial crisis of 1997-98. The repercussions of the Asian crisis eventually forced the Fed to lower short-term interest rates in the fall of 1998, after it had previously been leaning toward raising rates in order to forestall possible future inflation (although no actual inflationary threat could be discerned). In part, the Fed's hand was forced by massive inflows of funds seeking a safe haven in U.S. government securities, which were already reducing yields on long-term bonds. The Fed's action was also motivated by the effects of the Asian crisis on the U.S. domestic economy, which were being felt through declining export demand and rising import competition from countries with depressed economies and depreciated currencies. The capital inflows certainly constrained U.S. monetary policy, by pressuring the Fed to reverse its stance on interest rates, but again the influence went in the opposite direction of that implied in the contractionary bias argument: the Fed was induced to *reduce* interest rates, not to raise them, and it did so without coordination with the European or Japanese monetary authorities.

This change in the effect of international investment on interest rate policy can be explained in terms of Keynesian theory by a change in the nature of the self-fulfilling beliefs held by market participants. As Eatwell explains:

> In his *General Theory*...Keynes likened the operations of financial markets to a "beauty contest"....He had in mind a competition then popular in the British tabloid Sunday press in which readers were asked to rank pictures of young women in the order that they believed would correspond to the average preferences of the competitors as a whole. So in order to win, the player should not express his or own preferences, nor even the genuine preferences of average opinion, but instead should anticipate "what average opinion expects average opinion to be" (Keynes, 1936, 156). In the same way, the key to success in the financial markets is not what the individual investor considers to be the virtues or otherwise of any particular policy but what he or she believes everyone else in the market will believe everyone else will think. (Eatwell 1996b, 31)

Evidently, financial market participants have become convinced that unemployment rates below 5% and growth rates above 3% do not pose an inflationary threat in the U.S. economy of the late 1990s, contrary to the previously held view that there was a "natural" unemployment rate of about 6% and a "natural" growth rate of about 2%, which the economy supposedly could not improve upon without sparking accelerating inflation.[28] Of course, investors were reassured by the fact that monetary policy was under the control of a conservative Fed, chaired by inflation hawk Alan Greenspan, and by other indicators that were seen as favorable by financial investors (including a growing budget surplus, high corporate profits, and sluggish wage increases).

It remains true that U.S. macroeconomic policy in the 1990s has been conservative overall, with fiscal policy targeted on budget balance and monetary policy targeted on price stability. One could say that macro policies have been deflationary, since inflation is currently at its lowest rate in the U.S. in over three decades[29] (although some of this decline in inflation is due to exogenous forces such as falling commodity prices, including oil prices, in the 1990s). But this deflationary policy stance has thus far not prevented a continued economic expansion—the longest peacetime expansion in the postwar period, which has brought unemployment down to rates not seen since the 1960s. Moreover, investors have changed their beliefs about how much growth and how little unemployment can be permitted without risking higher inflation, and have thereby permitted the expansion of the U.S. economy to continue beyond what was previously believed to be possible. Indeed, financial investors seem to have been out ahead of the Fed in perceiving the reduced threat of inflation in the U.S. economy. While the Fed was still proclaiming itself "leaning" toward raising short-term interest rates in late 1997 and early 1998, investors could see the absence of any perceptible inflationary threat, which led to the inversion of the "yield curve" (the relationship between short- and long-term interest rates) as long-term bond rates came down below the overnight money market rate set by the Fed.[30] In effect, investors were betting that the Fed would reverse its policy and lower short-term rates, since long-term rates reflect market expectations about future short-term rates.

Similarly, financial markets do not always penalize governments that run large budget deficits. In the early 1980s, U.S. President Ronald Reagan's fiscal profligacy was rewarded with large capital inflows into the U.S., which helped to finance the budget deficit and (along with a tight monetary policy) boosted the value of the U.S. dollar between 1981 and 1985 (see Blecker 1992; Bosworth 1993). Financial investors, both domestic and foreign, not only tolerated Reagan's deficits but bankrolled them. Of course, there were reasons for this. Investors were attracted by the high real interest rates caused by the combination of tight monetary policy and loose fiscal policy, and they undoubtedly liked the anti-inflationary bias of the Fed's monetary policy. Investors may also like deficits caused by tax cuts and military spending more than deficits incurred to pay for social welfare benefits or public investment spending[31]—which could explain why financial markets later vetoed Bill Clinton's modest "stimulus package" in 1993 (see Woodward 1994). The Reagan example suggests that capital mobility can play a key role in skewing fiscal policy in directions favored by financial and corporate interests, but it does not support the notion that capital flows always veto expansionary fiscal policies.

Thus, while capital market liberalization does contribute to an anti-inflationary bias in monetary policy, and may even lead to somewhat higher real interest rates on average (recall the results of Grilli and Milesi-Ferretti 1995, cited earlier), it does not generally enforce a steady, relentless pressure on governments to adopt contractionary policies that keep growth perpetually slow and unemployment chronically high. Eatwell (1996b, 32) seems to accept this point when he notes that the disciplining effect of international capital markets has been "erratic." His argument implies a belief that governments eventually learn from their past mistakes (or those of other countries), and adopt deflationary policies in anticipation of (and in order to forestall) potentially destabilizing financial crises. Thus he writes, "It is *potential* volatility which creates the pressures on government policy" (Eatwell 1996a, 50, emphasis in original). However, this pressure is not consistently felt, and there is a constant temptation by governments to feel that they are exempt from conventional limits on sustainable policies.

Moreover, governments that feel thus exempt are not immediately punished for their hubris. As Thurow (1998) notes, "when countries have had a string of boom years megalomania sets in and their governments *and large investors* come to feel that ordinary economic rules do not apply to them" (emphasis added). In other words, investors themselves may participate in the suspension of belief in limits to growth, thus encouraging governments to pursue potentially unsustainable policies, and there seems to be very little "learning" from past experiences (how else to explain overinvestment in Mexico only 10 years after the debt crisis of 1982?). Thus, international financial flows do not seem to maintain the type of consistent pressure on policy makers assumed in either the "sound policy" or "contractionary bias" arguments. Rather, capital flows seem to operate something like a very elastic rubber band, which stretches out when pulled, but only up to a certain point and then snaps back or breaks. Investors may overinvest in a country with flawed or inconsistent policies, but eventually—when the disequilibria get too far out of line—the investors react and pull out their funds, thus precipitating a crisis. The capital flight, then, provides the "discipline," but only after the capital inflows encourage the unsustainable policies in the first place.

Increased cyclical instability

The difficulties with the policy discipline or bias argument suggest a somewhat different critique of how international capital mobility affects domestic growth and employment. Contrary to what is sometimes asserted, macroeconomic policies that are conventionally regarded as "prudent" and "sound" (such as budget surpluses, high real interest rates, and strong currencies) along with microeconomic policies of liberalizing and deregulating financial markets do not necessarily lead to chronically slow growth and high unemployment. Rather, such a constellation of policies frequently leads to an exaggerated boom-bust cycle arising out of the internal dynamics of the private sector.[32] Rapid growth can occur for several years, fueled by private consumption and investment spending sprees facilitated by net inflows of capital. As long as the boom continues, foreign investors effectively bankroll rapid growth, lured into complacency by their belief in the "credibility" of the orthodox policy package combined with the attraction of high rates of return on domestic assets.

Later, the unsustainability of the situation becomes clear, perceptions of risk heighten, and shrewd investors (both domestic and foreign) rush to the exits. A crisis ensues, followed by a sharp contraction and often a prolonged period of stagnation. One could certainly argue that the crisis is the "discipline" that brings growth to a halt. But the capital flows in while the boom is hot, and has already left (and does not eagerly return) while the economy cools down. In short, foreign investors may reward conservative fiscal and monetary *policies*, but they do not reward contracting or stagnating *economies*. Thus, international capital flows tend to reinforce both the upswings and downswings of the business cycle, i.e., they are "procyclical." As a result, financial market liberalization and the abolition of capital controls can foster greater cyclical volatility in both financial sectors and real economies. This point is stated succinctly by D'Arista (1996):

> In terms of macroeconomic policy, the most important and damaging effect of foreign portfolio investment is that it is procyclical. It responds to cyclical developments in national markets in ways that amplify the peak or trough and duration of the cycle. (D'Arista 1996, 11)

The evidence for this critique is strong, at least for the developing countries. Each of the economies that has recently undergone a financial crisis, from Mexico to Indonesia, had a prior economic boom fueled in large measure by significant net capital inflows into its "emerging" financial market. Billions of dollars of "hot money" poured into these countries in the early 1990s, prior to their financial crises.[33] While the details of each country's boom and the trigger for its collapse have varied, the one common feature in every episode is a boom-and-bust cycle that followed upon the liberalization of capital inflows and outflows along with deregulation of the domestic financial sector (see Bullard et al. 1998; Corbett and Vines 1998; MacLean et al. 1998; Kaminsky and Reinhart 1996; Rodrik 1998; A. Singh 1998; Taylor 1998a, 1998b; Wade 1998a, 1998b). All of these countries had more growth, more investment, and larger current account deficits as a result of their increased openness to capital inflows than they would have had otherwise. And each had a much harder fall and deeper crisis later because of the impact of the massive capital flight that followed the outbreak of a self-fulfilling panic by investors, both domestic and foreign.[34]

The procyclical nature of capital flows suggests that financial investors do not focus on "sound fundamentals" in nations' economic policies, as presumed in the policy discipline argument. If investors were motivated mainly by fundamentals, they would tend to operate in a more countercyclical fashion, cautiously withholding funds during booms and then reinvesting them in downturns, motivated by a belief that in the long run countries tend to follow a "natural" growth path and do not remain permanently either booming or depressed. Investors would recognize early on when currencies were becoming overvalued in real terms, and would not continue to plow money into countries where a future devaluation seemed inevitable. If that were the case, financial speculation would be largely stabilizing rather than destabilizing. The experiences referred to here suggest the opposite: that speculation largely follows self-fulfilling expectations rather than underlying fundamentals,[35] and therefore tends to worsen rather than to ameliorate cyclical fluctuations.

Theories of why capital flows have this procyclical tendency are still being developed and are an important area for future research.[36] Taylor (1998a, 1998b), building on the work of Frenkel (1998) and Neftci (1998) on Latin America and Asia (respectively), describes a model of how cyclical instability can arise in the private sector out of the internal dynamics of the financial system under an orthodox policy regime in a developing country with liberalized capital markets.[37] The model starts with a situation in which tight monetary policy has fostered high interest rates that create large spreads in favor of home country assets. Capital market liberalization then allows massive net inflows of funds that take advantage of these spreads, while a fixed exchange rate encourages investors to ignore exchange rate risk as long as the government is believed to be able to maintain the official peg. Spreads can be amplified in deregulated stock and bond markets when asset price bubbles develop and expected capital gains are high. The domestic financial sector borrows heavily in foreign currency from international lenders at short maturities. Meanwhile, those same financial institutions re-lend the borrowed funds for longer terms in domestic assets, either paper assets or real enterprises. The underlying quality of those assets is often weak and poorly evaluated by the creditors, possibly as a result of nontransparency of balance sheet positions or "crony" relationships between borrowers and lenders (although the latter are not a necessary feature of the story). There is a substantial downside risk of a devaluation causing asset values to collapse in foreign currency terms, in which case the financial institutions that are short in foreign currency could become illiquid or even insolvent. For a long time, all these risks are underestimated, but at some point the risks become increasingly apparent, investors (both domestic and foreign) panic, net capital inflows are reversed, and a financial crisis erupts.

These dynamics of the financial sector interact with the dynamics of the "real" economy. Easy credit made possible by re-lending funds borrowed from abroad encourages domestic spending—especially investment, which can lead to the creation of excess capacity in industry or other sectors (e.g., commercial real estate in Thailand).[38] In this situation, apparently deflationary policies are not contractionary in practice, since the huge capital inflows that they attract provide ample credit to domestic businesses. At the same time, the use of a nominal exchange rate peg as an "anchor" for the price level generally leads to a real appreciation of the currency, as domestic inflation, while reduced, usually still exceeds average foreign inflation. This in turn encourages imports of both consumption and investment goods, often facilitated by simultaneous trade liberalization, while making exports less competitive. The result is a worsening problem of excess capacity accompanied by a burgeoning deficit on merchandise trade. The trade deficit is then augmented by rising net outflows of interest payments on the growing international debts, resulting in a rapidly increasing current account deficit.

Rising trade deficits, increasing foreign debts, and mounting debt service obligations eventually cause investors to revise their expectations of the risk of currency devaluation upward. Meanwhile, investors begin to perceive the risks inherent in the asset market bubbles that have built up. As currency risk premiums soar and expectations of capital gains turn negative, the perceived spreads in favor of domestic assets (factoring in the increased risk premiums) vanish. Financial investors—often led by wealthy national citizens, who have the best information—start to flee domestic assets. The ensuing capital flight turns the expectation of a devaluation into a self-fulfilling prophecy, as the government is eventually forced to devalue.

The situation can be worsened if the government stubbornly refuses to devalue and tries to defend an overvalued peg with inadequate foreign currency reserves. This invites a speculative attack, which in the end usually results in a sharper devaluation and a more severe financial panic. The situation can also be aggravated if foreign lenders call in their loans (as Japanese banks did to their Korean borrowers in 1997), if a bubble collapses in a local asset market (as in the case of commercial real estate in Thailand), or if there are contagion effects from other countries (such as the effect of Russia's collapse in undermining confidence in Brazil in 1998). However the balance-of-payments crisis unfolds, it is far more severe as a result of the opening of capital markets to unrestricted inflows and outflows, which allows the disequilibria to become larger and last longer and then also exacerbates the intensity and duration of the crash.

Lastly, there is a feedback effect from the "real" sector to the financial sector. Even before the balance-of-payments crisis breaks out, there is typically a slowdown in growth as the government ratchets up interest rates and slows spending in an effort to stave off the impending crisis (Kaminsky and Reinhart 1996). These adjustments only make fragile financial institutions more shaky, as borrowers' incomes fail to keep pace with rising debt service obligations, making loan portfolios go sour at the same time as new infusions of borrowing are harder to obtain. When the crisis breaks out, real activity collapses further, as the government usually sends interest rates through the roof and adopts fiscal austerity measures (often, but not always, under pressure from the IMF). This move, however, only further weakens the financial sector, as the number of illiquid or insolvent firms rises and the proportion of nonperforming loans increases. The financial structure suddenly appears more risky than ever, sparking further flight from domestic assets. As a result, a country's currency can continue to plummet in spite of increased interest rates, especially in Asian countries where firms typically have very high debt-equity ratios (Radelet and Sachs 1998a, 1998b; Wade and Veneroso 1998a, 1998b). Due to all of these reciprocal feedbacks between the real and financial sectors, a country can endure a downward spiral of asset values and real activity that persists for a substantial period.

While the argument about increased cyclical volatility clearly has much resonance in light of recent events, it is also not without potential criticisms. There is a counter-argument implicit in other accounts of the Mexican and Asian financial crises, which put more emphasis on policy errors and domestic factors. One version of this argument claims that many countries have provided excessive amounts of deposit insurance and "lender-of-last-resort" intervention, which have exacerbated "moral hazard" problems and encouraged undue amounts of imprudent lending (McKinnon and Pill 1996). This story has an excellent theoretical pedigree, but exaggerates the extent to which most developing countries effectively guarantee investors and banks against losses (see Noland et al. 1998; Taylor 1998b). Another version of the argument focuses on the order of liberalization efforts. According to many experts, international capital flows should be liberalized gradually and markets for short-term capital should be opened only after other forms of liberalization and reform—such as liberalization of trade barriers, macroeconomic (fiscal and monetary) policy stabilization, liberalization of direct investment, and improved prudential supervision of banks—have been implemented (see Fischer and Reisen 1992; McKinnon 1993). In this latter view, capital market liberalization is still desirable, but only in countries that have achieved a certain level of development of their domestic financial systems, which makes them better prepared to handle the pressures of international financial flows.

Some analyses place more stress on specific policy mistakes by individual countries. For example, Mexico has been faulted for failing to devalue its currency sooner (Dornbusch and Werner 1994) or for allowing excessive monetary growth (Sachs et al. 1996b) before the December 1994 peso crisis. Many of the Asian countries have been blamed for problems of weak banking supervision and a lack of transparent accounting practices. But as Rodrik (1998) notes, few of these policy mistakes (he calls them "policy errors *du jour*") were recognized as serious problems in advance, none of them apply generally to all the countries that have had financial crises recently, and none of them can explain the severity of the crises. Rather, it appears that increased capital mobility has made the consequences of otherwise minor policy mistakes (or long-term structural weaknesses) far more severe and has exaggerated the underlying volatility of domestic economies.

Nevertheless, the increased cyclical volatility argument is most plausible for developing countries with underdeveloped internal capital markets and inadequate domestic banking supervision and financial regulation. While it is easy to see how capital mobility can foster instability in such countries, it is not clear whether capital mobility also worsens cyclical instability in more developed economies with more advanced mechanisms for prudential regulation of financial institutions. This is an important issue for the United States because of the magnitude of the net capital inflows that have pouring into this country in recent years, [39] which pushed up the value of the dollar in 1995-98 and have contributed to worsening current account deficits, asset market bubbles for stocks and bonds, and rising international debts (see Morici 1997; Blecker 1998a). The Frenkel-Neftci model summarized by Taylor (1998b) assumes "stylized facts" based on conditions in Latin America and East Asia, where financial regulatory systems were inadequate and currencies were pegged at unsustainable values. At a minimum, this model would require substantial revisions to be applicable to the U.S. economy, in which regulatory systems are more capable and the exchange rate is flexible. However, as the U.S. becomes more open to trade and investment flows and as the U.S. international debt position worsens, the possibility that the U.S. economy could be destabilized by international financial flows cannot be readily dismissed, and is an important topic for future research.

To the extent that liberalized capital flows worsen macroeconomic fluctuations, the presumption of beneficial effects of capital mobility on economic efficiency is undermined. The efficiency argument presumes that all resources (including labor and capital equipment) are fully employed, and that the only issue is where those resources can be deployed with the greatest productivity at the margin. However, if rapid reversals of capital flows contribute to overheated booms followed by severe depressions, capital cannot be presumed to be flowing in the most productive directions. On the one side, excessive amounts of capital may be deployed in places where they are not really needed or likely to offer high future returns during an overinvestment boom. On the other side, when investors flee a country in a panic, capital may fail to flow into locations and sectors where it could in fact be highly productive and offer attractive long-term returns. Thus, capital flows can exacerbate macroeconomic fluctuations while failing to enhance microeconomic efficiency.

Conclusions

There is little question that the drive to open national capital markets to unregu-lated flows of short-term portfolio capital was based on weak theoretical foun-dations and scanty empirical evidence—especially in less-developed countries with underdeveloped domestic financial systems. Although there are many nu-ances in the debate over capital market liberalization and many issues that re-quire more research and analysis, given what has long been known about the problems of information and volatility in liberalized capital markets, the rush to abandon all restrictions on capital movements was clearly premature. For countries with fixed exchange rates, large foreign currency debts, and inad-equate prudential regulation of domestic financial institutions, capital market liberalization was nothing short of irresponsible.

Instead of waiting for more evidence—or even considering the evidence that was already available—policy makers in the U.S. government and the IMF encouraged a headlong rush into a risky policy change.[40] And by pushing the same policy on so many countries at the same time, the capital market liberalizers unintentionally paved the way for the very contagion effects and correlated risks that they now profess to find so surprising. This point has now been tacitly conceded at the IMF and U.S. Treasury, where the new watchword is the need for more "orderly" financial market liberalization phased in along with domes-tic regulatory reforms (see, e.g., Eichengreen and Mussa 1998; Fischer 1998; Summers 1999).

Many elements in the critique of capital market liberalization appear to be strongly supported by the evidence. The argument that short-term capital flows are often based on self-fulfilling expectations rather than underlying eco-nomic fundamentals is now widely accepted. Also, it seems clear that capital market liberalization often fosters financial volatility that in turn causes or ex-acerbates real economic instability in developing countries. But the ways in which domestic economic policies are constrained by global financial markets turn out to be complex and subtle. Since the one thing that surely scares off financial investors is the risk of high inflation, policies that are regarded as anti-inflationary are a precondition for financial investors to bankroll rapid growth. But beyond that, there seems to be plenty of room for international capital flows to effectively support a range of specific policies, including policies that allow for periods of rapid economic growth—and policies that often turn out to be unsustainable in the long run. And some of the constraints that are often claimed to be imposed by capital mobility turn out to result from the *combination* of capital mobility with *other* factors, such as fixed exchange rates or large foreign-currency debts, rather than from capital mobility per se.

Ultimately, the constraints on policy are as much political and ideological as they are economic (Epstein 1993). An inability on the part of governments to adopt policies that undermine the interests of financial investors suggests that financial interests have gained greater influence at the expense of other economic interests, such as manufacturing, labor, and agriculture, not to mention environmental or consumer concerns. Moreover, financial interests may be linked to other powerful interests, such as "footloose" multinational corporations that seek to escape from national regulations in the various countries in which they operate. But in this respect, the economic constraint of capital mobility clearly interacts with the political constraints of power and ideology. In the words of Glyn (1998, 408), "the internationalization of finance...has increased the speed at which, the drama with which, and the costs imposed when financial markets bring retribution on governments whose policies are not deemed credible."

Chapter 2

International financial models and their policy implications

The Washington Consensus economic policies promoted by the IMF and the U.S. government are grounded in certain theoretical models of international financial markets and their impact on national economies. These models have strong implications for what kinds of monetary, fiscal, and exchange rate policies countries should adopt, and how the effectiveness of those policies varies depending on whether capital markets are open or closed. Like all economic theories, these traditional models of international finance are based on simplifying assumptions, and their relevance to contemporary conditions depends heavily on how well those assumptions mirror the essential aspects of more complex situations in today's world. As this chapter will show, the older generation of models that underlies the Washington Consensus policy approach rests on assumptions that fail to capture the salient features of today's globalized financial markets. In particular, these models ignore the potentially destabilizing dynamics of liberalized capital flows and unrestrained currency speculation that have sparked repeated financial crises and caused real economic turmoil. As a result, these models are obsolete and no longer provide reliable guides to policy.

This is not to say that the older theories are of no use. The traditional models still provide useful foundations for logical thinking about exchange rates and the balance of payments. The "fundamentals" of countries' money supplies, interest rates, budget deficits, and other macroeconomic variables emphasized in the older theories are still significant for explaining international financial flows and even for analyzing speculative behavior. However, the presumptions in the older models that international financial flows tend to be stable, that exchange rate changes are predictable, and that payments imbalances are easily corrected have all been overturned. Much new research, both theoretical and empirical, has shown that liberalized capital movements can have destabilizing effects on financial systems and real economies that were not contemplated in the older models. Moreover, exchange rate fluctuations are now recognized to be unpredictable based on any conventional model. And new theoretical models reveal why traditional cures for payments imbalances are often less effective, and have more undesirable side effects, than the older theories implied. This new research—some of it, ironically, produced in the research department of the IMF itself—has been largely ignored by policy makers who continue to rely on outmoded theories. As a result, it should not be surprising that the application of Washington Consensus policies has proved so ineffective for halting the spreading contagion of financial crises in the 1990s.

This chapter will survey the main strands in international financial modeling, from the earliest theories of automatic balance-of-payments adjustment to the most recent models of self-fulfilling bubbles and panics in foreign exchange markets. For the reader interested in global financial policy, there are two reasons to pay careful attention to these models. First, they give us tools for analyzing how much autonomy governments have over their economic policies, under a variety of conditions, in a world of liberalized capital flows. And second, these models constitute the framework of the policy conversation—the language of the expert debate over how countries should manage their monetary, fiscal, and exchange rate policies. If one wants to enter these debates and to develop alternatives to the Washington Consensus approach, one needs to be armed with an understanding of the theories that support alternative policy perspectives.

Before proceeding to the survey of models, a few caveats are in order. First, the ultimate objectives of international economic policies are actually aspects of domestic economic performance, such as sustainable growth, full employment, price stability, and living standards. However, international finance affects domestic performance in these areas through a set of intervening variables, especially exchange rates (i.e., the prices at which different currencies trade for each other) and the balance of payments (i.e., the payments for transactions in goods, services, and assets between residents of different countries). Therefore, our survey will be organized around a series of approaches to modeling exchange rates and the balance of payments, even though our ultimate concern is with the effects of policy on domestic economic performance.

Second, while we will explain the core logic of each model, we do not attempt to cover all of the mechanics and technicalities of the models—for these, the interested reader should consult a good international finance textbook.[1] Instead, we emphasize the policy messages of the models: what they tell us about global financial constraints on domestic macroeconomic policies, and how they inform our understanding of the policy options available to national governments and international organizations today. In order to keep the survey brief and accessible, it will be restricted to the simplest and most basic cases of the various models. While we will attempt to indicate some of the complexity and subtlety of each theoretical approach, some of the richness and flexibility of the models is inevitably lost in such a survey, and the interested reader is referred to the sources we cite for further details.

Finally, even the simple models surveyed in this chapter can be difficult to understand, and the discussion is inevitably dense at points. Every effort has been made to make the survey as accessible as possible to readers without advanced technical training in international economics. Also, a glossary has been included at the end of the book to explain some commonly used terms in discussions of global financial issues. Nevertheless, some background in macroeconomics and international economics is helpful for understanding this chapter, and the reader who finds it rough going may want to skim over some of the more difficult parts.

A typology of models

International financial theories can be grouped into four broad categories along two different dimensions, the balance of payments and the exchange rate, as shown in **Figure 2.1**. One dimension concerns whether, in their treatment of the balance of payments, the models emphasize the current account and monetary ("official") reserves or the capital account and private ("unofficial") asset markets. These items correspond to the three parts of a country's balance of payments: the current account includes trade in goods and services plus net income from foreign investment, migrant labor remittances, and transfer payments; official reserve transactions are purchases or sales of gold and currencies by central banks; and the capital account records all other foreign asset transactions (international borrowing and lending, and purchases and sales of all internationally traded assets other than central bank monetary reserves). The more traditional theories emphasized the first two of these parts and neglected the third, while more recent theories emphasize the third part, i.e., the capital account or asset transactions. The second dimension concerns the factors that are assumed to determine exchange rates, which may be either macroeconomic "fundamentals" (such as money supplies, interest rates, fiscal policies, income levels, and price levels) or autonomous dynamics of the financial markets themselves (such as herd behavior and self-fulfilling prophecies on the part of currency speculators).

Of course, any such effort to categorize theoretical models inevitably oversimplifies. For example, most of the models in the second row do have some elements (sometimes strong elements) of fundamentals built in. And some of the models in the upper-left box can allow for capital flows, although those models emphasize other factors. The typology is based on what are the most salient or distinguishing characteristics of each modeling approach.

Most of the theories are found in the first row and the lower-right hand box; there are only a few models that emphasize autonomous foreign exchange market dynamics without also emphasizing the capital account. Thus, the evolution of international financial theories has proceeded mainly across the first row, and then down the second column. Early models that focused on the current account (mostly merchandise trade) and monetary reserves domi-

FIGURE 2.1 Typology of international financial models

		BALANCE-OF-PAYMENTS ADJUSTMENT DRIVEN BY:	
		The current account and monetary reserves	The capital account and asset markets[a]
EXCHANGE RATES DETERMINED BY:	Macroeconomic fundamentals	• Specie flow mechanism • Elasticities approach • Absorption approach • Monetary approach • Purchasing-power parity	• Mundell-Fleming model • Asset approach and portfolio balance models • Exchange rate overshooting model • Intertemporal models of the current account • Balance-of-payments-constrained growth with capital mobility
EXCHANGE RATES DETERMINED BY:	Autonomous financial market dynamics	• Speculative attack models (first generation)[b]	• Random walk models • Long swings • Speculative bubbles • Speculative attack models (second generation)[b] • Contagion effects • Self-fulfilling panics • Financial fragility and debt-deflation crises

Notes:
[a] The term "asset markets" here refers to "unofficial" assets in the balance of payments, i.e., assets other than central bank reserve holdings of gold, foreign exchange, and government bonds. The Hume specie-flow mechanism and the monetary approach are excluded from this category because they incorporate only official reserve assets.
[b] All speculative attack models contain elements of self-fulfilling prophecies (which are a type of autonomous financial market dynamic), since a speculative attack can force a government to abandon an exchange rate peg before it would otherwise do so. However, these models also contain specifications of fundamentals, which influence the probability and timing of an attack. These models differ in regard to whether they include unofficial capital flows and whether a successful speculative attack can occur in the absence of some prior inconsistency in the fundamentals. See text for further discussion.

nated until the 1960s.[2] During the 1960s and 1970s, in response to the growing importance of international capital flows, new theories were developed that began to place more emphasis on international asset transactions and the capital account in the balance of payments, but these theories still assumed that exchange rates were determined by fundamentals. Since the 1980s, still newer models have been developed that not only emphasize asset markets and the capital account, but also allow for movements in exchange rates and other asset prices to be driven by speculative behavior that can be delinked to some extent from the underlying fundamentals. Our discussion will focus on these three types of theory, while making only brief reference to the fourth (lower-left) box in the figure.

Models without capital mobility

The earliest theories of the balance of payments and exchange rates focused on the merchandise trade balance, with monetary flows seen as accommodating trade imbalances.[3] These theories assumed that any adjustments that took place would tend to be self-equilibrating in the sense of tending to eliminate trade surpluses or deficits. Since these models mostly ignore capital mobility, they do not have direct implications for how such mobility does or does not constrain policy. Nevertheless, these models are significant for their claims about the self-correcting nature of international payments imbalances in the absence of capital mobility. Moreover, these models provided the building blocks for the later, more complete models with capital mobility. And, most importantly, *these simple models still form the basis for much policy thinking in today's world*, even though many of their results have been undermined by later theoretical developments that incorporate capital mobility and speculative behavior.

The specie flow mechanism

The earliest balance-of-payments adjustment model is the classical specie flow mechanism, attributed to Hume (1752).[4] In this model, if a country has a trade surplus, the surplus will be accommodated by a net inflow of gold bullion ("specie"), assuming a gold monetary standard. The net inflow of gold then increases the nation's money supply, thereby raising the price level (assuming that the "quantity theory of money" holds, i.e., the price level is proportional to the money supply). A higher price level in turn makes the country's products less competitive, causing exports to fall and imports to rise until the trade surplus is eliminated—at which point, the specie flows cease. The reverse series of steps occurs under a trade deficit, i.e., gold leaves the country, prices fall, and exports rise and imports fall until the deficit disappears.

This model was used to argue against the mercantilist view that governments should intervene to promote trade surpluses in order to increase national income and employment, on the basis that such surpluses could not be sustained. Essentially, the policy message was that a country should not worry about its balance of trade and cannot do anything about it anyway. However, the model is only valid under extremely restrictive assumptions, including the absence of international borrowing and lending (i.e., capital immobility) and the operation of the quantity theory of money (which in turn assumes perfectly flexible prices and perpetual full employment).

The elasticities approach

In the late 19th and early 20th centuries, it was recognized that these assumptions do not necessarily hold and hence the automatic adjustment promised by the specie flow mechanism would not necessarily work. In response to this recognition, the elasticities approach to the balance of payments analyzed whether a currency devaluation could be successful in improving a country's trade balance. To understand the elasticities approach, note that a country's trade balance (measured in domestic currency units) can be expressed as:

Trade Balance = Value of Exports – Value of Imports
= (Price of Exports **x** Quantity of Exports) –
(Price of Imports **x** Quantity of Imports)

A devaluation makes imports more expensive in domestic currency terms and thus raises the price of any given quantity of imports. Hence, assuming that the price of exports is fixed in domestic currency terms, relatively large changes in the quantities of traded goods (increases in exports and decreases in imports) are required to offset the higher price of imports and improve the trade balance.[5]

This approach shows that a devaluation can improve a country's trade balance, but only if the quantities of exports and imports respond sufficiently to the price changes brought about by the devaluation (which makes exports cheaper in foreign currency, and hence more competitive in global markets, and makes imports more expensive in domestic currency, so that domestic consumers buy fewer imports). In technical terms, the "elasticities"[6] of supply and demand for exports and imports (with respect to prices) have to be of the right magnitudes for a devaluation to be effective in increasing the trade balance. In the simplest version of the model, which assumes that prices are fixed in the seller's currency, costs of production are constant in each country,[7] and trade is initially balanced, the requisite condition for a devaluation to improve the trade balance is the Marshall-Lerner condition (named for the two economists who invented it, Alfred Marshall and Abba Lerner): the sum of the price elasticities of demand for imports and exports must be greater than one. Then, the increased quantity of exports and the reduced quantity of imports will outweigh the higher domestic currency prices of the imports, and the trade balance will improve. In more complex models (e.g., with increasing costs of production or an initial trade deficit), more complex conditions are required for the same result to obtain, but these conditions all depend on the magnitudes of the relevant elasticities.

The elasticities approach promised a fairly simple cure for a trade deficit: devalue the currency. For a country with a fixed exchange rate, this is simply a matter of increasing the official price of foreign exchange.[8] Alternatively, if a country has a flexible exchange rate, it was traditionally assumed that the currency would naturally depreciate in response to a trade deficit, since (in the absence of capital flows) a country with a trade deficit would also have an overall balance-of-payments deficit implying excess demand for foreign exchange. Excess demand for foreign exchange would tend to increase its price in relation to domestic currency, thus depreciating the latter. This idea was the basis for the widespread belief that letting currencies float would tend to eliminate trade imbalances. As we shall see later, however, this belief is not generally valid when capital is mobile.

Many economists were initially skeptical that the elasticities of supply and demand were of sufficient magnitudes for devaluations to be effective, leading to what was known as "elasticity pessimism." Subsequently, however, numerous empirical studies (e.g., Houthakker and Magee 1969; Cline 1989; Bosworth 1993) have found reasonably high price elasticities of demand for most industrialized countries' exports and imports that easily satisfy the Marshall-Lerner condition. Nevertheless, many developing countries have low price elasticities of demand for imports (since those countries lack domestic substitutes for many imported goods), as well as low price elasticities of supply and demand for primary exports (agricultural and mineral products—for which consumer demand tends to be inflexible, and supplies are sometimes hard to adjust). Such "rigidities" in how quantities of imports and exports respond to the price changes brought about by a devaluation can make devaluation ineffective and even counterproductive in developing countries, possibly even lowering the trade balance (especially when there is a large initial trade deficit and the trade balance is measured in domestic currency). Developing countries are also often very dependent on imports of crucial raw materials and basic consumption goods, in which case a devaluation significantly raises the costs of production (including nominal wages, if there is "real wage resistance"[9]). In this case, a devaluation causes domestic prices to rise and fails to stimulate exports.

Even in the industrialized countries, there are other problems with the elasticities approach. For example, the assumption that traded goods prices are fixed in the seller's currency is not generally valid. Exporters may "price to market," in which case there is only "partial pass-through" of the exchange rate change into the destination currency price.[10] An example of this occurred when the U.S. dollar depreciated and the Japanese yen appreciated in the late 1980s. Japanese exporters raised the dollar prices of their exports by a smaller percentage than the yen rose—thus effectively accepting lower yen prices and lower profit margins for their exports in order to prevent too large a loss of market share in the U.S. In this case, the quantity of U.S. imports from Japan did not fall by as much as it would have if the Japanese had kept their yen prices constant and passed through the entire cost of the higher yen to U.S. consumers.

But the point that originally stimulated the most criticism of the elasticities approach was the fact that it implicitly held the level of national income constant, and thus ignored the effects of a devaluation on national income and their feed-backs onto import demand. After all, if the trade balance improves, as one hopes following a devaluation, more income flows into the pockets of domestic workers and consumers—who are then likely to use some of this increased income to buy more imports. How can one then be sure that the trade balance will end up higher after all these effects of the devaluation are played out?

The absorption approach

These types of income effects were emphasized in the next generation of models, known as the absorption approach. The term "absorption" refers to a country's total domestic expenditures: the sum of total consumption spending, investment in new capital goods, and government purchases. Alexander (1952) noted that the trade balance (defined as exports minus imports) must equal the difference between a country's national income and its domestic expenditures, or, equivalently, its national saving minus its domestic investment. Thus:

Trade Balance   = Exports – Imports
                              = Income – Expenditures (absorption)
                              = Saving – Investment

To understand conceptually why all these differences must be equal to each other, one needs to realize that a country running a trade surplus must effectively lend to the rest of the world enough funds to cover the excess of the country's exports over its imports, while a country running a trade deficit must borrow enough from the rest of the world to pay for the excess of its imports over its exports.[11] What a country has to lend out is the extra income it is not spending, which must be equal to the extra saving it is not using to finance investment at home. In the case of a country that is borrowing, it must borrow to cover the excess of its expenditures over its income, which must be the same as the portion of domestic investment that is not being financed by domestic saving.[12] In all of this discussion, the trade balance is measured by the broad definition of the current account in the balance of payments (given above),[13] and "national saving" is defined as total domestic saving including the government budget surplus (which is negative if there is a budget deficit) as well as the private saving of households and corporations.

Once one understands these equations, one can see that a devaluation improves the trade balance if and only if it raises income relative to expenditures or, equivalently, raises saving relative to investment. This can occur, for example, if the devaluation makes imported consumption goods (and domestic substitutes) more expensive, and as a result consumers reduce their real expenditures.[14] Also, if the devaluation increases exports and aids import-competing industries, national income should rise, and as long as less than 100% of the increased income is spent, income will rise by more than expenditures. Higher income should also boost saving, hopefully by more than it boosts investment. Increased saving can also result from the redistributive effects of a devaluation: if a devaluation allows firms to raise prices and increase their profit margins, it reduces real wages of workers and redistributes income to corporations (and their stockholders and bondholders)[15] who are likely to save a higher proportion of their income than workers.[16]

The absorption approach shifted the emphasis in the analysis of balance-of-payments adjustment away from devaluation alone to devaluation combined with other policy tools. In particular, it led to a focus on "expenditure-reducing" policies (such as reductions in budget deficits) as complements to "expenditure-switching" policies (such as devaluation or import restrictions) for rectifying trade deficits. Both types of policy operate to improve the trade balance, but the former has contractionary macroeconomic effects while the latter (under the favorable conditions assumed in the elasticities approach) can have expansionary effects. In theory, then, these two types of policies can be combined in a judicious blend that leaves the national income of a country unchanged while the trade balance improves.[17] This double-barreled policy approach has become one of the cornerstones of IMF stabilization policies in countries experiencing balance-of-payments problems.

In practice, however, the combination of the two types of policies (devaluation and expenditure reduction) has often ended up being severely contractionary. This is largely because the devaluation part of the package often has depressing effects on aggregate demand that were not anticipated in the standard models, especially in developing countries where the relative price effects of devaluation often don't work as intended for the reasons noted earlier.[18] In these situations, the onus of adjustment falls mainly on expenditure reductions, either directly (e.g., via reduced government spending) or indirectly (e.g., via a devaluation causing a fall in real wages).

The absorption approach has thus been applied mainly to designing policies for deficit countries; hence the emphasis on expenditure-*reducing* policies. Conceptually, however, there is no reason why this approach cannot also be applied to surplus countries, where it implies that expenditure-*increasing* policies (such as fiscal expansion) are needed, along with currency appreciation. This point is important because a policy approach that focuses only on how the deficit countries should adjust leads to a contractionary bias in the global economy, as emphasized by Davidson (1996). If only a few small countries have deficits and reduce their expenditures, they may suffer recessions, while the global economy as a whole is little affected. But if a significant number of countries that collectively form a large part of the global economy are all acting to solve their deficits by reducing their expenditures simultaneously—as has occurred in East Asia since 1997—the result can be a serious drag on the entire global system. Thus, the absorption approach can be used to justify a different policy stance, focusing on the need for demand-side stimulus in the surplus countries (in today's world, mainly Japan and the EU) to maintain global aggregate demand and employment (see Blecker 1998a).

The monetary approach

The monetary approach[19] is based on the fact that, in a country with a fixed exchange rate, any imbalances in international transactions must ultimately be settled by flows of internationally accepted monetary assets, such as gold or hard currencies (e.g., U.S. dollars). In the simplest monetary approach model, which we will consider here, all international transactions are for goods and services; there are no private capital flows or international borrowing and lending.[20] In this situation, trade imbalances must be offset by monetary flows: surplus countries receive net inflows of money, while deficit countries have net outflows. If one further assumes that the public in each country has a certain amount of money balances (cash and bank deposits) that it wishes to hold to carry out its transactions, and that this "demand for money" can differ from the supply emitted by the country's central bank and banking system, then the difference between a country's demand for money and its supply of money must be met by a net inflow of money from other countries, which supplies the excess demand for money. Thus, a net inflow of money is the other side of the coin of a trade surplus (or, a net outflow indicates a trade deficit).

In this model, a country with an excess demand for money spends *less* (on goods and services) than its income, thereby running a trade surplus that brings in an inflow of monetary payments, which in turn increases the supply of money until it equals the demand (at which point trade is balanced). Alternatively, a country with an excess supply of money spends *more* than its income, resulting in a trade deficit that sends the excess money abroad—thus lowering the country's money supply until it equals the demand and trade is again balanced. Thus, monetary inflows or outflows automatically restore balanced trade by adjusting money supplies back to levels that are in equilibrium with the public's demand for money. This is similar to what is hypothesized in the specie flow mechanism, except that in the modern monetary approach the adjustments can take place entirely through changes in money supplies and expenditure levels, and do not require flexible prices.[21]

The monetary approach thus has a simple and clear policy message: since balance-of-payments problems are caused by excessive monetary creation, the solution lies in tighter monetary policy.[22] Again, for countries with balance-of-payments problems, this simple wisdom has become canonized in the IMF's standard policy package, which includes slower monetary growth and higher interest rates as key components. Indeed, combining the three "approaches" to the balance of payments just discussed, one can understand the rationale for the three key elements of any IMF stabilization package: currency devaluation (based on the elasticities and absorption approaches), fiscal austerity (based on the absorption approach), and monetary tightening (based on the monetary approach). Although the global economy has changed dramatically since these simple theories were invented, they continue to be the basis for the adjustment policies that the IMF and the U.S. government promote. Whether this trinity of stabilization policies is still appropriate in the contemporary global economy will be discussed further below.

Purchasing-power parity

The last theory in the first group (upper-left box of Figure 2.1) is the doctrine of purchasing-power parity (PPP), originally developed by Cassel (1922, 1928). The PPP hypothesis states that tradable goods should sell at equivalent prices in different countries, when the prices are converted to a common currency. This hypothesis is based on the assumption of commodity price arbitrage in competitive international markets: if a good is cheaper in one country than in another country, it will pay for traders to "buy cheap and sell dear" until neither country has a price advantage over the other. This mechanism can work either through exchange rate changes, if exchange rates are flexible (since the cheaper country's currency would be expected to appreciate), or through changes in goods prices, if exchange rates are fixed.

The "absolute" version of PPP implies that exchange rates should equal the ratio of the price levels in the home and foreign countries, for comparable goods and services. The "relative" version of PPP implies that changes in nominal exchange rates should exactly offset changes in relative price levels, which means that real exchange rates (nominal exchange rates adjusted for inflation at home and abroad) should remain constant.[23] Relative PPP is a weaker proposition because it does not require that goods and services sell for equivalent prices in all countries, only that the relative prices of goods and services in different countries stay constant over time.

Although the theory of PPP is not explicitly concerned with policy, it does have a strong policy implication. That is, this theory suggests that there are powerful, automatic forces tending to prevent persistent competitive advantages of one country over another and thus to correct imbalances in international trade. Hence, the implicit policy message of PPP is one of laissez-faire: if currency values are out of line, and international trade is imbalanced, governments need do nothing in response, since real exchange rates can be expected to revert to equilibrium levels at which overall competitive advantages are eliminated and balanced trade is restored.

Merely to state the logic of PPP, however, is to reveal the weakness of its fundamental assumptions. To begin with, trade barriers, transportation costs, and information problems prevent complete arbitrage of international price differentials. Secondly, while some goods may be "perfect substitutes" regardless of the country in which they are produced (e.g., a certain grade of crude oil), other goods clearly are not. If goods are differentiated in some qualitative respects (e.g., French versus California wines, or Japanese versus Korean cars), their prices cannot be expected to be uniform. Thirdly, many goods and services are not internationally traded, in which case average price levels (e.g., in terms of a consumer price index) need not converge even if prices of traded goods do converge.

Capital mobility further undermines the presumption of a tendency toward PPP, especially when combined with flexible exchange rates. When capital is mobile, exchange rates are determined by the demand and supply for foreign exchange for *all* types of transactions—including purchases and sales of assets (bonds, stocks, bank deposits, loans, etc.) as well as trade in ordinary goods and services. If the value of asset transactions far exceeds the value of trade in goods and services, as is presently the case, then exchange rates are determined primarily by the perceived relative advantages of investing in assets denominated in different currencies.[24] This asset-driven determination of exchange rates may pull a currency's value in the opposite direction of that required for PPP. For example, if Japanese investors decide to buy more U.S. bonds, the increased purchases of dollars push up the value of the dollar, even if Japanese goods are underselling U.S. goods and Japan has a large trade surplus with the United States.

Empirical tests of the relative PPP hypothesis have had mixed results.[25] There is universal agreement today that PPP does not hold in the short and medium runs—i.e., periods of up to five or 10 years—except for countries experiencing hyperinflation, compared with countries with more stable price levels. In the United States, the real exchange rate does not stay constant, as predicted by relative PPP, but rather has tended to move in close synchronization with the nominal rate since the dollar began to float in the 1970s. This tendency can be seen graphically in **Figure 2.2**, which shows that the real value of the dollar has closely tracked its nominal value since 1975. If relative PPP held, the real dollar index (the dashed line in Figure 2.2) would be flat. The fact that the dashed line fluctuates so widely means that the real purchasing power of the dollar over imported goods and services has varied over time, rather than remaining constant as implied by relative PPP.

For the long run (periods of several decades or more), there is some evidence that PPP held in the pre-1973 era of mostly fixed exchange rates and limited capital mobility. For the post-1973 era of mostly floating exchange rates and increased capital mobility, the evidence is mixed, and it is sensitive to the particular exchange rates studied and statistical methods used. Numerous studies using time-series methods have shown that real exchange rates have not generally been stationary (i.e., mean-reverting) since 1973. Bleaney and Mizen

FIGURE 2.2   Nominal and real indexes of the value of the U.S. dollar (quarterly, 1975 Q1 to 1998 Q4)

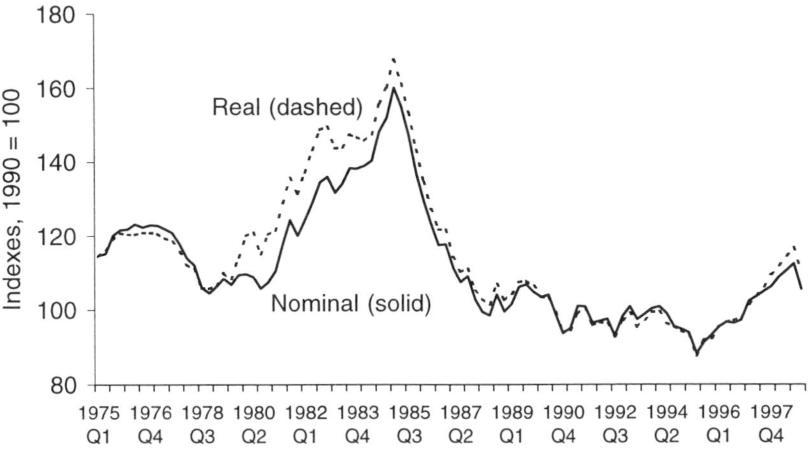

Source: International Monetary Fund, *International Financial Statistics* (various issues).

(1996) find that, while real exchange rates have not been stationary, they have fluctuated within relatively wide bands around their mean levels in the post-1973 period. If there is a tendency for exchange rates to revert to PPP levels, it is at best one that operates slowly and unevenly, and nothing that could be counted on to eliminate payments disequilibria within a socially acceptable time frame.[26]

Estimates of absolute PPP exchange rates (i.e., exchange rates that would equalize prices of goods and services across countries) are often notably out of line with estimates of equilibrium exchange rates that would stabilize current account balances or debt-to-GDP ratios (sometimes called "fundamental equilibrium exchange rates"[27]). For example, recent estimates (Williamson 1994; Wren-Lewis 1998; Wren-Lewis and Driver 1998; Bank for International Settlements 1998a, 103-4) show that the dollar should be moderately lower against the old German mark (and the new euro) and significantly lower against the Japanese yen just in order to stabilize U.S. trade deficits with Europe and Japan, compared with current market exchange rates—and the dollar would have to fall even further to reduce the U.S. trade deficit. However, PPP estimates show exactly the opposite, i.e., the dollar would have to rise in value against the mark (or euro) and the yen in order to achieve PPP. This suggests that PPP exchange rates can be quite misleading guides to policy. In the cases of U.S.-European and U.S.-Japanese exchange rates, any efforts to make actual rates move toward PPP levels would be a disaster, since they would result in explosive trade imbalances (i.e., larger and ever-growing U.S. trade deficits).

Conclusions on the early models

Early international financial models, which largely ignored capital mobility, promised a relatively easy and painless set of cures for international payments imbalances. Currencies would automatically adjust in the right direction to maintain balanced trade, if exchange rates were flexible, or could easily be manipulated to accomplish the same objective if they were fixed. Real output and employment need not be adversely affected by such adjustments. Countries that let their exchange rates float (or adopted "realistic" pegs for their fixed rates) and adopted "sound" macro policies (small budget deficits or budget surpluses and slow, steady monetary growth) were assured that all would be well in their international finances and their domestic economies. But as capital mobility became a more important factor in determining countries' balances of payments and exchange rates, this confidence in the stability of the international financial system was soon undermined—and economic theory has been struggling to keep up with the destabilizing effects of capital mobility ever since.

Fundamentals-based models with capital mobility

The surge in international capital mobility since the 1960s has brought forth a spate of new models that have sought to incorporate capital mobility into theories of exchange rates and the balance of payments. None of these models was intended to entirely displace the earlier theories that focused primarily on the current account. Rather, the intention was to construct more general models that would highlight the implications of capital mobility while still incorporating the insights of the earlier models. Indeed, the older models can be seen as special cases of the newer ones assuming that capital is immobile.

The Mundell-Fleming model

The first theoretical framework that highlighted the role of international capital mobility was the Mundell-Fleming model (Mundell 1963; Fleming 1962), which was essentially an open-economy extension of the dominant macroeconomic model at the time, the neo-Keynesian "IS-LM" model.[28] Mundell-Fleming is significant because it reflects the "conventional wisdom" on how capital mobility does (or does not) constrain the effectiveness of fiscal and monetary policies at the national level. While there are different versions of the model, we shall limit ourselves here to the most basic case of a small, open economy with perfect capital mobility, in which the world rate of interest is taken as given. Assuming further that the home country's assets (bonds) are perfect substitutes for foreign assets and ignoring all types of risk (e.g., country risk or exchange risk),[29] the interest rate on domestic bonds must equal the (given) interest rate on foreign bonds.

On these assumptions, the Mundell-Fleming model makes a striking set of predictions about how the effectiveness of monetary and fiscal policies (for increasing national income and employment in the short run) depends on the exchange rate regime. With a fixed exchange rate, monetary policy is powerless, because any effort to increase or decrease a country's domestic money supply is quickly and fully offset by the net outflows or inflows of monetary reserves that are required to maintain the exchange rate target (outflows when the money supply is increased, and inflows when it is decreased).[30] However, fiscal policy is very powerful with a fixed exchange rate and capital mobility, since a change in government spending (or taxes) induces a change in the money supply in the same direction as the fiscal policy shift (i.e., either expansionary or contractionary).

For example, starting from balance-of-payments equilibrium, a fiscal stimulus (i.e., a spending increase or tax cut) causes a balance-of-payments surplus by drawing in net capital inflows to finance the increased budget deficit.[31] The balance-of-payments surplus in turn causes a net inflow of monetary assets (hard currency reserves), which have to be accumulated by the central bank in order to maintain the fixed exchange rate (i.e., to prevent the home currency from appreciating in response to the greater supply of foreign currency). Essentially, the central bank emits more domestic money in exchange for the foreign currency it buys up, thus adding a monetary stimulus that complements the original fiscal expansion. Thus, with a fixed exchange rate, a country's money supply is effectively "endogenous"—i.e., determined by forces inside the economy (in this case, what the central bank has to do to maintain the fixed exchange rate)—and cannot be controlled independently by policy makers.[32]

These results are exactly reversed with a flexible exchange rate—in which case the money supply becomes "exogenous," or subject to control by policy makers. In this case, monetary policy is very powerful—in spite of the fact that a small country cannot control its own interest rate in this model—because of its impact on the exchange rate. A monetary expansion, for example, causes the currency to depreciate by increasing the supply of domestic money relative to the demand. The depreciation in turn improves the trade balance and thereby increases national income and employment, assuming that the conditions highlighted in the elasticities and absorption approaches are met and that the economy is operating below full employment to begin with.

However, a fiscal stimulus is completely ineffective with a flexible exchange rate, because the fiscal stimulus makes the exchange rate move in the wrong direction (appreciation). This occurs because the fiscal stimulus draws in capital inflows in order to finance the government's increased budget deficit. With the interest rate unable to rise due to perfect capital mobility, and with the central bank not intervening to buy up the excess supply of foreign exchange, the exchange rate (price of foreign exchange) must fall, and hence the domestic currency has to appreciate. The domestic currency rises until the fall in the trade balance exactly offsets the rise in the fiscal deficit, at which point there is no change in the level of national income.[33]

The standard conclusions of the Mundell-Fleming model can thus be encapsulated as follows:

> To summarize the conclusions regarding perfect capital mobility, there is a neat symmetry in the results. Under fixed exchange rates, fiscal policy reaches its peak effectiveness, but monetary policy becomes completely powerless. Under floating exchange rates, by contrast, fiscal policy loses all power, and it is monetary policy that reaches its peak effectiveness. (Caves et al. 1990, 597)

The Mundell-Fleming model suggests that the effectiveness of monetary policy depends mainly on whether exchange rates are fixed or flexible, not whether capital is mobile or immobile. Indeed, this model suggests that monetary policy is *most* powerful when capital is mobile and exchange rates are flexible, because in this case the rapid movements of capital in response to incipient interest rate differentials (which are presumed to be so rapid as to keep actual interest rates equal to world rates) make the exchange rate changes occur even more quickly than they would with immobile capital. The effectiveness of fiscal policy also depends on the exchange rate regime. In particular, fiscal policy is ineffective with a flexible exchange rate because the capital movements induced by a fiscal stimulus lead to a perverse exchange rate change that worsens, rather than eliminates, the trade deficit caused by the fiscal stimulus. This result highlights the fact that capital mobility can impede the kind of automatic adjustment of the trade balance that was featured in earlier models that ignored capital mobility.

However, the strong conclusions of the basic Mundell-Fleming model result from strong assumptions that do not generally hold in the real world. For example, the result that monetary policy is most powerful with perfect capital mobility and a flexible exchange rate assumes that the relevant elasticities are large enough for a depreciation to significantly improve the trade balance, which may not be true in all countries. Also, the simple Mundell-Fleming model assumes that domestic and foreign bonds are "perfect substitutes," in which case perfect capital mobility implies equalization of interest rates at a unique world level. But bonds from different countries are generally imperfect substitutes since they may embody different risks. When assets are imperfect substitutes, then—even with perfect capital mobility—nominal interest rates can differ across countries as a result of expectations of exchange rate changes and perceptions of country risk.[34] Since the results of the basic Mundell-Fleming model rest on the assumption that a small country with perfect capital mobility cannot affect its own interest rate, those conclusions need to be modified when more financial market complexity is added to the model.[35]

The basic Mundell-Fleming model also assumes that central banks allow net inflows or outflows of foreign exchange reserves to affect domestic money supplies. In reality, central banks that buy or sell foreign exchange reserves in order to manage exchange rates often "sterilize" those changes in reserves (i.e., neutralize their effects on the money supply) by selling or buying domestic reserve assets (government bonds) to offset the changes in foreign exchange reserves. If central banks sterilize, then the monetary repercussions of the Mundell-Fleming model with fixed exchange rates need not occur.[36] For example, a fiscal expansion will be less effective under a fixed exchange rate than the model predicts if the central bank sterilizes the inflow of foreign exchange reserves by selling government bonds, since this move will prevent a complementary domestic monetary expansion from occurring.

Also, some of the strong results of the Mundell-Fleming model depend on the implicit assumption that monetary and fiscal policies operate independently. For example, the ineffectiveness of fiscal policy with a flexible exchange rate and perfect capital mobility assumes that the central bank manages to hold the money supply constant in spite of the increased demand for credit stimulated by a fiscal expansion. If monetary policy is accommodative, or if the money supply is effectively endogenous (determined by the public's demand for bank credit, rather than controlled by the central bank's policy actions),[37] then the currency need not appreciate and the fiscal stimulus could have positive effects. Considering that central banks often do (at least partly) accommodate fiscal expansions when exchange rates are flexible, and that they often sterilize changes in foreign exchange reserves when exchange rates are fixed, the effects of fiscal policy need not differ so much between the two types of exchange rate regimes, as the simple Mundell-Fleming model implies.

The asset approach and the portfolio balance model

In the 1970s, dissatisfaction with the treatment of capital mobility in the monetary approach and the Mundell-Fleming model led to a broader "asset approach" to the balance of payments and exchange rates. The basic idea of the asset approach is that international investors may hold their wealth in a variety of forms, including different national currencies, bonds and other financial assets denominated in different currencies, and real assets (such as corporate equity or real estate) located in different countries. In general terms, the supplies and demand for all of these assets simultaneously determine the prices of the assets (including the exchange rates, which are the prices of the currencies) and the corresponding rates of return (e.g., interest rates on bonds). The asset approach literature contains a vast array of different models that cannot be summarized in a short space. We shall focus here on one influential model of this type, the portfolio balance model. This model has many extensions and applications, and only a basic version will be discussed here.[38]

In the basic version of the model, investors hold three assets in their portfolios: domestic money, domestic bonds, and foreign bonds. Domestic residents hold the foreign bond, but foreign residents do not hold the domestic bond. Usually, money is assumed to pay zero interest, while each type of bond has its own interest rate (the bonds are imperfect substitutes). The shares of total wealth held in each of the three assets depend on the interest rates on the two bonds: money demand depends inversely on both interest rates, while the demand for each bond depends positively on its own interest rate and negatively on the other interest rate. The exchange rate enters the model only in converting a given value of foreign-denominated bonds into domestic currency units. In the basic model, only positive stocks of the foreign asset are held; thus the consequences of foreign debt positions are not usually considered. For a small country, the foreign interest rate can be taken as given and the model can be solved for the domestic interest rate and the exchange rate (taking the stocks of the three assets as given in the short run).

The portfolio balance model can be used to analyze a variety of policy options, including monetary expansion (via open market purchases of either domestic or foreign bonds), monetary-financed fiscal expansion, and bond-financed fiscal expansion. The results are varied but, in general, show that *both* fiscal and monetary policies can affect *both* the interest rate *and* the exchange rate with perfect capital mobility (contrary to the Mundell-Fleming model, which assumes that neither kind of policy can affect the interest rate). In the short run, a monetary expansion generally lowers the interest rate and depreciates the currency. A fiscal expansion has more ambiguous short-run effects. A fiscal expansion raises the domestic interest rate if it is bond-financed and lowers it if it is money-financed. A money-financed fiscal expansion definitely depreciates the currency, while a bond-financed fiscal expansion can either appreciate or depreciate the currency depending on the degree to which domestic and foreign bonds are substitutes. Only in the case where the two types of bonds are close substitutes does one get the Mundell-Fleming result that the currency appreciates (which makes sense, since Mundell-Fleming assumes the extreme case of perfect substitutes).[39]

The portfolio balance model also provides an analysis of long-run adjustments in exchange rates and the current account. The dynamics of adjustment derive from the fact that a current account surplus (or deficit) leads to an increase (or decrease) in the holdings of the foreign asset, since the capital account consists of purchases (or sales) of the foreign bond. Thus, for example, if a country runs a current account deficit, the stock of foreign bonds will decrease gradually over time. As the supply of foreign bonds falls relative to the demand for those bonds, at a given foreign interest rate, the price of the foreign currency (the exchange rate) must rise, i.e., the home currency must depreciate. The currency depreciation will continue until a new long-run equilibrium is reached in which the current account is balanced.[40] Thus, the portfolio balance model predicts that stock-flow adjustments in the presence of capital mobility will generally move the exchange rate in the right direction to eliminate a current account deficit in the long run.

Although the portfolio balance model generated a lot of intellectual excitement when first proposed, it has since fallen into disfavor. The model seemed plausible in the 1970s, when the major country with chronic trade deficits (the United States) experienced a tendency for its currency to depreciate after the adoption of floating rates in 1973. However, more recent experiences have not been as kind to the model's predictions. In the period 1981 to 1985 and to a lesser extent from 1995 to 1998, the dollar tended to appreciate rather than depreciate in spite of large and growing U.S. current account deficits (see Figure 2.2 above). Undoubtedly, other factors have been at work, including some that could be analyzed using the portfolio balance model. For example, increased perceptions of risk in other countries have induced investors to want to hold more U.S. assets—especially very safe ones like treasury bonds—which pushes up the value of the dollar. Nevertheless, these experiences have undermined faith in automatic exchange rate adjustments as a means for eliminating current account deficits.

Formal statistical tests of the portfolio balance model have turned out poorly. A series of econometric studies has found that the effects of relative asset supplies on exchange rates are either statistically insignificant or have the wrong signs, compared with the predictions of the model (Hallwood and MacDonald 1994, 199-203). Yet, the basic conceptual approach of modeling investors' choices among alternative assets is so intuitively appealing that one wonders why better results have not been obtained.

A possible explanation for the poor predictive performance of the portfolio balance model is suggested by Taylor (1998c), who argues that the standard formulation of the model does not adequately specify the full array of assets that needs to be taken into account in analyzing international portfolio choices. Among other things, the standard version of the model ignores home country debt (i.e., foreign ownership of domestic bonds)[41] and also neglects crucial distinctions between different categories of asset owners (households, business firms, commercial banks, central banks, and governments). By providing a more complete accounting of asset ownership and more comprehensive wealth identities (based on work by Godley 1996) in a two-country framework, Taylor shows that many of the standard results of the simple portfolio balance model can be reversed. For example, in the standard model, a depreciation of the home currency increases the home country's wealth because it increases the domestic currency value of foreign bonds owned by domestic residents. But Taylor shows that a depreciation reduces home country wealth as long as foreign ownership of domestic bonds is greater than the domestic central bank's holdings of foreign currency reserves.

Taylor also shows that the portfolio balance model cannot explain all of the variables (interest rates and exchange rates) that its originators intended it to explain when the full array of assets is taken into account. In a two-country version of the model, Taylor shows that the asset market equilibrium conditions can determine only two out of the three key variables, the home and foreign interest rates plus the exchange rate.[42] Hence, if one wants to solve the model for both interest rates and the exchange rate, it is necessary to further specify the behavior of the exchange rate itself. In effect, this means that the strong predictions of the simple portfolio balance models about the stabilizing direction of exchange rate movements have a weak theoretical foundation. Taylor's more general model reveals the possibility of dynamically unstable cases in which exchange rates tend to move away from levels that would equilibrate current account balances, or may oscillate around equilibrium levels in a cyclical fashion. Overall, Taylor's work suggests that the standard portfolio balance model is too restrictive; however, his work also suggests that the basic approach of modeling portfolio choices between alternative assets is a good one that can be extended to more complete and realistic scenarios—including debts as well as assets.

Exchange rate overshooting

Another theory that emphasizes the role of the capital account is the exchange rate overshooting model developed by Dornbusch (1976). This model was motivated by the instability of floating exchange rates that was observed after the Bretton Woods system of "adjustable pegs" broke down in 1973. By the mid-1970s, it was evident that floating exchange rates tended to fluctuate rapidly up and down rather than to adjust smoothly to new equilibrium levels, and in the process there were noted short-run departures from PPP. This led to a search for theoretical models that could explain such volatility in floating exchange rates.

The basic concept of overshooting is that an exchange rate may move past its new long-run equilibrium level in the short run following a monetary policy "shock." Then, the exchange rate has to reverse direction as it subsequently adjusts to its new long-run equilibrium level. **Figure 2.3** gives a hypothetical example of overshooting in the U.S. dollar-U.K. pound exchange rate.

FIGURE 2.3 An example of exchange rate overshooting

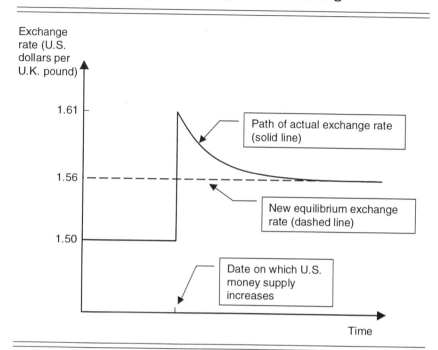

Note: See text for explanation.

In the figure, the exchange rate is steady at $1.50/£ until there is a sudden 4% increase in the U.S. money supply on a certain date (holding the U.K. money supply constant). This causes the equilibrium exchange rate to rise by 4% to $1.56/£ (shown by the dashed line in the figure).

Dornbusch argues that the actual exchange rate will not stop at the new equilibrium level in the short run, but instead will initially overshoot that level. The reason is that, in the short run, the increase in the money supply causes the domestic interest rate to fall. Assuming that the foreign interest rate is unchanged,[43] investors will be willing to hold domestic bonds if and only if they expect the home currency to *appreciate* by enough to compensate for the lower interest rate on domestic bonds. Dornbusch therefore invokes the assumption of "uncovered interest parity," which implies that the expected change in the exchange rate must be equal to the international interest rate differential.[44] In our example, for the dollar to be expected to appreciate, it must depreciate more in the short run than it has to in the long run. If we suppose (hypothetically) that the U.S. interest rate initially drops to 3 percentage points below the U.K. interest rate, and also assume that currency traders know that the true long-run equilibrium exchange rate is \$1.56/£, then the exchange rate must initially rise (i.e., the dollar must fall) by 3% *beyond* the new equilibrium level to approximately \$1.61/£ in order to create an expectation that the dollar will subsequently rise by 3%.

In order to guarantee this result, Dornbusch assumes that expectations are "consistent" in the sense that market participants have correct knowledge of the long-run equilibrium exchange rate. He also assumes that investors are "risk-neutral," in the sense that they don't care about the risk of the exchange rate not changing as expected, and therefore they don't require a risk premium to hold the foreign bond. Dornbusch further assumes that the goods market adjusts slowly (i.e., prices are rigid in the short run and adjust slowly over time), while asset markets clear instantaneously (i.e., interest rates and exchange rates immediately "jump" to market-clearing levels following a policy change). This is why the monetary stimulus causes the interest rate to fall and the exchange rate to over-shoot in the short run. However, as the price level gradually increases, the real effects of the monetary stimulus are gradually eroded (in technical terms, "real balances" fall back to their initial level), and the interest rate rises back to equal the foreign interest rate. As these long-run adjustments play out, the exchange rate gradually falls (i.e., the dollar gradually appreciates) until it reaches its new long-run equilibrium level (as shown by the solid line in Figure 2.3). As this long-run adjustment takes place, the price level eventually rises in the same proportion as the money supply increased and the equilibrium exchange rate rose, so that in the long run relative PPP holds and the monetary expansion has no real effects. In other words, in the long run, the nominal depreciation of 4% just compensates for a 4% higher price level at home and the real exchange rate is unchanged.

The Dornbusch overshooting model thus provides an ingenious theoretical explanation for short-run volatility in exchange rates. In spite of its impressive logical structure, however, this model rests on a number of dubious assumptions. Most empirical tests (surveyed by Mussa and Goldstein 1993; Hallwood and MacDonald 1994; and Marston 1995) have shown that the uncovered interest parity condition does not generally hold. The studies that have rejected uncovered interest parity generally imply that there are significant risk premiums that change over time, which the Dornbusch model ignores.[45] The assumption that money is neutral in the long run has been challenged by many Keynesian economists, who argue that changes in nominal price levels have lasting, long-term effects on real economic activity as a result of their effects on the real values of assets and debts (see Tobin 1980; Minsky 1986; Palley 1996).[46] The assumed consistency of investors' expectations of future exchange rates is also problematic, since the evidence indicates that expectations of exchange rate changes are frequently biased predictors of actual changes (see Frankel and Rose 1995). For these reasons, it is doubtful that Dornbusch's model explains the observed volatility of exchange rates.

Empirically, the Dornbusch model also seems flawed. This model predicts that, in response to a change in monetary policy, one should see a rapid, one-time jump of the exchange rate in one direction, followed immediately by a sharp movement in the reverse direction toward the new long-run equilibrium, as shown in Figure 2.3. In reality, the initial response of exchange rates to monetary policy changes seems to be more gradual and prolonged than the Dornbusch model predicts, and the predicted adjustments toward long-run equilibria in response to monetary policy shocks are often postponed longer than the model would lead us to expect.[47]

The intertemporal approach to the current account

All of the models with capital mobility discussed thus far (Mundell-Fleming, portfolio balance, and exchange rate overshooting) utilize what is broadly called the "income-expenditure approach." These are open economy extensions of traditional neo-Keynesian macroeconomic models based on the IS-LM framework. These models all combine elements of the older elasticities, absorption, and monetary approaches to exchange rates and the balance of payments, modified to take account of capital mobility. Since the 1980s, these models have been displaced in some academic circles by a new generation of models based on the assumption of intertemporal optimizing behavior by consumers, i.e., consumers rationally deciding how to allocate their earnings over different periods in their lifetimes (plus bequests to their descendants).

This intertemporal approach builds upon the observation in the absorption approach that a country's current account balance equals the difference between its national saving and its domestic investment, i.e., its net lending to the rest of the world (or net borrowing, if the difference is negative). While the neo-Keynesian models assume that consumers save and consume fixed fractions of their after-tax income, the intertemporal models assume that consumers' saving and consumption decisions in the present are determined by farsighted, rational plans for future consumption—including the consumption of future generations as well as the consumption of the current generation in retirement—and hence saving and consumption respond flexibly to economic incentives such as changes in interest rates.

In regard to policy implications, the intertemporal approach is marked by a striking paradox. On the one hand, advocates of this approach make strong claims for the normative superiority of their models for evaluating alternative policies:

> The Mundell-Fleming approach offers no valid benchmark for evaluating external balance. In practice, policymakers often strive to avoid a negative current account....however, efficient trade across time often calls for an unbalanced current account. The intertemporal approach identifies

circumstances, for example, a transitory fall in output or a rise in domestic investment productivity, that justify a current account deficit....The intertemporal approach to the current account offers a viable framework for assessing macroeconomic policy, one that must supplant the Mundell-Fleming model for normative questions. (Obstfeld and Rogoff 1995, 1794)

On the other hand, as advocates of this new approach are the first to admit, it has thus far had virtually no impact on actual policy making, which continues to be based on the older models. As Obstfeld and Rogoff (1995, 1794) concede, the Mundell-Fleming approach, "which ignores intertemporal choice and even intertemporal budget constraints, remains overwhelmingly dominant in policy circles." One reason for the negligible impact of the new models is that they are so complex that they do not yield simple policy rules that can be understood without an intimate knowledge of the models themselves. Although the intertemporal models yield very precise-sounding results about how fiscal policy affects interest rates, exchange rates, and the current account under various conditions,[48] they contain so many special cases and contingent results that even their advocates are hard-pressed to summarize their implications in terms that nonspecialists could understand.[49]

In fact, these models make too many far-fetched assumptions to be reliable guides to policy analysis. The amounts of information and computational capabilities that individuals would have to have in order to make the kinds of optimizing decisions contemplated in these models are utterly implausible (Taylor 1991). As Keynes (1936) taught, saving decisions are based on setting aside income for an uncertain future, not on definite plans for future consumption. Moreover, empirical evidence is not generally consistent with some of the predictions of intertemporal optimizing models, such as the implication that consumption growth should be an increasing function of interest rates and unrelated to income growth (see Carroll and Summers 1991). In addition, these models all assume Say's Law, which implies that output is determined only by supply-side factors and that there is always full employment of labor and other resources. Models that ignore the demand side in analyzing the dynamics of international investment are unlikely to yield useful results—especially since most empirical studies of investment find strong effects of demand-side variables (Blecker 1997). Overall, support for the intertemporal approach seems to rest more on the a priori beliefs of some economists in the ultra-rationality of human behavior and the efficiency of markets rather than any demonstrated relevance of these models for explaining actual data or informing policy choices.

Nevertheless, the advocates of the intertemporal approach make some valid points. Current account imbalances create net asset or debt positions that have implications for future payments balances and growth trajectories. Thus, it is important to analyze the long-term dynamic implications of current international borrowing and lending activities. The intertemporal theorists also deserve credit for taking a more subtle view of fiscal policy, rather than just focusing on the level of the budget deficit per se:

> A proper analysis of the effects of fiscal policies on the world economy cannot be carried out on the basis of a single aggregate measure of the fiscal stance such as the budget deficit. It must be based on more detailed and specific information on government spending and taxes. On the spending side, such information must specify the distribution of spending between tradable and nontradable goods and its intertemporal allocation. On the revenue side, the information must specify the characteristics of the tax system, including the timing of taxes and the types of taxes used to finance the budget. (Frenkel and Razin 1992, 309)

But these valid points can be appreciated—and modeled—without making the strong assumptions of the intertemporal models with regard to long-term consumer optimization and perpetual full employment.

Balance-of-payments-constrained growth

Although the intertemporal approach does not offer realistic models for policy analysis, it does raise important issues about the sustainability of international capital flows (lending and borrowing) and how such flows affect long-run economic growth. A more promising approach to modeling this issue is found in the literature on "balance-of-payments-constrained growth," originally developed by Thirlwall (1979) and extended to incorporate capital mobility by Thirlwall and Hussain (1982) and Moreno-Brid (1998-99).[50] This approach is concerned with external demand constraints on countries' ability to grow and how those constraints can be relieved by capital inflows. Essentially, this approach builds on the elasticities and absorption approaches to the balance of payments, but instead of using them to analyze the effects of a devaluation on the trade balance, it uses the same concepts to analyze how the growth of national income must be limited in order to prevent trade imbalances from growing too large.

The basic premise of this approach is that, since domestic growth generates a rising demand for imports, a country cannot grow too fast without generating a perpetually increasing trade deficit. The question then is how to specify this limit on a nation's long-term, average growth rate more precisely. Consider first the case where a country must keep its trade in goods and services balanced (on average) in the long run—either because capital is immobile, or because short-term capital inflows are easily reversed and cannot be sustained in the long run. In this case, according to Thirlwall's model, a country's growth must be limited by the rate of growth of its exports relative to the income elasticity of its demand for imports (i.e., how much imports grow in response to income growth) in order to prevent import expenditures from outstripping export revenues.[51] This result assumes that all of the adjustment burden falls on income growth and none on relative prices (real exchange rates)—either because relative PPP holds in the long run (so that relative prices and real exchange rates do not permanently change), or else because relative price effects on demand for imports and exports are negligible due to low price elasticities (failure to satisfy the Marshall-Lerner condition).[52]

This model can then be extended to show how long-term net capital inflows can relax the balance-of-payments constraint on growth by allowing countries to finance chronic trade deficits (and thus pay for additional imports) through sustained international borrowing. Thus far, there have been two approaches to analyzing this effect. Thirlwall and Hussain (1982) show that net capital inflows allow a country to grow faster than it could without such inflows, but only if the capital inflows grow more rapidly than export earnings (on average, in the long run). Moreno-Brid (1998-99) argues that Thirlwall and Hussain's approach does not constrain the net capital inflows to grow at a rate that is sustainable in the long run, because it allows those inflows to lead to a perpetually increasing debt burden (in the sense of a continuously rising debt-income ratio). Moreno-Brid proposes an alternative concept of long-run balance-of-payments equilibrium with capital flows, in which the ratio of the current account deficit to domestic income must remain constant (and the debt-income ratio stabilizes) in the long run. Moreno-Brid shows that sustainable net capital inflows (by this definition) allow a country to increase its growth rate as long as the country has an initial current account deficit and a relatively high income elasticity of demand for imports (i.e., imports respond strongly to income growth).

The balance-of-payments-constrained growth model with capital mobility explains the underlying reason why countries want capital inflows in order to boost their growth, i.e., to enable them to afford the additional imports that are required for more rapid growth. This model also makes it clear that the growth-stimulating effects of capital inflows are sustainable only as long as the capital inflows themselves are sustainable—not if capital inflows ebb and flow in a boom-bust cycle. However, even with Moreno-Brid's extensions, the model still does not include a full analysis of the financial market dynamics that determine whether net capital inflows are sustainable in the long run. As Moreno-Brid writes, a more complete analysis requires "adding behavior[al] specifications of the main debit and credit items of the capital account of the balance of payments and examining the macroeconomic impact of changes in their flows as well as in their respective stock positions" (1998-99, 286).[53]

Taylor (1997) provides a more explicit model of the dynamics of international debt accumulation. Taylor's model of two countries with international lending and borrowing incorporates the well-known condition that international debt burdens are sustainable only if the growth rate of output exceeds the interest rate. His model also reveals a number of other conditions that affect whether international lending is a stable process or leads to explosive debt burdens.[54] This paper is only a beginning, however, and much more work is needed to understand the impact of international debt dynamics on economic growth and instability.

Conclusions on fundamentals-based models

All the models we have covered so far analyze exchange rates and the balance of payments based on underlying economic fundamentals such as interest rates, national income and expenditures, fiscal and monetary policies, and price levels. The predictions of these models vary widely, as we have seen. The earliest models, which ignored capital mobility, tended to focus on the price competitiveness of internationally traded goods and services, as well as the effects of fiscal and monetary policies on flows of income and expenditures. These models generally taught that trade surpluses or deficits would lead to offsetting movements in either money supplies or exchange rates, which would smoothly and automatically restore balance-of-payments equilibrium with balanced trade—or else that simple policy responses (such as devaluations of pegged currencies) could easily and painlessly eliminate payments imbalances.[55]

Such simple verities were then supplemented with—and partly overturned by—the various models that incorporated capital mobility. The Mundell-Fleming model showed how the exchange rate could move in the opposite direction from what is required for current account balance, if a country attracts large enough capital inflows to sustain chronic current account deficits. The portfolio balance model revealed that the effects of fiscal policy on exchange rates depend not only on the openness of domestic capital markets, but also on the degree to which domestic and foreign assets are substitutes for each other. The exchange rate overshooting model showed that capital flows could lead to exaggerated fluctuations in exchange rates and interest rates, taking price rigidities and exchange rate expectations into account. The balance-of-payments-constrained-growth model showed how capital inflows can relax the constraints on countries' growth imposed by rising demand for imports, but only if those inflows are sustainable in the long run.

All of the preceding analyses presume that exchange rates are essentially *predictable*, based on some underlying fundamental factors. While the models give different views on which fundamentals should be emphasized, they all imply that exchange rates should move in predictable directions in response to changes in those factors. Even the overshooting model, which emphasizes exchange rate *volatility*, still assumes that exchange rate fluctuations are predictable based on known fundamentals such as money supplies and interest rates. Moreover, this presumption of predictability is not just an intellectual exercise; it is an essential aspect of the analysis underlying all of the policy implications of the models. For example, the Mundell-Fleming result that a fiscal stimulus is ineffective with perfect capital mobility and a flexible exchange rate is valid *only* if the model is correct in forecasting that such a stimulus causes the currency to appreciate. But the record of all these models in predicting exchange rates is quite poor, as we shall see in the next section.

Models of speculative behavior and financial instability

After more than 25 years of experience with floating exchange rates since the collapse of Bretton Woods in 1973, international financial economists have been forced to admit that their ability to predict exchange rate movements using fundamentals-based models is at best limited, and at worst nil. We have already discussed the fact that efforts to predict long-run movements in exchange rates by PPP have produced only mixed results. For shorter-term movements in exchange rates, the fundamentals-based models have had even less predictive success. In an exhaustive survey of the empirical literature on exchange rates,[56] two top international economists conclude that:

> no model based on such standard fundamentals like money supplies, real income, interest rates, inflation rates and current account balances will ever succeed in explaining or predicting a high percentage of the variation in the exchange rate, at least at short- or medium-run frequencies. (Frankel and Rose 1995, 1707-8)

What is broadly known as the "asset market approach" to exchange rates suggests a reason *why* they are so unpredictable. That is, since exchange rates are prices of assets (national currencies), their prices depend above all on expectations about future events that will affect the values of those assets—including expectations of future policies as well as the actions of other agents in the markets. "News" that causes such expectations to be revised therefore leads to sudden and dramatic short-term movements in exchange rates, while as long as current expectations are confirmed market participants will continue to bet in the same direction. This asset market perspective forms the basis for a number of efforts to explain what drives fluctuations in exchange rates, if they are not responding in a predictable fashion to the traditional fundamental variables.

Random walks and long swings

An important benchmark in the econometric literature on exchange rates is the finding that they cannot be predicted better than the "naive" assumption that they follow a statistical "random walk." A variable follows a "random walk" if its value in one time period equals its value in the previous period (which is called the "lagged" variable) plus a random change, which can be either positive or negative. Thus, the finding that exchange rates follow random walks implies that the best predictor of a current exchange rate is its own previous value, regardless of the current or past values of any of the fundamentals (money supplies, interest rates, etc.). As Frankel and Rose summarize the evidence,

> By the early 1980s..., some early apparent empirical successes in the literature had been overturned and key empirical findings began to turn negative, a state of affairs that continues through the present day. The most profound negative result was produced by Meese and Rogoff (1983a,b), who compared the predictive abilities of a variety of exchange rate models. Their key result was that no existing structural exchange rate model could reliably out-predict the naive alternative of a random walk at short- and medium-run horizons, even when aided by actual future values of the regressors. This extremely negative finding has never been entirely convincingly overturned despite many attempts. The simple random walk model of the exchange rate has become the standard benchmark for empirical exchange rate performance, no matter how uninteresting it is per se. (Frankel and Rose 1995, 1690-91)

To be sure, some researchers, using some statistical methods for some datasets for some countries and time periods, have reported results where some particular model can outperform a random walk (see Hallwood and MacDonald 1994, 179-80, for citations). But these results have generally required considerable "tweaking" of the data and are very sensitive to the datasets and modeling specifications used. Moreover, the predictions thus obtained may only marginally improve upon a random walk model—and beating a random walk is a rather weak standard of predictive ability. Overall, current research shows that no fundamentals-based model can reliably forecast short-term exchange rate changes better than a random walk model in most countries most of the time.[57]

This conclusion undermines *all* of the standard analyses of the effects of macroeconomic policies or other parameter changes on exchange rates in the fundamentals-based models discussed above. Consider what would happen to the U.S. dollar if, for example, the United States improved its competitiveness, or cut taxes, or lowered interest rates. While there are many models that give very specific predictions about these effects (including careful qualifications based on different conditions and assumptions), the empirical results suggest that the best answer in every single case is that *we just don't know for sure.* The dollar could go up, down, or nowhere, in response to any of these changes in fundamentals. And if we don't know how these changes will affect the exchange rate, we can't be sure how they will affect ultimate policy targets such as growth rates or inflation rates.

Nevertheless, the random walk model should not be taken too literally. It is useful as a statistical benchmark for evaluating the predictive powers of alternative models, not for its own sake. Indeed, there is evidence that fluctuations in exchange rates are more complex than a simple random walk process, even if exchange rates are largely independent of fundamentals in the short-to-medium run. For example, Engel and Hamilton (1990) find persistent movements in the U.S. dollar that can be characterized as "long swings." That is, the dollar tends to trend upward (or downward) for periods of several years, before reversing itself and moving the other way (as can be seen in Figure 2.2 above). Technically, what Engel and Hamilton do is to test the hypothesis of "segmented trends" in the value of the dollar against the alternative hypothesis of a simple random walk. Engel and Hamilton's results show that the segmented trends hypothesis gives better out-of-sample forecasts than the random walk for three different bilateral exchange rates (the U.S. dollar with the German mark, French franc, and British pound) for up to three or four quarters. However, Engel (1992) found that the long swings model was not superior to the random walk model for a number of other exchange rates.

The long swings view of exchange rates is just as destructive of fundamentals-based models as the random walk view. In either view, exchange rates are largely determined by some autonomous process in the foreign exchange market itself, rather than by the predictable influence of fundamental macroeconomic variables and policies. Nevertheless, the long swings view suggests the need to investigate the reasons for persistent movements of exchange rates in one direction or the other, as well as to identify factors that can cause reversals in those trends.

Speculative bubbles and herd behavior

The most popular explanation for persistent deviations of exchange rates from levels consistent with the fundamentals is the notion of speculative bubbles. A speculative bubble emerges when investors buy one currency and sell another based solely on the expectation that the first currency will appreciate relative to the other. If a sufficient number of speculators act in this manner, based on a common set of expectations (including the expectation that most other market participants share the same view of which way the exchange rate will go), the demand that is thus created for the currency that is expected to appreciate actually causes that currency to rise in value. Thus, a speculative bubble in a foreign exchange market is a case of "self-fulfilling expectations" in which investors follow "herd behavior," as discussed in Chapter 1.

Speculative bubbles are nothing new, of course. A long historical literature has documented—and debated—past episodes of speculative frenzies or "manias" in everything from Dutch tulip bulbs in the 17th century to the New York stock market in the 20th century (see, e.g., Kindleberger 1989; White 1990). In recent years, economic theorists have focused much of their attention on how speculative bubbles in asset markets can be reconciled with the postulate of "rational behavior" (see, e.g., Blanchard and Watson 1982; Rosser 1996, 1997).[58] For present purposes, however, the issue of whether bubbles are generated by rational or irrational behavior is of secondary importance; the key question, rather, is whether there are bubbles in foreign exchange markets that make exchange rates deviate persistently from the levels implied by macroeconomic fundamentals.

Interest in applying the bubble concept to exchange rates burgeoned with the sustained appreciation of the U.S. dollar in the early 1980s, shown in Figure 2.2 above, which to many observers seemed to go beyond a level that could be explained by the fundamentals. To be sure, there were plenty of reasonable fundamentals-based explanations of why the dollar *started* rising in the early 1980s. These explanations included increased U.S. interest rates (relative to other countries), expansionary fiscal policy (in line with the Mundell-Fleming model), tax cuts that attracted foreign investors, and increased foreign risk premiums (the "safe haven" argument). But the dollar *continued* to rise for several years, and even *accelerated* its climb in late 1984 and early 1985, well after most of these changes had occurred, and even after some of them had reversed themselves (for example, the U.S.-German interest differential peaked in 1984, while the dollar did not peak until 1985). Moreover, the dollar's rise continued in spite of one fundamental indicator that it should depreciate (according to the portfolio balance model): large and rising current account deficits.

Although the U.S. experience in the mid-1980s is consistent with a bubble explanation, proving that a bubble actually occurred is not a simple matter. In order to test that hypothesis, one has to determine whether the exchange rate persistently moved away from a level that would be consistent with the fundamentals—and this requires specifying a model of the relevant fundamentals. In technical terms, any statistical test for a speculative bubble really tests the "joint hypothesis" of the assumed model of the fundamentals *and* the presence of a bubble. In plain English, if we are not sure what is the correct model of the fundamentals, then we cannot be sure that we have reliable evidence for the alternative hypothesis of a bubble. Thus, one classic econometric study of this question modestly concludes that its "results are *consistent* with the *possible* existence of bubbles in exchange markets" (Meese 1986, 369, emphasis added).

Krugman (1985, 1987) examined whether there was a bubble in the U.S. dollar in the mid-1980s. He constructed a simulation model to test whether the level the dollar had reached by early 1985 was sustainable, given the exchange rate expectations implied by the interest rate differential between the U.S. and other countries.[59] Krugman's model showed that, if the dollar fell only gradually from that level (as implied by the modest interest differential), the U.S. would have faced continued large trade deficits for many years and an exploding international debt. Believing such a debt explosion to be unsustainable—because it would create a risk of U.S. default that would deter foreign investors from continuing to accumulate U.S. assets—Krugman concluded that the markets must have been underestimating the degree to which the dollar had to fall. Thus, the markets were making "a massive mistake" (Krugman 1989, 108); investors were simply ignoring fundamentals that were painfully obvious to anyone who cared to look for them. Therefore, at least part of the dollar's rise toward its 1985 peak must have been due to a speculative bubble, and "when the market realizes that the dollar must fall more rapidly than previously believed, the result is the bursting of that bubble" (Krugman 1989, 94).[60]

Thus, in spite of the difficulties in proving the existence of exchange rate bubbles, the preponderance of evidence supports the conclusion that such bubbles do occur. The conclusion that exchange rates often follow bubbles instead of fundamentals does not imply that we can ignore the fundamentals, however. Understanding the relevant fundamentals is crucial not only for diagnosing whether a speculative bubble exists, but also for predicting the necessity of a bubble eventually bursting. Thus, Frankel and Rose (1995) argue for the development of "a theory of endogenous speculative bubbles," which in their view must explain three things: (1) how exchange rates can deviate from equilibrium values and speculative bubbles can arise, (2) how speculative bubbles are propagated and prolonged once they have begun, and (3) how the fundamentals eventually reassert themselves and cause the bubble to burst. In this view, modeling of macroeconomic fundamentals remains important, not for predicting short-term movements in exchange rates but rather for understanding long-term limits on exchange rate fluctuations. While this view makes sense, it leaves open the question of whether the traditional models of the "fundamentals" surveyed above are the right ones to use for this purpose, a point to which we shall return below.

Speculative attacks on pegged exchange rates

While speculation can generate bubbles in floating exchange rates, it can also destabilize fixed exchange rates—broadly defined to include crawling pegs, joint floats, and other hybrid systems, as well as fixed nominal parities. A speculative attack occurs when currency traders who fear that a currency will be devalued (or allowed to float) decide to sell the currency, thus forcing the central bank to spend down its reserves and adjust other policies (e.g., raising interest rates) in defense of the peg. In many cases, speculators can attack a currency with borrowed funds, i.e., borrow a currency and then immediately sell it. If the attack succeeds, the authorities are forced to abandon the peg, in which case the expectation of a devaluation becomes a self-fulfilling prophecy—and the speculators profit handsomely (e.g., because they can repay their loans at a lower cost after the devaluation). Speculative attacks are not new; the assault on the British pound that forced the devaluation from \$2.80/£ to \$2.40/£ in 1967 is just one example. But interest in speculative attacks has exhibited a veritable bubble of its own in the 1990s, after a wave of incidents starting with the runs on the British pound and Italian lira in September 1992, and continuing with the Mexican peso crisis of December 1994, the various Asian currency crises in 1997-98, the Russian ruble crisis of August 1998, and the Brazilian devaluation of January 1999.[61] Moreover, capital market liberalization now allows speculative attacks to occur much more quickly and with greater force than before.

Theoretical models of speculative attacks are placed along the second row of Figure 2.1, because they all incorporate a certain element of self-fulfilling prophecies. At a minimum, all of these models imply that a government can be forced to devalue (or float) the currency *sooner* than it would have to in the absence of the speculative attack; some of the models imply even more strongly that a speculative attack can force a government to devalue (or float) when the exchange rate peg would otherwise be sustainable indefinitely in the absence of the attack. However, all of these models also incorporate a specification of the "fundamentals," which determine whether an exchange rate peg is sustainable and influence the likelihood of a speculative attack occurring and succeeding.

The first theoretical model of a speculative attack was produced by Krugman (1979). The specification of the fundamentals is quite simple, with no internationally traded assets except the domestic and foreign currencies themselves (thus, this is the one model that fits into the lower-left box in Figure 2.1). Domestic money creation is driven entirely by the monetization of government deficits, i.e., "printing money" to pay for deficit spending. With a fixed exchange rate, any domestic money created to finance a government deficit will be offset to some extent by a loss of foreign exchange reserves as the monetary authority is obligated to defend the currency peg. If reserves fall to zero, the government will of course be forced to abandon the peg even if there is no speculative attack. However, rational speculators correctly anticipate that the country must have a burst of inflation after the reserves run out. Fearing a capital loss from holding domestic currency, speculators start to get out of domestic money before reserves actually run out. Moreover, speculators who fear that other speculators will start to sell off domestic currency are driven to do so further in advance. Thus, a speculative attack will inevitably occur (and succeed) at some point in time before reserves would otherwise run out.

In Krugman's model, the speculative attack makes the expected abandonment of the peg occur *earlier* than it would in the absence of the speculation. Otherwise, however, the *cause* of the speculative attack is an inconsistency in the fundamentals that is recognized by rational speculators with perfect foresight: the government is running a budget deficit financed by an amount of monetary creation that makes the pegged exchange rate unsustainable. If the government balanced its budget, no speculative attack could occur. Furthermore, a larger initial stock of reserves can delay a speculative attack and prolong the life of the peg. Other early models of speculative attacks (e.g., Flood and Garber 1984a; Obstfeld 1984), while based on more complex formulations incorporating capital mobility, also shared this characteristic that such attacks occur only when a fixed exchange rate is inconsistent with the underlying policy fundamentals.

Later models of speculative attacks have shown that such attacks can occur even if there is no inconsistency in the fundamentals that would otherwise require an eventual abandonment of the peg. The first such model applied to fixed exchange rates[62] was developed by Obstfeld (1986), whose work demonstrated

> the existence of circumstances in which balance-of-payments crises may indeed be purely self-fulfilling events rather than the inevitable result of unsustainable macroeconomic policies. Such crises are apparently unnecessary and collapse an exchange rate that would otherwise have been viable. (Obstfeld 1986, 72)

In Obstfeld's original model, the trigger for a speculative attack is "the expected adoption of an inflationary domestic-credit growth rule in the event the fixed exchange rate collapses" (76). Later models in this vein differ in their details,[63] but they generally show how rational speculators can make the costs of maintaining a peg too high for government officials, even when the policies in place do not otherwise make a devaluation necessary.

Thus, the theoretical models require a sharp distinction between situations in which the fundamentals are so bad that an exchange rate peg is unsustainable and situations in which the fundamentals are not that bad but a speculative attack could still succeed if one is launched.[64] In reality, however, fundamentals can be multidimensional and hard to interpret, especially if there is uncertainty about the "true" model of the economy (as noted by McKinnon and Pill 1996). The empirical literature on speculative attacks (e.g., Frankel and Rose 1996; Kaminsky and Reinhart 1996; Kaminsky, Lizondo, and Reinhart 1997; Martínez-Pería 1997; Reisen 1998b; Tornell 1998) has focused on identifying conditions that can predict when such attacks will occur. Some indicators of the likelihood of speculative attacks include foreign exchange reserves, international debts, bank lending, budget deficits, current account deficits, money supplies, real exchange rates, and interest rates. While these studies do find correlations between such indicators and the likelihood of speculative attacks, they do not provide clear and unambiguous thresholds for when the fundamentals are bad enough to allow an attack to be successful or to make one inevitable.

Contagion effects

Contagion effects occur when, in the aftermath of a currency crisis in one country, speculators look around for countries in similar circumstances that may be vulnerable to a speculative assault, but where the inconsistencies in the fundamentals were not severe enough to induce a speculative attack on their own. Calvo and Reinhart (1996) find evidence that the Mexican crisis of 1994-95 caused contagion to other financial markets, especially in Latin America. There are also strong reasons to suspect contagion as a cause of financial crisis in the spread of the "Asian flu" in 1997-98 (see Radelet and Sachs 1998a, 1998b; Rodrik 1998; MacLean et al. 1998; A. Singh 1998; Wade 1998a, 1998b; World Bank 1998). After the successful attack on the Thai baht in July 1997, speculators attacked several other currencies in rapid-fire succession, including the Malaysian ringgit, the Indonesian rupiah, the Philippine peso, and the Korean won. In each case speculators found problems to exploit, from weak banks in South Korea to "crony capitalism" in Suharto's Indonesia. But in none of these cases was a currency crisis expected based on the country's own internal policies and external situation *prior* to the Thai crisis. Moreover, these countries differed in their respective fundamentals. Most of them had budget surpluses, high saving rates, and low inflation rates (World Bank 1998). Many of these countries had growing current account deficits and rising international debts, but in most cases these seemed to be within bounds that required only minor adjustments at most.[65]

The coincidence of so many crises in such diverse countries in such a short period of time creates a prima facie case for the presence of contagion effects. The question then is what causes the contagion to spread. One common factor in all the developing countries that suffered financial contagion in the 1990s is that they all had recently liberalized capital markets (see Kaminsky and Reinhart 1996; MacLean et al. 1998; Taylor 1998a, 1998b; Rodrik 1998). As discussed in Chapter 1, capital market liberalization facilitated overborrowing in foreign currencies, which led to the emergence of vulnerable financial positions that invited speculative attacks. The implication is that financial liberalization per se makes speculative attacks more likely to be contagious.

Contrary to this interpretation, the IMF and U.S. administration have attributed the spread of currency crises in the emerging market countries to inadequate domestic financial regulation, including problems of nontransparent business accounting, weak banking supervision, and "crony capitalist" relations between borrowers and lenders. As discussed earlier, these characteristics are long-standing features of those economies that would not have caused a spate of financial crises in the absence of large inflows of foreign funds that destabilized the domestic financial systems. It is telling, in this regard, that several Asian countries that have *not* fully liberalized their capital accounts—notably China, India, and Taiwan—have thus far escaped from the worst contagion effects, even though their fundamentals are not beyond reproach and they have some of the same internal problems of nontransparent financial positions and crony capitalism that are found in the countries that have suffered currency crises. At most, weak domestic financial systems seem to be a necessary but hardly a sufficient explanation of contagion effects; a better explanation is the explosive *mix* of capital market liberalization with inadequate domestic regulation.

Much of the academic research on contagion effects has focused on whether they are caused by genuine weaknesses in policy fundamentals or by self-fulfilling prophecies in financial markets. One interesting study is by Tornell (1998), who claims to show that contagion effects can be explained by "fundamentals" alone. According to Tornell's statistical evidence, contagion effects following both the Mexican and Thai crises can be explained by the interaction of three factors: real exchange rate overvaluation, inadequate foreign currency reserves, and bank lending booms. Countries that had greater real exchange rate appreciations and larger bank lending booms were more likely to experience currency crises—but only if their foreign currency reserves were relatively low so that they could not ward off an attack.

Tornell's evidence is compelling, but his definition of "fundamentals" is too broad. For example, lending booms can reflect speculative frenzies in asset markets and are more likely to occur when capital markets have been liberalized.[66] Also, Tornell measures the adequacy of foreign currency reserves relative to the broadly defined money supply, M2 (which includes most kinds of bank deposits). But the ratio of reserves to M2 may incorporate the effects of speculative excesses in countries where banks have overlent (since increased bank lending leads to increased bank deposits and hence a higher M2). Furthermore, all of his results are contingent on a prior wake-up call from an initial crisis (Mexico in 1994 or Thailand in 1997), without which speculators might not have focused on the weaknesses in other countries' finances. Tornell's findings confirm that contagion effects are not irrational, in the sense that speculators select currencies for attack based on genuine, observable weaknesses. But his results do not disprove that the weaknesses that speculators exploit can result at least partly from self-fulfilling expectations in volatile financial markets.

Self-fulfilling panics

The financial crises of the 1990s have also generated interest in a new class of models of self-fulfilling panics. In the Mexican case, for example, standard models of speculative attacks cannot account for the magnitude and severity of the financial crisis that ensued *after* the peso was allowed to float in December 1994 (Sachs et al. 1996b). After all, if the problem was just a pegged exchange rate that was inconsistent with the fundamentals, one would expect the post-float exchange rate to settle quickly at a level more consistent with the fundamentals that would assuage foreign investors and end the crisis. Instead, in Mexico, as well as in several later cases, the stampede of investors taking their money out of the country accelerated dramatically *after* the peg was abandoned. As a result of this herd behavior, currency values plummeted to levels far below anything that could have been predicted beforehand on the basis of conventional measures of the degree to which these currencies were overvalued. For example, Dornbusch and Werner (1994) estimated that Mexico needed a 20% devaluation of the peso in order to correct the country's growing trade deficit. Only a year later—after the peso actually fell by about 60% (from about US$0.32 to US$0.13)—a chastened Dornbusch admitted that, "To virtually any observer, the sheer vehemence of the collapse and the extent of disruption in capital markets remain a surprise" (Dornbusch et al. 1995, 220).

These considerations have prompted new models of self-fulfilling panics, in which investors overreact to the underlying problems in a country in a way that exacerbates those problems. Such a panic is analogous to an ordinary bank run, in which depositors who fear that a bank will collapse rush to withdraw their deposits, potentially precipitating the feared event. When a generalized financial panic erupts, investors flee a wide range of domestic assets (e.g., bonds and stocks), and the currency goes into a free fall with no predetermined lower limit.

Several theories have been proposed for why such panics can emerge. As mentioned in Chapter 1, Calvo and Mendoza (1996) argue that the international diversification of global investors' portfolios reduces the incentives for investors to gather information about the individual countries in which they invest:

> highly diversified investors have lower incentives to acquire information than investors with fewer investment opportunities. This in turn results from the fact that as the number of countries in which to invest rises, the marginal gain from information-gathering eventually declines. Outcomes in which the equilibrium response to news is a self-fulfilling panic become plausible, and the behavior of policy-makers becomes as important as their policies (i.e. a poorly handled devaluation can have disastrous effects). (Calvo and Mendoza 1996, 251)

According to Calvo and Mendoza, this problem of a lack of incentives to acquire adequate information on any specific country leads to exaggerated reactions by investors when their expectations of any particular country's situation are revised downward. Of course, an ill-informed financial panic usually follows an equally ill-informed boom in foreign investment, which creates a financial position that is vulnerable to a sudden shift in perceptions.

The empirical literature has made some progress in identifying factors that can precipitate financial panics. For example, Goldstein and Calvo (1996) emphasize the maturity and currency composition of government borrowing, rather than the total amount of deficit spending financed by borrowing, in explaining the unusual severity of the 1994-95 Mexican crisis. In 1994, rather than making the adjustments it needed to (e.g., by devaluing sooner), the Mexican government tried to assuage wary foreign investors by issuing dollar-indexed, short-term bonds called tesebonos. Thus, while a moderate devaluation of the peso might have been sufficient to correct Mexico's current account (trade) deficit, it could not reassure investors that the Mexican government would be able to meet its short-term debt service obligations in foreign currency—if anything, the Mexican government's assumption of the exchange risk inherent in the tesebonos made investors more fearful of a default after the peso initially fell. The result was a panic that worsened *after* the initial devaluation in December 1994.

Goldstein and Calvo (1996) also identify a sharp decline in the ratio of foreign currency reserves to the broadly defined money supply M2 (which consists mainly of banks' deposit liabilities) as another warning sign of an impending panic.[67] The idea is that if bank depositors panic and try to send their assets abroad (as wealthy Mexicans did prior to December 1994), foreign currency reserves will be drained as deposits are cashed in and exchanged for foreign currencies. Thus, a fall in the ratio of reserves to M2 indicates that reserves are inadequate to handle a sudden, massive capital flight—and investors who realize this will turn the threat of such a panic into a self-fulfilling prophecy. Goldstein and Calvo and many others also argue that weaknesses in the banking system can make a country more vulnerable to the outbreak of a panic, since banks with large proportions of bad loans on their books will be more likely to fail when interest rate increases or currency collapses make it harder for borrowers to service their debts. Thus, the analysis of panics, like the analysis of contagion effects, has led to a focus on weaknesses in financial conditions in addition to inconsistencies in more traditional policy fundamentals.

Models of financial fragility and debt deflation[68]

As the preceding discussion makes clear, the analysis of financial crises has increasingly shifted toward identifying problems in countries' financial positions (e.g., their debt structures, banking systems, and asset markets) rather than in their traditional policy fundamentals (e.g., budget deficits, exchange rates, or monetary growth). These analyses reveal why some policy approaches are not working as intended. Especially, high interest rates that are supposed to restore investors' confidence often have the opposite effect of heightening financial panics (and further depressing falling currencies), because high interest rates increase default risks for both highly indebted firms and highly exposed banks. This phenomenon calls for new theoretical models of international finance in which the debt positions of business firms and the balance sheets of financial intermediaries are given greater prominence.

Some foundations for such an approach can be found in the work of American economist Irving Fisher (1933) on debt-deflation crises and Polish economist Mikhal Kalecki (1937) on default risk. Both of these theories were conceived during the Great Depression of the 1930s. Fisher and Kalecki's ideas were later revived and extended by Hyman Minsky (1982, 1986) in an effort to understand postwar financial crises in the U.S. economy.[69] Minsky's theory of "financial fragility" has been summarized as follows:

> Within the Minskyian framework the business cycle is characterized by the gradual emergence of "financial fragility," and this fragility ultimately causes the demise of the upswing....The business cycle upswing is characterized as a period of "tranquility" during which bankers, industrialists, and households become increasingly more "optimistic." In the real sector this translates into increased real investment, while in the financial sector it shows up in the form of an increased willingness to borrow, an easing of lending standards, and an increase in the degree of leverage of debtors. Effectively, there is a progressive deterioration of balance sheet positions measured by [increased] debt:equity ratios, accompanied by a progressive deterioration of debt coverage measured by [increased] debt service:income ratios. It is in this sense that there is growing financial fragility. These circumstances, then, either directly give rise to the end of the boom when firms fail to meet their debt obligations, or they create the conditions in which the economy becomes vulnerable to any small negative shock. (Palley 1996, 201-2)

A number of economists have produced formal models analyzing Minskyian financial fragility, mostly applied to closed (domestic) economies. For example, Taylor and O'Connell (1985) and Taylor (1991) construct models that emphasize fluctuations in business confidence and investment spending.[70] Palley (1994) offers a model that stresses the evolution of consumer borrowing and household finances. All of these models imply that debt accumulation can engender chronic business cycle instability under certain conditions. In particular, they show that high debt burdens and high interest rates increase financial fragility and exacerbate cyclical instability. These models could potentially be extended to incorporate international capital flows and their effects on domestic borrowing, debt accumulation, and cyclical volatility.

Another type of theory examines how financial factors impact real production and employment in the economy. Greenwald and Stiglitz (1993) point out that traditional economic models assume away financial risks in the way they treat firms' production decisions, and argue that more realistic models need to take financial risks into account.[71] Greenwald and Stiglitz's model shows that firms' production and investment decisions can be negatively affected by increased perceptions of bankruptcy risk, such as occur during financial crises. Greenwald and Stiglitz also conclude that downward wage and price flexibility can worsen, rather than ameliorate, cyclical instability of real output. This point was made earlier by Caskey and Fazzari (1987), who showed how downward flexibility of nominal wages can lead to increased output losses in a recession in an economy with a highly indebted financial structure. Since debt service obligations are fixed in nominal terms, the threat of bankruptcy increases when nominal wages and the price level fall and hence firms' nominal revenues are reduced.

While these models analyze the effects of falling nominal wages and prices in a closed economy, their logic could be extended to various issues that arise in open economies with liberalized capital markets.[72] For example, consider the case of falling prices for primary commodity exporters, which have affected countries such as Russia and Brazil. Since commodity prices are usually denominated in U.S. dollars or other hard currencies, global commodity price deflation reduces exporting firms' revenues and increases those firms' financial fragility. Another example is that currency depreciation can increase bankruptcy risks for firms that have borrowed heavily in foreign currency—unless the depreciation brings in enough extra export earnings to compensate, which requires highly price-elastic demand for the firms' export products. Also, the Greenwald-Stiglitz framework implies that increasing interest rates in an effort to stabilize a country's currency can instead destabilize the real economy by worsening bankruptcy risks.

The key contribution of these new models is to recognize that financial instability can have profound negative effects on real production and investment that were not anticipated in earlier models. These real effects in turn feed back upon and amplify financial instability by increasing risks of default or bankruptcy and thereby worsening the financial fragility of firms and banks. While the theory in this area requires much more work (and empirical testing), it already has clear implications for rethinking the way that international financial policies impact real domestic activity. For example, instead of emphasizing interest rate differentials and exchange rate risks as in the traditional models (e.g., portfolio balance and exchange rate overshooting), we need to take account of how policies affect default risks for firms and banks. In particular, the fact that high interest rates increase default risk explains why raising interest rates in countries in crisis (such as Russia and Brazil) often fails to accomplish its intended goal of stabilizing their currencies.

Conclusions

The new models of international finance show that global financial markets contain inherent sources of instability—and that the endemic instability in the financial sector also infects the real economy, with potentially severe consequences for employment, investment, growth, and equity. Yet, most of the policy discourse to date ignores these recent advances in theory and relies instead on older models that assume that global financial markets are more predictable and stable than they actually are. Even when the new models are considered, they are usually interpreted in a narrow fashion as merely suggesting a need for providing better information to investors and enhancing domestic supervision of financial institutions. With policy thinking still circumscribed by adherence to obsolete models (and tepid applications of the new ones), it is no wonder that the policies promoted by the U.S. government and the IMF for countries in crisis have so abysmally failed to stem the raging tide of financial contagion.

The remainder of this concluding section discusses the implications of the new models of global finance for the two questions that motivated the theoretical survey in this chapter. First, what do the new models imply about how global finance constrains domestic economic policies? And second, what do the new theories imply about how countries should manage their own economic policies in order to achieve more stable, equitable, and balanced growth than they have achieved under the Washington Consensus? This discussion then sets the stage for considering more specific proposals for global financial reform in the next chapter.

Self-fulfilling prophecies and policy constraints

The implications of the various models of self-fulfilling prophecies in exchange rates (speculative bubbles, attacks, contagions, and panics) for how global finance constrains domestic policies are not as simple and straightforward as the implications of the fundamentals-based models. The new models do not yield simple rules that determine when monetary and fiscal policies are more or less effective. In fact, the new models suggest that the apparently precise results of the older models are misleading, because the effects of a shift in fiscal or monetary policy in an economy that is open to speculative pressures depend on the market psychology prevailing at the time and are unpredictable based on any general model. For example, the Mundell-Fleming prediction that a fiscal stimulus is highly effective in a country with a fixed exchange rate and liberalized capital markets may be exactly wrong, if the fiscal stimulus generates expectations of a future devaluation and therefore induces speculators to take money out of the country (instead of pouring it in, as the model implies).

In a larger sense, however, the unpredictability of international financial flows that is highlighted by the new theoretical models can be considered a severe constraint on individual nations' ability to pursue autonomous economic policies. Governments that have to fear unpredictable reactions of global financial markets may be reluctant to try policy innovations that might upset investors' expectations. When capital markets are wide open, almost any policy shift—liberal, conservative, or otherwise—can invite instability, either by provoking an unsustainable bubble by attracting too much foreign capital, or else by spooking international investors and causing panic-stricken withdrawals of capital. As a result, national governments have inherently less scope for pursuing their own policy directions when their capital markets are wide open to speculative capital movements. Once one recognizes that free movements of capital are more often driven by self-fulfilling prophecies than by long-term fundamentals, one is driven to the conclusion that liberalization of capital markets ties the hands of policy makers to some extent *regardless* of traditional economic distinctions (such as whether they have fixed or flexible exchange rates or whether their countries' bonds are close substitutes for foreign bonds).

This is not to say that there are not important differences between countries in terms of how vulnerable they are to externally imposed constraints. Holding other factors constant, larger countries like the United States are less tightly constrained than smaller countries like Mexico, simply because the amounts of money that can flow across international borders are much more likely to overwhelm a small economy's capacity for adjustment. Moreover, for a country of any given size, factors such as the magnitude and composition of its external debts, the degree to which it depends on imports, and the strength of its financial regulatory apparatus can influence how much autonomy its government has to choose policies in the national interest. The new theoretical models and empirical studies support the view that currency speculators consider these types of factors in deciding whether to attack a given currency or whether to panic after a devaluation. Hence, countries that are in worse condition by these criteria are going to be more tightly constrained than other countries would be as a result of liberalized capital flows. Nevertheless, all countries find their room for maneuver constricted to some extent by the pressures of maintaining credibility with international investors—even if the pressure is not always consistent or contractionary, as noted earlier.

The models of self-fulfilling expectations of investors add an important new dimension to policy discussions: the crucial role of information about countries' true financial conditions (e.g., the solvency of their commercial banks or the adequacy of their central banks' foreign exchange reserves). In many of these models, uncertainty over the true state of a country's finances can increase the likelihood of a financial crisis occurring. Thus, the new models lend support to calls for more "transparency" and "surveillance" in financial institutions, business accounting, central bank reporting, and government budgeting. More broadly, the new models highlight the need for enhanced prudential regulation of domestic financial institutions in order to avoid the creation of unsustainable financial positions that invite speculative attacks. Solving information problems by improving transparency and supervision is an important part of many proposals for a new financial architecture, which are discussed in Chapter 3.

Although the new models support the need for greater transparency, they do not imply that more information or better supervision can eliminate all financial instability. Even where information is good and banks are well regulated, speculators can still attack currencies perceived to be misaligned or induce (and subsequently burst) bubbles in floating exchange rates. Indeed, even well-regulated asset markets, like the New York Stock Exchange, are subject to bubbles and busts. Better regulation and more information may temper the worst excesses of speculative crises by reducing the most extreme forms of herd behavior based on scanty information in emerging financial markets. But since the general ebbs and flows of speculative capital cannot be contained by greater transparency and surveillance alone, these types of reforms do not necessarily buy most countries much in the way of enhanced policy autonomy.

For this reason, the new models of international financial instability lead us inexorably to consider stronger types of reforms of the global financial architecture. The new models imply that speculative pressures can exacerbate underlying sources of instability in any economy, no matter how transparent or well-regulated, and can even foster instability in economies that would otherwise remain stable. Therefore, countries that wish to reduce their exposure to such unnecessary volatility may be justified in taking measures to reduce their openness to speculative inflows and outflows of funds. In other words, countries need to consider so-called "speed bumps" such as limits on short-term, reversible capital flows and taxes on foreign exchange transactions, policies that could help to discourage speculative bubbles, attacks, and panics. For example, if speculators cannot freely borrow a currency and then sell it short, they will have a much harder time attacking a pegged currency. And if investors cannot freely and quickly move massive amounts of funds into and out of countries with flexible exchange rates, they will not be able to produce huge bubbles on the upside or violent panics on the downside. Countries that use capital controls or exchange controls to relieve these sorts of pressures can thus buy some measure of greater autonomy for their domestic economic policies. In particular, such controls can potentially allow countries to avoid the need for high interest rates and draconian fiscal cutbacks to maintain credibility with wary foreign investors at the cost of producing severe recessions and hardships (Krugman 1998a, 1998b). Specific proposals for accomplishing this goal will be discussed in the next chapter.

Rethinking sound macroeconomic and financial policies

The older models of international finance implied a fairly clear prescription of "sound fundamentals" for macroeconomic policies: conservative fiscal policies and slow monetary growth, combined with exchange rates that were either flexible or fixed at competitive levels, would ensure the achievement of equilibrium in a country's balance of payments. Even some of the newer models still have a strong emphasis on macroeconomic fundamentals, usually defined more or less along these traditional lines, as an effective defense against speculative attacks or panics. Yet, as one studies the evolution of international financial modeling, one sees that definitions of sound fundamentals have become increasingly murky and that the ability of traditionally defined sound fundamentals to deter destabilizing speculation has increasingly come into doubt.

Even in terms of the traditional models, different policy objectives may be in conflict with each other, making it unclear which policies are fundamentally more sound. Consider, for example, whether countries like Brazil and Mexico should strive to peg their exchange rates at high levels or should let their currencies float and depreciate. If such countries try to keep their nominal exchange rates fixed, they have to offer high interest rates that stifle domestic growth, and they may suffer rising current account deficits if their currencies become overvalued in real terms (because domestic inflation exceeds foreign inflation). But if these countries devalue or float their currencies, they risk rapidly increasing inflation at home and higher costs (in domestic currency terms) of servicing their foreign debts. In such situations, policy makers are damned if they do and damned if they don't. There is no unique set of fundamental policies that allows such countries to escape from this dilemma, which results from the basic trade-off that a high currency value is useful for suppressing inflation and stabilizing prices, while a low currency value is better for external competitiveness and internal growth.[73]

But even leaving such conflicts in objectives aside, we have seen that speculative attacks can occur even against currencies whose (fixed) exchange rates are otherwise sustainable in the absence of an attack. Bubbles can develop in countries whose macroeconomic policies are generally regarded as entirely sound—often in response to the maintenance of high interest rates and nominal exchange rate anchors usually thought to be signs of a credible anti-inflationary policy. Contagion effects and self-fulfilling panics can force severe adjustments in countries whose policies might otherwise require only modest corrections. While one can argue generally that keeping exchange rates from being overvalued or amassing large reserves of foreign currencies are helpful measures for reducing the likelihood of speculative attacks, the fact remains that there is no magic bullet of so-called sound fiscal and monetary policies that effectively prevents such attacks from occurring in a country that is open to unfettered capital flows.

Indeed, economists concerned with explaining financial crises have increasingly recognized that traditional concepts of sound fundamentals (based on variables such as monetary growth or budget deficits) are inadequate for explaining when and where such crises break out (e.g., Reisen 1998b; Goldstein and Calvo 1996). These economists put more emphasis on factors such as the maturity and currency composition of government borrowing, rather than the total amount of deficit spending financed by borrowing, in explaining speculative attacks and financial panics. There is also an increasing recognition that the weaknesses that lead to a financial crisis may stem from private sector behavior rather than from public policy decisions. The Asian crisis in particular has led to a new appreciation of the crucial role of bad loan portfolios of banks and large debt positions of corporations in exaggerating financial crises and economic meltdowns.

Putting these ideas together, it is clear that countries' *financial positions* can make them vulnerable to a much more severe crisis than what their basic *macroeconomic policies* would lead us to expect. One response is to broaden the definition of the fundamentals to include indicators of financial fragility, which is essentially the approach taken by Tornell (1998), but this approach drains the concept of fundamentals of all meaning. Alternatively, it seems better to recognize that the distinction between macroeconomic fundamentals and financial factors has become increasingly blurred, and that the main reason why the older models have failed so badly is that they did not adequately incorporate the financial dimension into their analyses. Rather than a continuation of the elusive search for ideal fundamentals, what is needed is more creative thinking about how to design both macroeconomic policies and financial sector regulations in ways that can help to contain volatile financial flows and promote more stable and equitable growth.

The Washington Consensus view that countries should simply adopt "sound" fiscal and monetary policies and otherwise "get the government out of the way" is flawed and should be abandoned. Contrary to the conventional wisdom, what is needed may be *more* government management and regulation of the economy, especially interventions designed to contain short-run speculation and overlending booms, as well as to foster more stable, long-term flows of capital into developing countries. By reenacting capital controls and adopting other measures to contain speculative pressures, countries may be able to escape from the bind of having to maintain credibility with foreign investors and to adopt macroeconomic policies (e.g., lower interest rates and higher social spending) that better serve their national interests. Governments also need to find ways to manage their exchange rates in a more stable fashion and to coordinate macroeconomic policies internationally in order to discourage speculative pressures. And the U.S. government and the IMF need to reconsider the failed policies that they continue to promote in countries suffering financial crises. The next chapter discusses specific policy options for accomplishing these goals.

Chapter 3

Achieving financial stability and global prosperity: the policy agenda

The official proposals for a "new financial architecture" that have thus far come out of the U.S. government and various international summit meetings are modest in scope. They also have a few key features in common. First, the proposals have focused on the need for internal regulatory reforms in developing countries with emerging financial markets so that these countries can be better prepared to handle massive inflows and outflows of investment funds. Second, they emphasize the need for greater "transparency" in the accounting practices of both private firms and public agencies and improved "surveillance" of individual countries by the IMF and other agencies, in order to provide investors with better information on which to base their decisions. Third, they assume that liberalization of capital markets is both inevitable and desirable, and they aim simply to cure the worst excesses of financial instability. In a nutshell, the official designs for a new architecture would serve mainly to make the world a safer place for short-term investors.

Based on the arguments in the preceding chapters, we conclude that reforming domestic financial systems and increasing transparency and surveillance—while certainly helpful for countries that wish to participate in global financial markets—are not sufficient to contain the volatile financial flows that have plagued the global economy in recent years. Capital markets are inherently characterized by information problems that no amount of transparency or supervision can eliminate. Moreover, the diversity of national experiences and economic conditions makes it doubtful that one type of financial system developed in the West would function well in all countries around the world. Nor is it clear from the existing evidence that countries that prefer to opt out of the system of liberalized capital flows will be worse off as a result. And the official new architecture proposals ignore the fact that the Washington Consensus view of sound macroeconomic policies is plagued by flaws that have invited speculative capital flows and are currently producing a deflationary bias in the global economy. Thus, we find the conventional new architecture proposals that focus on internal reforms in emerging markets to be deficient.

Alternatives to these conventional new architecture proposals have come from two sides: one group that emphasizes creating new international institutions to manage the global financial system, and another group that emphasizes restricting international capital flows in order to increase national policy autonomy. These two groups share a distrust of the current system of unregulated capital movements, but disagree on the best means of reforming that system. As we shall argue below, this need not be an either/or choice; both institutional innovations and capital controls can be parts of a broader approach to a new financial architecture.

The first group argues that major new international institutions are needed in order to stabilize global financial markets—and that with such new institutions, global financial markets would work more in the public interest. Although there is some overlap in the intended functions of the proposed new institutions, they can be classified into three main types: a world central bank, an international financial supervisory institution, and an international monetary clearinghouse. Supporters of these new institutions claim that they would fulfill missing functions from the international financial system, such as providing a true international lender of last resort, enforcing more prudent banking standards on member countries, and stabilizing international currency values. In addition, some of these institutions are intended to counteract the deflationary bias in current international adjustment policies by providing an institutional mechanism responsible for maintaining an adequate level of global aggregate demand.

The second group argues for limitations on international flows of short-term capital in order to restore greater policy autonomy for national governments. This group includes advocates of international transactions taxes, such as a "Tobin tax" on foreign exchange transactions, as well as supporters of renewed capital controls to prevent destabilizing inflows and outflows of speculative hot money. These types of policies are also seen as helping to reduce volatility in international currency markets and other financial markets. But above all, capital controls and transactions taxes are desired in order to insulate national governments from the pressures of having to maintain credibility with foreign (and domestic) investors—and thus to allow individual countries to pursue more expansionary policies.[1] In particular, closing capital markets allows countries to control both their interest rates and their exchange rates, something they cannot do with open capital markets (according to the policy "trilemma," discussed in Chapter 1).

The proposals for new international institutions provide visionary insights into what it would take to manage global financial flows in the public interest. In principle, new global institutions could do much to stabilize currency values, reduce financial turbulence, and stimulate more stable and balanced growth throughout the world. Nevertheless, the political prospects for creating major new global institutions are dim at present. Most countries today seem unwilling to accept major new limitations on their sovereignty—with the partial exception of regional monetary unions, which will be discussed below. Such reticence is not irrational, since countries that want more autonomy from the pressures of financial speculators may be justifiably wary of ceding authority to new international bureaucracies. Also, there are enormous difficulties of governance and accountability that would have to be solved in order to prevent any new institutions from becoming as closed and unresponsive as the IMF is today.

Nevertheless, since the failures of the existing international financial institutions are an important part of the problem in the global economy, fixing or replacing those institutions must be part of the solution. An important place to start is with the IMF, which plays a powerful role today in responding to financial crises and influencing the direction of national economic policies. In this chapter, we present a comprehensive plan for fundamental reform of the IMF, in terms of both changing the type of economic policies it promotes and making it more accountable to the people in the countries it serves. We also discuss the more "visionary" proposals for new international institutions, which could potentially create the foundations for a better-managed global economy in the future.

In addition to reforming the IMF or creating new institutions, we believe that it is also essential to adopt appropriate measures to regulate and restrict capital flows. Capital controls can dampen the excessive and easily reversible flows of short-term, speculative funds that have devastated small, vulnerable economies—and which foster other forms of instability even in larger, more insulated economies (e.g., by causing gyrations in exchange rates among the industrialized countries). We are especially interested in policies that could limit short-term capital flows and prevent rapid shifts in inflows and outflows, while promoting more stable and long-term-oriented capital flows into those countries that want them.

But even regulating capital flows and reforming international institutions together are not enough. Much of the economic turmoil of the 1990s reflects underlying problems with the fiscal, monetary, and exchange rate policies that countries have followed. In some cases, policies have been inconsistent or unsustainable, thus inviting speculative attacks. In other cases, policies appeared to be sound (at least in terms of the Washington Consensus) but in fact fostered an environment in which overinvestment booms and speculative bubbles could emerge—and then collapse. In several key situations, changes in interest rates or fluctuations in exchange rates in the U.S. and other industrialized countries have had serious repercussions for other countries, such as Mexico and Thailand—repercussions that were not taken into account by policy makers in the former countries. The current approach to rectifying financial crises encouraged by the IMF and the U.S. administration—with its emphasis on fiscal and monetary austerity to solve balance-of-payments crises and restore investor confidence—imparts a contractionary bias to the entire world economy that threatens to spark a global recession. And the rash of competitive devaluations by one country after another in the 1990s has only worsened, rather than contained, the spreading contagion of financial crises around the world.

For all of these reasons, the global financial architecture cannot be secure from crises and instability unless it also rests on a solid foundation of exchange rate management and macroeconomic policy coordination. Thus, we concur with Will Hutton when he writes,

> The heart of a new financial order is maintaining stability in the value of the dollar, yen, and mark [or now the euro]. The governments that issue these currencies must accept that monetary and fiscal policy need to be closely coordinated....This triangular relationship needs to become the core of a new Bretton Woods system of bracketed but flexible exchange rates, protected against speculative currency flows by some form of turnover tax on financial transactions....Capital controls should be introduced where necessary. Such a financial order would ultimately mean lower real interest rates, longer time horizons, less financial speculation, and more real investment and growth. (Hutton 1996, 12)

Based on this overarching vision, this chapter will critically review the entire menu of proposals for a new financial architecture, which is summarized in **Table 3.1**. This list starts with the conventional proposals for making capital markets work better, and then continues on to four additional areas: (1) regulating capital flows; (2) reforming international financial institutions; (3) managing exchange rates; and (4) coordinating macroeconomic policies.[2] As the preceding discussion indicates, these are not four separate areas of policy design, but rather four closely interlinked and mutually supportive areas for policy reform. For example, capital controls cannot prevent all instability in exchange rates, and no exchange rate system can bring about stability in currency values unless it is accompanied by a consistent set of macroeconomic policies. Similarly, any approach to reforming international financial institutions (or creating new ones) must incorporate a view of the types of macro policies that those institutions should promote.

Numerous specific policies have been proposed within each of these areas. In what follows, we shall evaluate the pros and cons of each major policy approach and seek to identify the types of measures that have the greatest chances of success. In this discussion, we are guided by a belief that no one type of policy by itself offers a panacea for curing the current financial turmoil, and that different approaches may work better for different countries. Thus, a new financial structure needs to be built upon a solid foundation of action in all of these interrelated areas, with flexibility for individual countries to shape their own futures in accordance with their own values and priorities.

Making capital markets more efficient

As discussed in Chapter 1, the two main arguments in favor of capital market liberalization are the gains from a more efficient allocation of global saving and the opportunities for international investors to diversify their risks. In order for capital markets to fulfill these objectives, investment decisions have to be based on full information—or at least sensibly formed expectations—about the true returns to (and risks of) alternative investments in different countries and sectors. If investors are not well informed, or if expectations are based on something other than the long-term prospects for alternative investment opportunities, or if investors do not properly assess likely risks as well as prospective returns, liberalized international capital markets cannot be expected to achieve the twin objectives of efficiently allocating capital and diversifying investors' risks. Thus, in their proposals for a new international financial architecture, supporters of open capital markets have emphasized improving the information set used by investors and increasing the incentives to properly evaluate risks.

Official proposals for a 'new architecture'

Several recent international summit meetings attended by leaders from various groups of countries (such as the G-7 and G-22)[3] have produced statements about a new financial architecture that are essentially intended to make capital markets work more efficiently. The proposals discussed at these meetings were developed by finance ministries and central banks, not by wider representatives of national governments or civil societies. Thus, all such statements reflect a least common denominator approach that emphasizes financial interests and is unlikely to deviate substantially from the views of the U.S. Treasury. These official pronouncements are important both for their intrinsic content and for what they reveal about the limits of official thinking on these issues to date.

The official new architecture proposals generally emphasize the following five points.[4] First, they support greater transparency and disclosure of financial positions in both the public and private sectors. For example, central banks should disclose their true foreign exchange reserves, banks should reveal their off-balance-sheet activities (e.g., derivatives trading), and business firms should publish reliable accounting statements. Second, they urge the IMF to improve its surveillance of member countries' financial positions and issue a Transparency Report that would monitor countries' compliance with the new transparency requirements. Third, they call for the adoption of common prudential regulations (e.g., capital adequacy requirements, deposit insurance mechanisms) for banks and other financial intermediaries that would raise emerging markets up to the industrialized countries' level of financial supervision. Fourth, they recommend the development of new means of encouraging private lenders to make proper assessments of country risk and to take such risk into

TABLE 3.1 Menu of policy options for global financial reform

Official "new architecture" proposals: making capital markets work better
Increased transparency and disclosure for financial institutions
Improved surveillance by the IMF and other international agencies
Strengthened prudential supervision by domestic regulatory agencies
Better crisis resolution and prevention policies
  • reduction of moral hazard in IMF bailouts
  • bailing in of creditors, i.e., induce them to keep lending in a crisis
  • more orderly debt workouts and bankruptcy procedures
  • lending into arrears and in advance of crises
Improved risk management
  • private or public credit insurance

Regulating capital flows: cooling down the hot money
Tobin tax on all foreign exchange transactions
  • alternative foreign exchange taxes, e.g., Mélitz's 100% short-term foreign
    exchange profits tax
Capital controls and exchange controls in developing countries
  • Chilean-style reserve requirements on short-term capital inflows
  • Malaysian-style exchange controls to prevent currency speculation
  • stronger restrictions on short-term capital inflows or outflows
Regulation of capital flows in industrialized countries
  • prudential regulations on capital outflows, e.g., risk-weighted capital charges
    on pooled funds
  • restrictions on short-term inflows to discourage "safe-haven" investment
    during financial panics abroad
Creation of more stable channels for development finance
  • closed-end mutual fund for emerging market economies

Reforming international institutions
Abolition of the IMF?
  • why we need international financial institutions
Proposals for new international institutions
  • a world central bank
  • an international supervisory institution (board of overseers or world financial
    authority)
  • an international monetary clearinghouse
Fundamental reform of the IMF
  • new leadership
  • more democratic governance and accountability
  • a broader mission: macroeconomic prosperity and social justice
  • redesigning rescue packages
    – shifting of adjustment burden more onto creditors via "haircuts," debt
      relief, etc.
    – less stringent and more appropriate conditionality for debtors, including
      greater local participation
    – separate short-term goals of crisis remediation from long-term objectives
      of systemic reforms

TABLE 3.1 Menu of policy options for global financial reform *(cont.)*

Stabilizing exchange rates
Traditional alternatives
- flexible rates
- fixed nominal rates
  - currency boards
  - dollarization
- fixed rates with real targets (adjustable pegs)
- other types of managed rates (e.g., crawling pegs)

Compromise system of managed rates
- target zones with wide, crawling bands
- targets consistent with sustainable current account imbalances
- targets adjusted for inflation and growth differences
- bands that are "hard," with automatic and massive intervention to support them (either by national central banks or an international exchange stabilization fund)

Optimal exchange rate policies varying by type of country:
- target zones for the major currencies (the dollar, euro, and yen, plus other G-7);
- freedom of developing countries to experiment with exchange rate policies that meet their needs

Coordinating macroeconomic policy
Motivations
- to support target zones for exchange rates and discourage speculation
- to give policy makers more autonomy from financial market pressures

Williamson-Miller plan (for major industrialized countries)
- average interest rates targeted on global demand
- interest rate differences between countries targeted on exchange rates
- fiscal policies used for adjusting individual economies to meet national objectives

Modifications and qualifications
- targeting of demand policies on full employment at an acceptable inflation rate
- abandonment of rigid deficit reduction targets to make fiscal policies more flexible
- use of other instruments of credit control to supplement interest rate policy, which would be constricted by the coordination policy
  - e.g., reserve requirements at banks and other financial intermediaries, possibly shifted to assets (loans) rather than liabilities (deposits)

Guiding principles for policy coordination today
- lower average world interest rates to revive growth and prevent deflation
- depreciation of the U.S. dollar in order to reduce the U.S. trade deficit
- pursuit of expansionary demand policies in Europe and Japan to revive their growth and reduce their trade surpluses

account in lending decisions. And fifth, they propose better methods of crisis resolution, including: allowing the IMF to lend into arrears (i.e., to lend to countries that have temporarily suspended debt service but which are making good faith efforts to negotiate with their creditors); coordinating the responses of diverse groups of creditors; adopting more orderly debt workouts and bankruptcy procedures; and trying to "bail in" creditors by encouraging them to continue lending to countries in crisis.

A similar package of proposals is the "Halifax II agenda" of Goldstein (1998).[5] Goldstein's proposals are noteworthy because the author is a former deputy director of the research department at the IMF, and hence his views give some indication of how far a former IMF insider is willing to go in modifying the global financial architecture. His proposals, which go only modestly beyond the official positions of the G-7 and G-22, cover the following areas:[6] (1) reducing moral hazard in deposit insurance and bailout policies; (2) strengthening prudential supervision of banks and other financial institutions in developing economies; (3) increasing the amount of transparency and disclosure in international financial markets; (4) making IMF surveillance more effective; and (5) improving risk management in global financial markets. Within these five areas, Goldstein has many particular suggestions, including: restricting bailouts of uninsured large creditors of banks; providing for more orderly and flexible debt rescheduling or renegotiation in countries with unsustainable debt burdens; having the IMF and World Bank monitor countries' compliance with the Basle Core Principles for banking supervision, while giving countries financial incentives to adopt those principles; strengthening the Core Principles in regard to transparency requirements, bankruptcy laws, and risk management; providing more complete data on the maturity and currency composition of countries' external debts; making public the IMF staff's evaluations of individual countries' policies and prospects; and establishing international auditing standards and supervisory institutions to detect risk problems in financial institutions in industrialized countries as well as developing countries.

These types of proposals emphasize the need for individual countries to reform their domestic financial systems in order to better prepare themselves to meet the challenges of liberalized capital flows. In other words, the conventional new architecture proposals assume that the goal is to create a system of open capital markets, and the main issue is what countries with less-developed financial institutions and practices need to do in order to benefit more from participating in that system. This essentially puts most of the onus of international financial reform on the most vulnerable countries—and effectively requires them to make themselves over in the image of the United States or Western Europe.

Credit insurance schemes

One specific approach to improving risk management in the global financial system is the idea of credit insurance for international lenders. Although the idea of international credit insurance has not received much official support, we include it in this section because it aims at making global capital markets work more efficiently. In this approach, lenders would still charge risk premiums to borrowers to cover the perceived risk of default, as they do now, but lenders would also pay for additional insurance that would fully cover their losses in the event of an actual default. As Mann (1999) argues, the risk premiums ordinarily built into interest rates cover only average probabilities of default in normal times, but do not adequately insure against rare events such as major financial crises.

To solve this problem, Mann proposes the creation of voluntary private credit insurance on international loans and other foreign assets. Lenders who choose to pay for insurance against default risk would not have to sell off their positions in debtor countries when the latter have debt-servicing problems— thus discouraging herd behavior and nipping financial panics in the bud. Since "[s]lowing down the race to the exits could dramatically alter the self-fulfilling nature of some financial crises," Mann (1999, 3) argues that such insurance would reduce systemic risk and make IMF bailouts less necessary. However, she does not explain why private credit insurance has not already become widely available if it would be profitable for the private sector (e.g., banks or insurance companies) to make it so.

Another insurance proposal comes from international financier and speculator George Soros (1997). Soros' intention, like Mann's, is to make lenders pay more attention to risk and bear more of the costs, and to reduce herd-like stampedes of capital out of countries in times of financial distress. Unlike Mann, Soros assumes that the private sector would not provide such insurance and hence a public agency is needed. Soros therefore advocates a public institution called the International Credit Insurance Corporation, which would be "a sister institution to the IMF" and which would "guarantee international loans for a modest fee." The insurance would cover borrowing up to a certain ceiling for each debtor country, to be determined on the basis of economic and financial data supplied by those countries. Loans over the ceiling would not be prohibited, but they would not be guaranteed either, and they would likely include significant risk premiums for the borrowers.

To the extent that lenders would actually buy credit insurance—either voluntarily in Mann's plan or by lending under the ceilings in Soros' plan— herd behavior would be reduced and financial panics would be mitigated. Nevertheless, both of these proposals for credit insurance suffer from a similar defect, stemming from the fact that not all lenders would be required to take out insurance. Thus, lenders willing to bear the risk might forego purchasing voluntary insurance (under Mann's scheme) or lend over the ceilings (under Soros' proposal), in the hope that they would still be bailed out in a crisis because they would be considered "too big to fail." Since the insurance fund would have to cover the losses of the guaranteed loans in countries that ran into trouble, the likely result is that the "good" lenders who volunteer to buy the optional insurance (Mann) or who stay within the ceilings for the mandatory insurance (Soros) would end up paying higher premiums to cover the greater risks created by the actions of the "bad" lenders—who would not share any of the burden.[7] Thus, these proposals do not offer reliable guarantees against investors who are willing to bear extra risks and don't want to pay for the insurance—and it is precisely those investors who are likely to do the most damage.

There is another key problem with these credit insurance proposals, which Mann acknowledges but does not solve. She observes that lenders would be more willing to buy (voluntary) private insurance if public bailouts were not available. At a minimum, then, her plan would require the IMF to credibly commit itself in advance to refrain from bailing out creditors as much as it has in recent crisis situations. However, she also concedes that "it is unrealistic to suppose that there will be no international lending of last resort" by the IMF, which suggests that incentives to buy optional insurance may be lacking. Soros tries to solve this problem by making the insurance mandatory, but this in turn raises difficult questions about how the ceilings would be determined and which lenders would qualify for the insured loans (see Eichengreen 1999, 87). For all these reasons, it would be unrealistic to rely too heavily on credit insurance schemes for stabilizing the global financial system.

The limits of the official proposals

For countries that want to maintain open capital markets, the conventional new architecture proposals make a certain amount of sense. Providing more information and improving risk management could lead both foreign and domestic investors to be more cautious, which would help to relieve some of the pressures that lead to financial crises. But improved transparency and surveillance are not sufficient to eliminate the inherent volatility of short-term financial flows. As Stiglitz (1998) and Eichengreen (1999) argue, information problems are intrinsic to even the most open and best-regulated financial markets, and no amount of "transparency" can eliminate them. Moreover, there is no guarantee that making more information available will lead investors to utilize it in making their decisions—especially since investors have often failed to heed readily available information about individual countries' vulnerabilities in the past. Making better information available does not guarantee that investors will focus more on long-term, productive investments as opposed to short-term, speculative gambles. Thus, the obsession with transparency and surveillance in the official new architecture proposals can serve to distract us from exploring other types of policies that may be needed to contain financial volatility.[8]

In addition, the official proposals ignore the difficulties in getting culturally and economically diverse countries to effectively harmonize their financial practices and regulations—and they do not consider whether some countries would rather not participate in the world of liberalized short-term capital movements. For example, the nontransparent financial systems of the Asian countries fueled several decades of record-breaking growth performance (see, e.g., Zysman 1983 on Japan; Amsden 1989 on Korea; and Wade 1990 on Taiwan). While those financial systems may need to change as those countries become more developed,[9] it would probably be better for them to evolve in nationally appropriate directions rather than to be torn down and replaced by Western-style financial systems. The fact that the Asian countries are being pressured to open up their financial institutions to purchase by foreign investors (e.g., multinational banks) suggests that this process is being driven by powerful foreign interests rather than by what is really in the region's long-term best interests.

The conventional new architecture proposals also do not address the constraints that financial liberalization can place on policy makers (in fact, they seem to welcome these constraints as providing sound policy discipline), and they do not question the content of Washington Consensus macroeconomic policies or IMF stabilization programs. None of these proposals considers the possibility of adopting a more coherent regime of managed exchange rates or (with one common exception[10]) more direct measures for controlling volatile capital flows.

The bottom line is that, even if the conventional new architecture proposals were successful in achieving smoother functioning of global capital markets, they would not be adequate to ensure better global outcomes in terms of growth, equity, and stability. These proposal are founded on a narrow vision of what is good for the soundness and functionality of the financial sector itself. But the goal of economic policy should be to promote economic growth that improves living standards for ordinary workers and citizens around the globe, not to maximize the gains of the already wealthy. Moreover, such growth needs to be sustainable in every respect—economically, socially, and ecologically—and the benefits of such growth need to be shared equitably both among countries and among different groups within countries. An efficient and stable financial system should be a means to this end, not an end in itself. In order to make financial markets serve these larger objectives, it is necessary to consider a wider range of reforms than has been contemplated in the conventional conception of a new financial architecture.

Regulating capital flows

In order to pursue these broader goals, and especially to give national governments a greater ability to manage their own economies, it is essential to slow down the rapid movements of short-term hot money that have proven so destabilizing in global financial markets. Thus, Palley (1998b, 1) writes that "The task is to make this money 'cold,' in the sense of getting investors to invest on the basis of economic fundamentals." In this regard, the objective is not to return to a world of mostly closed capital markets—although developing countries that lack adequate institutions and regulations for handling capital mobility need to retain the option to impose substantial limits on capital flows. Rather, the objective is to try to channel capital flows toward longer-term investments that are more stable and that contribute more toward real economic growth. This requires different degrees and forms of capital market openness, depending on a country's level of development and the soundness of its domestic financial system. Or, in other words, "it is a matter of designing an institutional structure that enables the world economy to get the maximum benefit from capital mobility, while containing its costs" (Palley 1998c, 12).

This objective requires carefully targeted restrictions on capital flows that can discourage destabilizing, short-term flows of funds while encouraging more long-term, productive investments—restrictions that are sometimes referred to metaphorically as "speed bumps" or "sand in the wheels." While the gross amount of capital flows would undoubtedly be lower under many of these proposals than it is at present, it is entirely plausible that the long-term, average net capital flows would be larger and that all capital flows would be more stable and more oriented toward longer-term development needs. Also, since many of the pressures on monetary policy come from short-term interest arbitrage or short-term currency speculation, reducing the mobility of short-term funds could do much to relieve policy constraints and to discourage speculative attacks. In what follows, we discuss several specific proposals for discouraging short-term, speculative capital flows.

Taxing foreign exchange transactions
One of the most popular ideas for limiting currency fluctuations and stabilizing financial markets is the notion of taxing foreign exchange transactions, which would lessen the incentives to carry out speculative currency trades. Of these, by far the most well-known proposal is the Tobin tax.

Tobin tax. Named for Nobel laureate James Tobin, who first proposed it (Tobin 1974, 1978), the Tobin tax would be a small percentage levy on all foreign exchange transactions.[11] Such a tax (usually proposed to be on the order of about 0.1% to 0.5%) would significantly lessen the profit margins on short-term currency trading (so-called "round tripping") while having minimal effects on the returns to long-term international investments. Hence, a Tobin tax would discourage the short-term capital movements that have exacerbated exchange rate instability.

While the Tobin tax is a good idea, there are a number of practical problems that would have to be addressed in enacting and implementing it. The tax would have to be fairly universal in coverage in terms of both the types of international financial transactions to which it applied and the locations where the tax was collected, in order to avoid various forms of evasion (such as shifting foreign exchange transactions to offshore tax havens or inventing new ways of trading in currencies that circumvent conventional foreign exchange markets). Monitoring costs would not be trivial, and there might be a need for an international organization such as the IMF to supervise the collection and disbursement of the tax. But there are enforcement problems with any tax, and those connected with the Tobin tax do not appear to be insuperable barriers to its adoption. If anything, a Tobin tax might be considerably less intrusive than some of the other proposals for discouraging short-term capital flows discussed below, which require much more micromanagement of financial institutions' behavior as compared with simply levying a tax on their currency exchanges.

Then there is the question of how to allocate the revenue, which most estimates suggest would be considerable—at least \$100 billion per year and perhaps more than \$200 billion, even assuming a reduced volume of exchange transactions as a result of the tax (see Felix 1996). Some proposals envision spending the money at the international level, such as for multilateral development assistance or environmental protection efforts. Alternatively, part of the tax revenue could be allocated to national governments in order to give them incentives to enact and enforce the tax. Yet another possibility would be to dedicate some of the revenue to an international financial institution to be used to stabilize currency markets (e.g., by creating currency reserves that could be used for foreign exchange market intervention to maintain exchange rate targets). Although it is hard to promote new tax proposals in the current political environment, and it could be difficult to get a sufficient number of countries to agree on a consistent tax policy, the lure of the potential revenue that could be used to address various global problems could help to create a political constituency for adoption of a Tobin tax.

Many economists (e.g., Davidson 1997; Morris and Shin 1998; and Haq, Kaul, and Grunberg 1996) have pointed out that such a small transactions tax would not stop speculators from betting on large expected exchange rate changes. Thus, a Tobin tax should not be expected to eliminate the possibility of speculative attacks on currencies perceived to be seriously misaligned, such as the Thai baht in 1997. But this does not mean that such a tax is of no use. A Tobin tax would seriously discourage short-term round tripping based on small spreads, a practice that accounts for a large proportion of daily foreign exchange transactions. This tax could therefore significantly reduce the volume of short-term currency trading and hence would diminish excess volatility in currency values. A Tobin tax could also enhance the ability of national monetary authorities to intervene in currency markets and to maintain socially desired targets for exchange rates—as long as the targets are not too far out of line with the markets' sense of long-run, sustainable exchange rates. Thus, while a Tobin tax is not a complete answer to international financial turmoil, it does have a useful role to play in the larger package of policy initiatives discussed here, and may be essential for aiding in the establishment of target zones for exchange rates, as advocated below.

Foreign exchange profits tax. An alternative to the Tobin tax is the 100% tax on foreign exchange profits from short-term financial transactions, proposed by French economist Jacques Mélitz (1994). According to Mélitz's proposal, the tax would be levied on "all foreign exchange profits resulting from the sale of assets or the cancellation of debts that were carried for less than one year." The tax would be paid on the aggregate net profits of all foreign exchange transactions by an individual over a year, regardless of where those transactions took place (thus, offshore transactions would not be tax exempt for residents of any country that adopted the tax). Mélitz argues that his tax is superior to Tobin's in the case where only some countries adopted the tax, because each country could effectively tax its own residents' foreign exchange profits regardless of where the transactions took place (whereas Tobin's tax would be collected at the location where the transaction occurred). Mélitz hopes that his tax would be so successful at eliminating speculation that it would collect very little tax revenue, although this might lessen its attractiveness to governments.[12] However, Mélitz admits that a Tobin tax is potentially superior for fighting a speculative attack on a single currency, since it could discourage nonresidents from speculating against that currency in offshore markets—but only if the Tobin tax were universally adopted.

Capital and exchange controls

Historically, countries have used a wide range of types of capital and exchange controls, including restrictions on repatriation of investment income by foreign residents, restrictions on (or prohibitions of) domestic ownership of foreign assets, restrictions on (or prohibitions of) foreign ownership of domestic assets, restrictions on currency convertibility, and restrictions on international banking activity. Capital controls are often specific to particular types of investments, such as direct investment by multinational enterprises, short-term money market funds, pooled funds and derivative instruments, bank loans and deposits, and portfolio capital (e.g., investments in equity shares and bond markets).[13] Exchange controls often vary depending on the intended use of the foreign exchange or the type of agent who wishes to acquire it.

As discussed in previous chapters, capital controls open up space for greater domestic policy autonomy, especially in countries that have fixed or managed exchange rates, high openness to trade, and large international debt positions. Nevertheless, capital controls do not guarantee that policy autonomy will be used wisely, and they do not prevent unsustainable policies from failing. Since any type of controls can be evaded and the amount of evasion responds positively to incentives to move funds across borders, it is important to accompany such controls with other policies (such as interest rate and exchange rate targets) that reduce incentives for circumvention. Nevertheless, capital controls have proved effective in reducing capital flight from developing countries during past financial crises (Pastor 1989, 1990). Such controls do not necessarily increase growth rates, but they do not reduce them either, and they can help to contain financial volatility and to foster lower real interest rates (Rodrik 1998; Grilli and Milesi-Ferretti 1995).

Clearly, the rush to remove all capital controls has gone too far too fast, especially in developing countries with poorly developed internal regulatory and supervisory systems for their financial institutions. Even the IMF and U.S. Treasury now tacitly admit this, with their new emphasis on promoting "orderly" capital market liberalization (see, e.g., Eichengreen and Mussa 1998; Fischer 1998; Summers 1999). Nevertheless, capital controls should not be imposed willy-nilly, and the precise type and strength of controls that are required will vary from country to country. As Keynes (1933, 239) long ago realized, capital controls can be essential for allowing countries to embark on "politico-economic experiments...that...appeal to different national temperaments and historical environments."

In this vein, the type of controls that make sense in a country trying to maintain some kind of state-managed development (e.g., China) will differ from the type that are required in a country pursuing a more market-oriented path (e.g., Chile). Rather than try to fit all countries into the same mold, it is better to let countries choose their own level and style of controls. Excessively tight controls, which create large incentives for evasion and can lead to the growth of black markets and rent-seeking behavior, should be avoided everywhere. Even in countries that are moving in the direction of liberalization, however, the order of liberalization is critical. Serious scholars of the subject (e.g., McKinnon 1993; Fischer and Reisen 1992) argue that the liberalization of short-term external capital inflows should be one of the last stages—after long-term equity and direct foreign investment have been liberalized and after adequate prudential supervision and regulation of domestic financial institutions have been instituted.

Chilean reserve requirements. The Chilean case provides an interesting example of both the usefulness and the limitations of capital controls targeted on short-term inflows, as well as of how such capital controls interact with other policy levers, in a country that has adopted a largely liberalized overall approach to economic development. Starting in 1991, Chile adopted an unremunerated reserve requirement on financial inflows held in the country for under one year. Under this plan, foreign investors have to place a certain percentage of the funds in a non-interest-bearing account (see Aninat and Larraín 1996; Agosin and Ffrench-Davis 1998.)[14] This restriction on short-term capital inflows was part of a package of policies designed to prevent overvaluation of the Chilean peso, which would have thwarted the country's export-oriented growth policies, while encouraging more long-term capital inflows for development purposes.[15] The whole policy package rested on a foundation of fiscal austerity, which made international competitiveness and trade performance critical for sustaining aggregate demand and economic growth.

The results of the Chilean experiment have been mixed. On the positive side, Chile has enjoyed a relatively high proportion of direct investment to portfolio investment throughout the 1990s, a result that is often attributed at least partly to the reserve requirements on short-term inflows. Chile succeeded in obtaining moderate and stable net capital inflows throughout most of this decade (Blecker 1998a), although some of the net inflows were absorbed in the form of increased reserves at the central bank and thus did not contribute to domestic capital formation (Agosin and Ffrench-Davis 1998). Chile managed to avoid the extremes of currency overvaluation and unsustainable current account deficits that precipitated speculative attacks and currency crises in Mexico and Thailand. Indeed, Chile has successfully resisted severe contagion effects from both the Mexican and Asian crises—the country has not had a major financial crisis—and the lack of large, short-term liabilities in foreign currency has been helpful in this regard. However, Chile's resistance to the Asian flu can also be attributed to its well-developed domestic banking regulation and prudential supervision, which assisted in preventing the emergence of risky financial positions of the Asian variety.

In spite of these successes, Chile's experience with controls on short-term capital inflows has not proved entirely satisfactory. High interest rates and expectations of currency appreciation created such large spreads in favor of Chilean assets in 1995-96 that short-term capital inflows increased markedly, in spite of the reserve requirements (Agosin and Ffrench-Davis 1998). The high interest rates were fostered in part by the sterilization of the foreign exchange reserves acquired by the central bank, which required sales of government bonds that depressed their prices and increased their yields. The exchange rate ended up remaining close to the bottom end of the government's wide crawling band (i.e., at the highest value permitted for the value of the peso) through early 1997, so that the exchange rate was effectively fixed and monetary policy autonomy was not enhanced. There is also some econometric evidence that the overall level of short-term inflows was not effectively reduced, which implies that investors may have been able to shift capital inflows into instruments that were (legally or otherwise) exempt from the reserve requirements (Valdés-Prieto and Soto 1998). Moreover, Chile did suffer some contagion effects from the Asian crisis, which led to a depreciation of the peso in mid-1997. By early 1998, Chile found itself having a hard time attracting capital inflows and responded by lowering (eventually to zero) the percentage of required reserves. Overall, the literature on the Chilean reserve requirements concludes that they were more effective in the short term after their initial adoption than in the long term.

The Chilean experience certainly suggests that carefully targeted capital inflow controls can be a useful device for lessening financial volatility and encouraging capital to take a long-term perspective. But the Chilean experience also suggests other lessons about such controls, i.e., they cannot be effective on their own, they need to be accompanied by other measures, they do not automatically enhance policy autonomy, they do not fully insulate a country from external financial pressures, and their effectiveness may erode over time. Small countries like Chile may find it simply impossible to control the huge tides of funds that may wash onto their shores or back out to sea. The Chilean experience thus points out the need to consider other, tougher restrictions on capital flows and foreign exchange.

Malaysia's capital controls.[16] The Malaysian experience shows concretely how tougher capital controls and exchange controls can be used to stabilize an economy. Even before the Asian flu infected Malaysia, the government had restricted private firms' international borrowing by requiring them to demonstrate a capacity to earn enough foreign exchange to service their debts. This meant that Malaysian firms never assumed the kind of short-term liabilities in foreign exchange that made firms in other countries, such as Thailand and Korea, so vulnerable to a currency crisis.

After speculators attacked the Malaysian currency (the ringgit), the Malaysian government imposed strong exchange controls, essentially making ringgit held outside the country inconvertible into foreign exchange (after October 1, 1998) and restricting the amount of cash (national or foreign currency) that Malaysians could take abroad. In addition, Malaysia instituted a temporary (one-year) prohibition against repatriation of earnings by foreign investors on portfolio investments held in the country for less than one year. However, no restrictions were placed on inflows and outflows of capital for commodity trade and long-term investment. Finally, Malaysia also made it compulsory for exporters to turn in foreign currency earnings to the central bank in exchange for ringgit at the new pegged exchange rate.

These exchange controls effectively eliminated overseas holdings of ringgit. This in turn allowed Malaysia to set a new pegged exchange rate and to defend it more easily, since there could no longer be any speculation against the ringgit in offshore markets or short-term capital flight from inside the country. As a result, Malaysia could stabilize its currency while simultaneously lowering its interest rates in order to rejuvenate the domestic economy—thus avoiding the depressing effects of high interest rates used to defend currencies in other crisis countries such as Korea and Brazil. This was a forceful demonstration of one feasible solution to the international policy trilemma discussed in Chapter 1: closing the capital market to short-term flows allowed the country to control both its exchange rate and its interest rate. While the long-run success of Malaysia's policy remains to be demonstrated—and the fact that it is associated with an authoritarian and repressive political regime may lessen its appeal—so far, the low interest rate policy has been successful in stimulating a domestic economic recovery.

Controlling capital outflows from the industrialized countries. The hot money that destabilized financial markets in Mexico, East Asia, Russia, Brazil, and other developing countries came mainly from the rich, industrialized countries. For example, American mutual funds and pension funds invested heavily in emerging markets for stocks and bonds in Asia and Latin America, while Japanese banks lent heavily in Korea and other East Asian countries. Unregulated hedge funds like Long-Term Capital Management (LTCM) invested heavily and with highly leveraged positions in risky assets like Russian government bonds. The behavior of these large, institutional investors was an important contributing factor in the wave of financial panics and contagion effects. Once the institutional investors realized that they were in danger of sustaining significant losses in certain countries (from currency depreciations, asset price declines, or debtor defaults), they were obliged by their fiduciary responsibilities to pull their funds out immediately—which then only exacerbated the declines in currency values and asset markets. In the case of bank lending, the decision of Japanese banks not to roll over short-term Korean debts was the spark that set off the latter country's financial crisis. If institutional investors could be restrained from overextending themselves in lending to risky emerging markets in the first place, the latter would not be subject to such large destabilizing shifts in capital flows.

This aspect of the problem calls for prudential regulation of capital outflows from the industrialized countries. One innovative proposal by D'Arista and Griffith-Jones (1998) is to impose risk-weighted capital requirements on the foreign investment positions of U.S.-based institutional investors such as mutual funds. Institutional investors would be required to place deposits of cash reserves in commercial banks in proportion to the risks in their overseas investments, as assessed by standard regulatory authorities. The deposits would earn interest, but at rates below the rates of return on the funds' other investments. Since these compulsory capital charges would be placed on all types of financial institutions, pooled funds would lose some of the advantages they currently have over banks, which are already subject to capital adequacy requirements. This mechanism would lessen the incentives for all financial institutions to take overly risky and excessively leveraged positions in foreign financial markets. However, this proposal addresses only one source of volatile capital flows—U.S.-based pooled funds—and needs to be accompanied by other measures to discourage other types of capital outflows from the U.S. and other countries.

Aside from discouraging excessive capital outflows from the industrialized countries, another approach is to channel capital flows to developing countries into forms that do not require liquidation of positions when the confidence in the recipient countries falters. Along these lines, D'Arista (1998) proposes the creation of a public, closed-end mutual fund for developing countries, run by a respected international institution such as the World Bank, and "capitalized by purchasing and holding government securities of the major industrial countries" (24). The rationale for creating a closed-end fund (in which the number of shares is fixed, and only their value fluctuates) is to avoid the problems that are created when open-end funds (like mutual funds) have to liquidate positions in order to honor redemptions when shareholders sell their shares. As D'Arista explains,

> As a closed-end fund, the proposed fund's shares could be bought and sold freely in many markets and currencies. Although the value of the fund's shares would fluctuate, it would not have to sell the underlying portfolio in response to a fall in the price of its shares. This would protect emerging markets from the abrupt fluctuations in capital flows that have been associated with foreign portfolio investment in the 1990s....The proposed fund's investment objectives would focus on the economic performance of enterprises and countries rather than short-term financial performance. (D'Arista 1998, 24)

This is an interesting proposal, and probably worth pursuing, but one should note that investors would be free to choose whether to use this fund as a vehicle for investing in emerging markets. Also, share prices of the closed-end fund could fluctuate dramatically, as is already the case for individual country closed-end funds that have exhibited bubble behavior (see Ahmed et al. 1997; Rosser 1997), and share price instability could discourage investment in the proposed fund. The proposed fund would create a channel for promoting stable, long-term capital inflows into developing countries, but it would not guarantee that large amounts of funds would actually flow through that channel.

Other types of controls. The case for trying to control short-term capital outflows from industrialized countries and inflows into developing countries seems clear. Reverse regulations—controls on capital outflows from developing countries and inflows into industrialized countries—are more controversial today, but they should not be rejected out of hand. Certainly, industrialized countries with more sophisticated regulatory mechanisms and more transparent financial practices can tolerate more open capital markets than can developing countries that lack these protections. Nevertheless, the openness of the U.S. and other industrialized countries to capital inflows contributes to economic volatility both at home and abroad. Domestically, capital inflows can contribute to asset market and exchange rate bubbles—and subsequent collapses—in the U.S. or other industrialized countries, just as they do in less-developed nations. The U.S. has repeatedly suffered from large trade deficits and attendant losses of jobs in traded goods sectors (especially manufacturing) due to overvaluation of the dollar caused by large capital inflows (see Morici 1997; Blecker 1992, 1998a). At the same time, the availability of the U.S. as a wide-open "safe haven" for foreign investors increases the threat of capital flight from *other* countries. Rather than allowing panic-driven flights of capital into the U.S., it would be better to encourage capital already invested in developing nations (including the savings of domestic residents) to be more patient in a crisis and to wait for a recovery (which would also help a recovery to occur). Thus, controls on capital outflows from developing countries and inflows to the U.S. could help to stabilize global financial markets and prevent excessive fluctuations in the value of the dollar and the U.S. economy.

Speed bumps: part of the solution

In the end, it is clear that various kinds of capital controls, foreign exchange taxes, and related restrictions (so-called "speed bumps") can potentially be useful in slowing down the rapid inflows and outflows of hot money in global financial markets and lessening their destabilizing impact on national economies. International transactions taxes such as a Tobin tax (or, less likely, a Mélitz tax) could help to restrain speculation-induced fluctuations in floating exchange rates, but are unlikely to prevent speculative attacks on currency pegs perceived to be misaligned by wide margins. For countries that want to retain some measure of autonomy over their monetary policies and to avoid being overwhelmed by the raging currents of global financial flows, it is essential to enact controls on short-term capital flows. However, the exact nature and degree of such controls has to be linked to the specific economic structure and overall policy regime in a particular country as well as the global situation, and as a result we cannot prescribe a single model of capital controls for all countries. Finally, there is much that the major industrialized countries (led by the United States) could do to lessen the volatility of capital flows into and out of smaller and less-developed countries, especially by placing more prudential controls on short-term capital outflows and by reducing the incentives for capital to flee from the latter type of countries in times of crisis.

Taxing speculative transactions and controlling capital flows are important parts of the solution to global financial instability—but they are far from a complete solution. A more comprehensive package of reforms also needs to include an institutional framework to protect the global economy against financial crises; an exchange rate regime to stabilize currency values at levels consistent with larger economic objectives; and a macroeconomic policy approach to foster a more stable pattern of global growth. We now examine each of these items in turn.

Reforming international institutions

The financial crises of the 1990s have generated considerable debate over the appropriate institutional framework for managing the global financial system. Much of this debate concerns the actions and policies of the IMF, which has repeatedly been in the forefront of responding to financial crises—and which has been accused of making those crises worse instead of preventing them. This section briefly reviews the criticisms of the IMF (many of which have been covered in previous chapters) as well as the proposals either to abolish the IMF or else to replace or supplement it with a new set of more powerful international institutions. In the course of this review, we consider the deeper questions about what kinds of international financial institutions are needed and what kinds of policies they should pursue. At the end of this section, we offer our own proposals for fundamentally reforming the governance and practices of the IMF.

Criticisms of the IMF

The IMF was created at the Bretton Woods conference in 1944 to help avoid another global economic depression in the post-World War II period.[17] The IMF was intended to extend credit to countries with short-term balance-of-payments problems in order to enable these countries to continue meeting their obligations to foreign creditors. By providing such credit, IMF intervention was supposed to prevent the debtor countries from having their growth choked off by foreign exchange constraints (i.e., an inability to obtain hard currencies to pay for imports) under the Bretton Woods system of adjustable currency pegs.[18] Although the Bretton Woods exchange rate system was abandoned in 1973, many smaller and less-developed countries still maintain some form of fixed or pegged exchange rates, and the IMF has maintained an active role in lending to these countries in times of financial crisis.

Indeed, the IMF has evolved into an institution that largely lends to, and evaluates or promotes policies in, developing countries and transition economies.[19] Financial markets have come to regard the IMF as an important judge of the credibility of a nation's policies, and hence its willingness to endorse a particular country's policies can be key for ensuring the continuity of private capital inflows. Contrary to the original intentions of its founders, the IMF has long been led by conservative economists generally imbued with a free market, monetarist orientation toward policy. As discussed earlier, the IMF (with the blessing of the U.S. Treasury) has prescribed a package of "sound" macroeconomic policies and liberalized financial markets combined with improved prudential supervision and greater transparency as the cure-all for financial crises in developing nations.

While the IMF's policies have been controversial for a long time,[20] its failure to prevent the spread of financial crises around the world in the late 1990s has led to more widespread criticism by prominent economists and political scientists (e.g., Calomiris 1998; Feldstein 1998; Friedman 1998b; Kissinger 1998; Radelet and Sachs 1998a; Sachs 1998b, 1998c). Today's critics charge that the IMF's bailout policies have actually exacerbated the recent financial crises since the Mexican peso collapse of 1994-95—both in the sense of making individual crises worse than necessary and in the sense of spreading the contagion to additional countries.

Although different critics emphasize different points, the charges against the IMF include the following:

- imposing excessively harsh austerity policies that unnecessarily depress a country's economy as a condition of obtaining bailouts;

- inviting speculative attacks by encouraging countries to maintain indefensible exchange rate targets with unsustainably high interest rates;

- worsening moral hazard problems by repeatedly bailing out foreign investors who take imprudent risks (and thus encouraging them to overinvest again);

- exacerbating financial panics by announcing that countries with temporary illiquidity problems and fundamentally sound economies were suffering from deep structural flaws;

- pushing capital market liberalization on countries that lack the requisite internal institutions and regulations to manage the resulting capital inflows;

- unduly interfering with domestic institutions and practices that are unrelated to the IMF's core mission of solving balance-of-payments problems;

- prescribing macroeconomic and financial policies that ignore structural features of national economies and that fail to take account of their likely social and political effects; and

- worsening inequality by making ordinary workers and citizens bear the burden of adjustment through increased unemployment and reduced incomes, while bailing out wealthy creditors (both domestic and foreign).

The economic logic behind these charges has been discussed extensively in previous chapters and will not be repeated here. Rather, we turn here to discuss the three leading options for what to do about the IMF: abolish it, replace it, or reform it.

Abolish the IMF?

Calls for abolishing the IMF have come primarily from strong supporters of free market capitalism (e.g., Friedman 1998; Schwartz 1998). These economists argue that private investors in liberalized capital markets should be penalized in a crisis by taking significant losses in asset values and investment income, and that the threat of such discipline is essential to induce investors to be more cautious and prudent. In this view, IMF bailouts interfere with the normal workings of the free market and foster a problem of "moral hazard." That is, investors who believe that they will be bailed out whenever their investments are endangered are likely to make too many highly risky investments in the first place. Thus, bailouts of countries in crisis only encourage more imprudent lending that eventually leads to more crises down the road. If only the IMF would get out of the way, this argument implies, market discipline would work its magic, and the problem of overlending to risky countries would soon disappear.

This view is flawed for two reasons. First, market discipline works only at a potentially severe social cost: borrowers are cut off from new funds, and thus can be forced to accept draconian cuts in their incomes and expenditures, while lenders' losses can be so great as to precipitate widespread failures of financial institutions, which in turn can cripple the functioning of the entire economic system. It was exactly these kinds of problems with market discipline that originally led to the establishment of lender-of-last-resort intervention by central banks in individual countries and IMF bailouts at the international level. Second, precisely because the costs of pure free market adjustment can be so high, there is an almost inevitable tendency of financial regulators to adopt a "too-big-to-fail" attitude and bail out endangered financial institutions. As a result, a prior commitment not to engage in bailouts is unlikely to be realistic or credible. Even without an IMF, for example, leading central banks might feel obligated to assist countries in financial distress (just as the U.S. Federal Reserve orchestrated a private bailout of the LTCM hedge fund, even thought it had no legal authority to do so).

If bailouts are inevitable, it seems prudent to have an institution in charge of them and to regulate how that institution carries out its rescues of financially strapped nations. Moral hazard is potentially a serious problem in financial rescue efforts, however, and crisis intervention needs to be designed in ways that minimize it. The key to minimizing moral hazard problems is to make sure that creditors bear a large share of the adjustment burden in a financial crisis, as will be discussed in more detail below.

Abolishing the IMF without creating any new institution in its place would take us back to the 19th century of unregulated capitalism with frequent and recurrent crises, not forward to a 21st century of more stable and equitable growth. Indeed, the current global financial turmoil demonstrates more than ever that the world needs international institutions to regulate and manage financial markets and to improve macroeconomic performance. A capitalist market economy cannot operate in a social vacuum; it requires a sound foundation of legal regulations and social protections in order to contain the destructive side of its creative forces (Polanyi 1944). Although we are far from having a totally integrated global economy, international interdependency and interlinkages—especially in the financial area—have reached a point where the world cannot afford a vacuum in international policy coordination and the ability to act to contain crises. The needs for prudential regulation by supervisory agencies and lender-of-last-resort intervention by central banks have long been recognized in national economies like the United States. As the world economy becomes more integrated, it must evolve the same sorts of regulatory institutions that have proven crucial—and effective—for regulating financial markets in individual nations (see Minsky 1982, 1986). The question, then, is what kind of international institutions are needed and how they should operate, given that that there is no world government in charge of the world economy and political power remains in the hands of individual nations.

New international financial institutions

If international institutions are needed and the IMF is not doing the job, an obvious alternative is to construct new institutions that could more effectively stabilize the global financial system. Most proposals for new global financial institutions can be grouped into three categories: a world central bank, an international supervisory institution, and an international monetary clearinghouse. Although in practice there is some overlap in the functions intended for the proposed new institutions, they have conceptually distinct roles, and we shall discuss each type separately. We discuss only the first two types of institutions here; international monetary clearinghouses (or, more modestly, exchange stabilization funds) are discussed in the next section on exchange rate management. Also, while most of these proposals call for new global institutions, other proposals call for creating smaller, regional institutions; these proposals will be discussed separately.

*A **world central bank***. The notion of creating a world central bank arises from an understanding of the inherent limitations of the IMF for dealing with global financial problems. Although the IMF is often referred to as a "lender of last resort," by analogy to a domestic central bank, the IMF is not in fact a central bank and cannot perform all of the lender-of-last-resort functions that a national central bank can perform. All the IMF can do is to loan money[21] to governments of countries that have balance-of-payments problems and debt crises, in exchange for conditions imposed on the countries' macroeconomic and exchange rate policies (and sometimes on broader financial and regulatory policies, such as capital controls). It cannot take over and manage failed national financial institutions that have contributed to the countries' financial difficulties, or even force domestic regulatory authorities to do so. It also cannot engage in expansionary monetary policy—i.e., it cannot directly inject liquidity into an economy by buying up public debts—although it can replenish a country's foreign exchange reserves, which helps to relieve the contraction of liquidity in a crisis.

Those who favor a world central bank argue that the IMF's lack of true central banking powers renders it incapable of reacting in a positive way to an international financial crisis of the magnitude witnessed in 1997-99. Because of the limitations on the IMF's role, it is naturally led to prescribe policies that emphasize domestic adjustments by individual countries in crisis—the standard package of currency devaluation, fiscal austerity, and monetary tightening derived from the elasticities, absorption, and monetary approaches to the balance of payments as discussed in Chapter 2. These standard policy levers can solve an isolated balance-of-payments problem in a single country—albeit at the cost of sparking a domestic economic downturn (and often much social pain and suffering). But these policies are globally dysfunctional when applied to a large group of countries at once.[22] Simultaneous devaluations by large numbers of countries cause competitive problems for other countries (both from increased imports and reduced exports), possibly leading to competitive devaluations or protectionist responses that can cause a downward spiral of global purchasing power. And fiscal and monetary contraction in large groups of countries depresses global aggregate demand, possibly provoking an international recession. Thus, instead of functioning as a true global lender of last resort, the IMF ends up draining demand stimulus from the international system just when it is needed most. One of the side effects of this lack of true lender-of-last-resort intervention is the fact that the U.S. economy is pressured to provide the demand stimulus for the entire world as the "market of last resort"—a role that is untenable in the long run both socially (because of the losses of jobs and incomes at home) and financially (because of the future debt problem it creates—see Blecker 1998a).

Yale School of Management Dean Jeffrey E. Garten advocates a global central bank that would see the need for global reflation in these circumstances and act accordingly. As he explains it,

A global central bank could provide more money to the world economy when it is rapidly losing steam. For example, it could buy the bonds of the Central Bank of Brazil, thereby injecting hard currency into that country when it most needs the help (like right now). It would have the ability to buy a country's debt at steep discounts, a crucial need now because in countries like Thailand and Venezuela debts are piling up and preventing new lending and new investment. (Garten 1998)

Garten's world central bank would involve a number of difficulties, both technical and political. The technical difficulties include above all its financing, which could come from credits extended by national central banks, or from a dedicated source of tax revenue (such as a Tobin tax on foreign exchange transactions or a modest tariff on trade in goods and services). The governance of a global central bank—and the whole question of how much authority national central banks would cede to it, and whether they would be willing to do so—is an even more difficult problem. Garten suggests that the bank be governed collectively by the major industrialized countries and representative developing countries, but this is clearly an unresolved issue in his proposal.

Another proposal for an international central bank (ICB) comes from D'Arista and Schlesinger (1998). The ICB's assets would consist of its member countries' government debt, and its liabilities would consist of the member central banks' currency reserves. The ICB would be able to conduct open market operations in any country's bond markets and could thus inject liquidity directly into a national banking system through open market purchases. D'Arista and Schlesinger also envision that all international payments would be cleared through the ICB, with each country's residents able to settle their obligations in their own currency under a system of adjustable exchange rate pegs (thus, the ICB serves as a monetary clearinghouse as well as a central bank). Essentially, the ICB would put foreign exchange markets out of business, thus closing down the casino in which currency speculators place their bets. This is an ingenious and visionary conception of how the world could achieve a quasi-monetary union without adopting a single currency, but most governments are unlikely to cede so much power to a new global institution in the foreseeable future. It should also be noted that the ICB would not eliminate the exchange risk arising from the fact that exchange rates would be adjustable; this risk would still be borne by anyone with outstanding international obligations.[23]

An international supervisory institution. While the proposals for a world central bank focus on the need for a true international lender of last resort, proposals for an international supervisory institution address another missing function in the global financial system: a regulatory agency capable of enforcing common prudential standards on financial institutions around the world. This idea builds upon the basic new architecture concept of making capital markets work better, but adds an institutional dimension that is lacking from conventional new architecture proposals that do not specify how greater transparency and improved risk management would be enforced.[24]

One vision of such a new institution comes from Henry Kaufman, who calls it a "Board of Overseers of Major Institutions and Markets." This board would

> ...set forth a code of conduct for market participants to encourage reasonable financial behavior. It would supervise risk-taking not only by banks and other financial institutions that have always been regulated and supervised but also by new participants in the global markets. It would be empowered by member governments to harmonize minimum capital requirements, to establish uniform trading, reporting and disclosure standards and to monitor the performance of institutions and markets under its purview. (Kaufman 1998)

Another plan for an international supervisory institution comes from John Eatwell and Lance Taylor, who propose a "World Financial Authority" (WFA) that would grow out of an expanded role for the existing Bank for International Settlements (BIS). The BIS is a little-known institution in Basle, Switzerland, which serves as a clearinghouse for transactions between central banks and also promulgates prudential standards for national banking systems (such as the Basle Core Principles). The WFA would be "a body that develops and imposes regulatory procedures" as well as "a forum within which the rules of international financial cooperation are developed and implemented" (Eatwell and Taylor 1998a). Eatwell and Taylor argue that countries would voluntarily want to join the WFA and submit to its regulations because the WFA stamp of approval would become essential for attracting international investment. They also suggest that the WFA would be given authority to oversee the activities of the IMF and World Bank— to keep them "transparent" and hold them "accountable"—and would "monitor and mediate the imposition of capital controls by national governments" (Eatwell and Taylor 1998b, 1998c). However, as in many of these proposals, it is not clear to whom the WFA itself would be accountable or how it would be governed.

Regional alternatives. Instead of creating new global institutions, an alternative approach is to create new institutions for managing international financial flows at the regional level. Indeed, there are already powerful forces pushing toward greater regional economic integration, especially in Europe, East Asia, and the Americas. Europe is the most advanced area in terms of institutionalizing its integration process, with the formation of an economic and political union in the European Union (EU) and a monetary union (with somewhat fewer members) in the European Monetary Union (EMU). The Americas have only a few subregional trade agreements (NAFTA, Mercosur) and a vague commitment to form a continental free trade area in the future, while Asia merely has a forum for intergovernmental cooperation in the ASEAN group. These differences are understandable, given Europe's longer history of integration efforts and the more similar levels of economic development prevailing within Europe compared with Asia or the Americas.

Policy makers in other regions will be watching the EMU to see if it can serve as a model for regional coordination of monetary and exchange rate policy. Monetary integration in other regions would probably take different forms from the EMU's creation of a new regional currency. In the Western Hemisphere, the U.S. is so hegemonic that the most likely scenario is other countries simply "dollarizing" their economies (i.e., accepting the U.S. dollar as local currency, or issuing a domestic currency that is legally tied to the dollar in a one-to-one ratio). In Asia, the rivalries between the major countries are sufficiently strong (and the countries are so diverse) that a coherent currency bloc may not be politically feasible for many decades to come.

While the EMU may serve as a model, however, it also suggests several important cautions (see Allsopp and Vines 1998). The most important issue is who controls the regional central bank and how it sets its common monetary policies. In the European case, the European Central Bank (ECB) was deliberately set up as an independent body that would be unresponsive to the concerns of member countries so that it could focus on making the euro a strong currency with low inflation. This means that high interest rates and high unemployment have been the price that countries have had to pay for joining the EMU. A second issue concerns the lack of regional supervision of financial institutions or a regional fiscal policy within the EMU, which will make it hard to compensate for any local difficulties that ECB policies create (i.e., if high interest rates cause widespread bank failures or depressed business conditions in a particular member country).

The European example does suggest that, as countries within a region converge in structure and aspirations, and as the need to manage the ongoing integration process becomes more apparent, countries may be more willing to surrender some of their sovereignty at the regional level than they are at the global level. Especially, countries are likely to feel that they will have more input into a regional monetary authority than they could ever have in a global institution, and hence are likely to find regional institutions less threatening to their national sovereignty than a global central bank or supervisory institution. Nevertheless, the structure of the ECB suggests that small countries need to be cautious about assuming how much voice they will have in a regional organization dominated by a few larger nations. Latin American countries need to be especially cautious about dollarizing their economies if this would mean surrendering their monetary policies to the U.S. Federal Reserve, which does not take their needs into account in setting its interest rate targets.[25]

Aside from regional monetary unions, a less-intrusive possibility is the creation of regional funds for stabilizing financial markets that could compete with the IMF. Early in the Asian crisis in 1997, Japan proposed setting up an Asian mechanism to bail out the countries in crisis. This proposal was quashed by a negative reaction from the U.S. Treasury, which wanted to have more control over the response to the Asian crisis by giving the IMF (where the U.S. largely calls the shots) a monopoly on managing the response. Given the IMF's flawed handling of the Asian crisis, proposals for regional stabilization funds should be reconsidered.

Wade and Veneroso (1998a, 1998b) argue for the creation of an Asian Monetary Fund (AMF). They point out that the Asian countries as a whole (led by Japan, China, and Taiwan) still have enormous financial strengths, such as large foreign currency reserves and positive external creditor positions. The Asian countries also have a good understanding of the region's unique structural characteristics, such as the high debt ratios of corporations and the long-term relations between borrowers and lenders that are now derided as "crony capitalism"—relations that served Asia well for many decades and that have been poorly understood by the outside world. Hence, Wade and Veneroso reason, an AMF would have both the resources and the information to do a better job of assisting those Asian countries that get into financial trouble. They also hint that an AMF would be more sympathetic to strategies that partially closed off Asian countries to Western financial flows, such as the Malaysian exchange controls. After all, several leading Asian countries (especially China and Taiwan) never liberalized short-term capital flows in the first place—and these countries have remained much more insulated from the Asian contagion than their neighbors with more open financial markets.

Wade and Veneroso also argue that the AMF could offer the IMF competition in the sense of testing whose policy solutions work better. Presumably, a regional fund like the proposed AMF could inject liquidity into countries with financial crises more quickly, and with less inappropriate conditionality, than the IMF. Had such a fund existed in 1997, the authors suggest, the Asian crisis might never have spread so far or led to such large collapses in real production and employment. More broadly, regional stabilization funds controlled by their member governments with less interference from Washington might have a better sense of how to handle local situations and prevent them from blowing up into major global crises. However, it is not clear how realistic this approach is outside of Asia, where enough countries have sufficient financial strength to make intra-regional rescue packages feasible.

The prospects for new financial institutions. The proposals for new global financial institutions contain valuable insights into more sensible ways of managing and regulating international financial markets. Especially, a world central bank would be extremely useful because it would provide an institutional mechanism for injecting liquidity directly into countries that need it in times of financial distress. This could help enormously to counteract the deflationary pressures that result from individual countries having to contract in order to cure their own payments deficits. The other proposals regarding international supervisory oversight and payments clearing are even more visionary, but still need more work to flesh out how they would operate and what benefits they would bring.

However, any evaluation of proposed new institutions must consider their political feasibility. The Bretton Woods institutions (the IMF and World Bank) were created at a time when the international system was emerging from a global depression and a world war—and when two countries (the United States and United Kingdom) could basically decide the outcome of the process (with a single country, the United States, largely getting its way). While it will not necessarily take an international crisis of those dimensions to pave the way for new international institutions, it would probably take a global crisis much more severe than what the world has thus far experienced since 1997. The prospects for creating new institutions are currently much better at the regional level, where countries are more similar and could expect to have more voice in the operation of new organizations. But if recent history teaches us anything, it is that global conditions can change rapidly. Therefore, those who are concerned with promoting global prosperity and stability need to continue working on long-term visions for more comprehensive international financial institutions.

At the same time, it is important to recognize the potential danger in creating new overarching global institutions that would seek to impose a uniform regulatory regime or monetary policy approach on all nations. The international economy is far from being perfectly integrated or homogenized. The diversity of national structures and development levels suggests a continued need for some degree of autonomy in designing optimal financial systems and monetary policies for different types of countries. Some of the promoters of new global institutions insist that their proposed new organizations would enhance national autonomy by freeing countries from the dictates of short-term investors and currency speculators. However, any autonomy gained through this channel could be fleeting if the new institutions ended up enforcing their own harsh discipline on their member countries. The history of the IMF and World Bank amply demonstrates how international institutions can evolve very far from the intentions of their founders and end up imposing their own agendas on vulnerable nations.

This brings us to the deep and difficult questions that would have to be addressed about the governance and accountability of any new institutions. These questions have not been resolved in a satisfactory way at the IMF and World Bank, which continue to be largely creatures of U.S. government policy—especially (in the former case) the policies favored by the Treasury Department and Wall Street financial interests.[26] To create new institutions without solving these problems would run the risk of creating a new and even more powerful set of unresponsive global bureaucracies, which could be "captured" by the vested interests in Wall Street and other financial centers just as the IMF has.

Fundamental IMF reform

If the world does need international financial institutions, yet is unlikely to get new ones in the immediate future, it is vital to focus on reforming the most important such institution that already exists: the IMF. In this section, we propose four practical ways in which the IMF could be transformed into a more responsive and functional institution for global financial management within a period of a few years: (1) replace the current leadership and put the organization in temporary receivership; (2) open up its organizational structure to allow for greater accountability and more democratic governance; (3) change its long-term mission to put more emphasis on macroeconomic prosperity and social justice; and (4) redesign rescue packages to better meet the needs of individual countries and to shift more of the adjustment burden from debtors to creditors.

New leadership. The current leadership and bureaucracy of the IMF have failed miserably at their primary task of stabilizing countries' balance of payments and preventing the spread of financial contagion at an acceptable social cost. If the government of any democratic country had failed as much in its economic policies as the IMF has failed in country after country, that government would long since have fallen or lost an election. Therefore, the first condition for reforming the IMF is that its entire top leadership should resign or be fired, including not only the political leadership, but also the top economic advisors (essentially, the equivalent of the resignation of the government in a parliamentary political system, which would include the departure of the finance minister and his or her staff).

Since much of the IMF's ideology and practices are entrenched in its bureaucracy, many of its senior staffers should also be induced to leave. Golden parachutes should be prohibited, but with reasonable conditions some early retirements of long-term staffers could be justified. At the same time, there are many good people on the IMF staff—especially in the Research Department, which has often produced scholarship that forthrightly analyzes the sources of instability in the global financial system and the costs of capital market liberalization (including some of the innovative research cited in Chapter 2). Innovative thinkers who are not wedded to the current policy line should be identified and promoted from within where possible, while new blood should be brought in from the outside.

To make this happen without unduly undermining confidence, the IMF should be placed in temporary receivership by the major governments of the world, including developing countries as well as industrialized nations. A respected financial leader—someone with a pragmatic bent and without a strong ideological agenda—should be placed in charge. He or she should recruit top specialists in international finance and macroeconomics—academics, policy analysts, and financial specialists—who have visions for reforming the IMF and its operations, to serve on a temporary board of overseers. The World Bank, which has become a source of relatively progressive thinking on global economic needs under President James Wolfensohn and chief economist Joseph Stiglitz, should be represented on the board of overseers.[27] The current monolithic viewpoint at the IMF should be replaced with a diversity of perspectives, including views from different parts of the globe as well as different parts of the political spectrum. This receivership should be only temporary, and should function as a transitional authority toward the new structure outlined below.

Accountability and governance. The IMF must be subject to more democratic control, and its policy making should be opened up to more public scrutiny and peer review. As Palley (1998c, 24) puts it, "Just as the IMF has insisted on increased transparency in government and in financial markets, so too its decision making [should] be made transparent." Sachs (1998b, 21) proposes that the IMF should make all its current program documents and the archives of its past programs public, in order to open up IMF policies to "public debate and critical scrutiny." Of course, governments may resist making outside analysis of their economic situation public, but governments that refuse to allow such scrutiny should be denied access to IMF loans and bailouts. Publication of internal IMF documents and country studies is important partly for allowing peer review and public discussion of the IMF's own analysis and advice; it may also give financial markets more advance warnings of countries' problems that would inhibit the build-up of unsustainable financial positions based on underestimates of country risks. Such ideas for making the IMF itself more transparent have been accepted in principle by the G-22 (see U.S. Council of Economic Advisers 1999, 269-70), but much remains to be done to implement and enforce this in practice.

In addition, more democratic control of the IMF by all member countries is needed to make it serve the interests of the whole international community, rather than the dictates of what Bhagwati (1998, 7) calls the "Wall Street-Treasury complex." Of course, political reality dictates that the United States and other large industrialized nations, who foot most of the IMF's bills, will continue to have a large influence. But voting on the IMF's board should be changed, for example, by allocating a larger proportion of the votes to developing countries than they currently receive. A diversity of perspectives from Europe, Japan, and developing nations is essential to ensure that the IMF understands and responds to a variety of needs beyond those of large investors in the major financial centers of a few industrialized countries. To ensure that this happens, power in the IMF should be shifted away from the current "interim board" (which largely defers to the top administrators, who in turn defer to the U.S. Treasury) to a permanent board of directors with a more equitable allotment of voting rights and a greater role in determining the Fund's policies.

A more representative board could also play a greater role in oversight of IMF operations and policies. For example, the board could institute a formal "process of external review and evaluation of past programs," as advocated by Sachs (1998b, 21). Regular external reviews of IMF programs and policies should be conducted to prevent the kind of insular and defensive view that has enveloped the Fund up to the present. This external review process could incorporate evaluations of IMF programs for their impact on poverty, equity, the environment, and long-term development needs by the World Bank or other international organizations.

Finally, it will be hard to reverse the conservative bias in IMF policies if its governance is merely opened up to a wider range of finance ministries and treasury departments, which generally tend to be exceptionally cautious and are often subservient to financial interests. Therefore, the IMF needs input from a broader range of sources in its member countries, including nonfinancial officials and nongovernmental organizations (NGOs) concerned with labor, industry, agriculture, the environment, and other interests as well as finance. This involvement will help to ensure that the IMF begins to pursue a wider set of social objectives, as discussed under the next point. Some limited input along these lines was legislated as part of the congressional deal that approved an $18 billion extension of U.S. contributions to the Fund in 1998; this arrangement created a broad-based advisory board to the U.S. Treasury secretary in regard to the U.S. position at the Fund. But such broader input needs to be institutionalized at the IMF itself.

A broader mission. The IMF is a public institution charged with overseeing the international payments system in the public interest. Many of the problems with the IMF's role stem from an overly narrow conception of the public interest it is supposed to pursue, focused solely on stabilizing international financial markets and promoting anti-inflationary policies. The IMF needs to redefine its overarching mission as promoting sustainable global growth with full employment and an equitable distribution of income in its member countries. Its interventions in countries with balance-of-payments problems should be designed with these larger objectives in mind, rather than having these objectives sacrificed to serve financial interests that want to salvage the value of their investments while imposing the costs of their imprudent lending on debtors.

This broader mission for the IMF has two components, a macroeconomic element and a social dimension. On the macroeconomic side, in order to avoid unnecessary losses of global jobs and production, the IMF should take responsibility for international oversight of the global level of aggregate demand—

thus playing part of the role that a global central bank would play if one were created. The IMF should monitor aggregate demand conditions and report on situations where there is an undue bias toward deflation and contraction in the global economy (just as it now monitors undue inflationary biases). The IMF needs to worry about avoiding global recessions or depressions just as much as it worries about avoiding global inflation. Stiglitz (1998, 14) endorses such a shift in global policy objectives when he writes,

> macroeconomic stability—as conceived by the Washington consensus— typically downplays stabilizing output or employment. Minimizing or avoiding major economic contractions should be one of the most important goals of policy. In the short run, large-scale involuntary unemployment is clearly inefficient—in purely economic terms it represents idle resources that could be used more productively. The social and economic costs of these downturns can be devastating....

There will always be times when individual countries go into recessions, as well as occasions when balance-of-payments problems cannot be solved without some contraction of domestic economic activity (although the amount of contraction should be limited as much as possible). The problem today is that the simultaneous adjustment of many countries in crisis by cutting their domestic expenditures is having significant contractionary spillover effects onto other countries. Therefore, there is a need for an international body to step in and call for simultaneous reflation by those countries that are best able to expand their economies, especially those with unemployed resources and trade surpluses (currently, Japan and most of Western Europe). Such a coordinated injection of demand could greatly alleviate the adjustment burden on the deficit countries, allowing them to rectify their payments imbalances with smaller reductions in domestic incomes and expenditures. But coordinated demand expansion requires an institution capable of monitoring global economic conditions and identifying the need for demand stimulus by particular countries—and in the absence of a global central bank, this task should be carried out by the IMF.

An objection could be raised that too much of a focus on maintaining global demand could distract the IMF from its core purpose of rectifying international payments imbalances—and could prevent the imposition of needed adjustment policies. But this is a false opposition. First, the original intention of the IMF (in the vision of John Maynard Keynes and Harry Dexter White) was precisely that having an institution to lend to countries with balance-of-payments problems would help to maintain global demand and prevent another Great Depression. It is therefore a complete perversion of the IMF's original mission for it to solve balance-of-payments problems in ways that threaten, rather than support, the maintenance of global prosperity. Second, there is no reason to think that a regime of restricted demand, high unemployment, and slow growth is one that ultimately serves the interests of financial stability itself. As discussed in Chapter 1, financial investors want to invest in countries that are prosperous and booming—the problem has been that they overdo this, not that they want to invest in countries that are depressed and stagnant. This is not to say that all pain and sacrifice can be avoided in cases of financial crisis, but policy responses need to be designed to minimize income and employment losses, limit business cycle downturns, and revive economic growth.

On the social side, human rights and democratic freedoms are a legitimate concern of a global financial institution like the IMF in places where the lack of these contributes to corruption and cronyism in business enterprises and financial markets (e.g., Indonesia or Russia). Support for core labor rights (such as freedom from child labor or the right to organize) and improved labor standards (such as reasonable minimum wages and enforced health and safety regulations) should be incorporated into IMF policy as offsets to other policies (e.g., currency devaluations or fiscal austerity) that tend to cut real wages and hurt workers. Moreover, if excessive competition over export markets is a cause of currency crises, part of the solution must lie in expanding internal markets. This in turn requires more wage-led growth, which cannot occur when workers' rights are systematically abused and minimal standards are not enforced (see Palley 1998a, 1998b). Finally, there is increasing concern over the environmental impact of the IMF's stabilization policies—for example, when countries are induced to exploit their natural resources more intensively in order to export their way out of debt crises. Consequently, the enforcement of environmental protection efforts is also a crucial offset to other components of the IMF's activities.[28]

An objection could also be raised that broadening the IMF's mission in this way would involve the Fund inappropriately in dictating domestic social policies and thus would violate countries' sovereignty (a position implicitly adopted by Bullard et al. 1998). Interestingly, the same argument has been made (e.g., by Feldstein 1998) about the fund violating national sovereignty in other areas, such as mandating how countries should reform their banking systems or open their capital markets. The important point here is one of consistency. If the IMF could somehow keep itself completely out of the business of influencing countries' internal policies, it would be reasonable to insist that it overlook issues of human rights, labor standards, and environmental protection as well as issues of banking regulation, macroeconomic policies, and financial practices. But this is simply not possible.

Even by carrying out the narrowest conception of its mission—i.e., assisting countries in solving balance-of-payments crises—the IMF is necessarily involved in promoting policies that have profound effects on income distribution, living standards, and environmental conditions. For example, the traditional trinity of IMF-supported adjustment policies—currency devaluation, fiscal austerity, and monetary contraction (higher interest rates)—typically cuts real wages, increases poverty, and widens inequality—and sometimes induces environmentally destructive practices by citizens reduced to destitution. When the IMF gets involved in broader areas of market-oriented "reform" (such as privatization of state enterprises, deregulation of industry, and liberalization of trade and finance), it is unavoidably endorsing policies that have strong biases in terms of who benefits and who loses.

In short, the IMF cannot do its job without affecting social outcomes in one way or another. Its policies are never socially neutral. Especially if the IMF is going to set standards for countries to participate in the modern world of global finance (e.g., in regard to financial transparency, banking regulation, bankruptcy laws, and so on), it needs to have a more balanced set of criteria for determining what a "modern" country's social standards should be. Moreover, the IMF does not have to act alone in these areas: as social and environmental standards come to be accepted parts of international trade negotiations, other institutions such as the International Labor Organization (ILO) and World Trade Organization (WTO) may develop institutional capabilities for monitoring and enforcing labor rights, human rights, and environmental protection around the world. The point is that the IMF must become another pillar for seeking to harmonize social standards upward throughout the world, instead of a force for undermining them through harsh austerity conditions and market liberalization efforts. Thus, respect for basic human freedoms and labor rights, as well as reasonable efforts to upgrade labor and environmental standards, should become part of the long-term policy reform package that the IMF insists on for member countries to qualify for assistance.

Redesigning rescue packages. The repeated failures and high costs of IMF rescue packages in recent years call for new thinking about what policies those packages should contain—which in turn requires recognition of the changed causes of financial crises. In the early postwar years when capital was largely immobile, balance-of-payments crises could be attributed solely to inconsistent macroeconomic policies and misaligned exchange rates, and traditional cures emphasizing monetary and fiscal responses along with currency devaluation were more appropriate. In today's world of highly mobile capital, this type of policy approach is no longer adequate.

In a world where balance-of-payments crises can be imported via volatile capital flows, and where speculative attacks and panics can greatly exaggerate any underlying policy weaknesses, a new approach to IMF intervention is called for. The guiding principle should be that IMF interventions should focus on rescuing the affected countries, not on bailing out the imprudent investors who caused the problems in the first place. This does not mean that debtor countries can or should escape all costs of adjustment, or that genuine policy weaknesses should not be corrected. But the primary purpose of rescue packages should be to get the countries back on their feet and restore their ability to participate in international commerce and meet the needs of their citizens as quickly as possible.

In order to minimize the costs imposed on groups in the debtor countries who were not responsible for creating the financial crisis in the first place, a substantial part of the adjustment burden should be shifted onto creditors. This requires two major types of changes in bailout policies: first, forcing creditors to take more of a "hit"; and second, modifying the conditions that debtor countries are required to meet (so-called "conditionality"). The first type of change would help to reduce the moral hazards created by IMF intervention, while the second type would ameliorate the often regressive distributional impact of its stabilization policies.

There have been several worthwhile proposals for limiting the degree to which creditors benefit from country bailouts. One useful idea is what has come to be known as "conditional haircuts" (see, e.g., Shadow Financial Regulatory Committee 1998). As originally explained by Richard N. Haass and Robert E. Litan,

> A possible solution is for the IMF to condition its assistance on countries' penalizing all lenders of foreign currency in the event IMF intervention is required. In particular, the model legislation that each country could adopt would require (as long as an IMF rescue is in effect) that creditors automatically suffer some loss of their principal when their debt matures and is not rolled over or extended. (Haass and Litan 1998, 5)

Helfer (1998, 5) further specifies that the write-downs or "haircuts" would be required for "foreign currency denominated interbank loans" and that "Ideally, the haircuts would be equivalent to the discounts that markets impose on a country's sovereign debt just prior to the IMF rescue." The option for creditors to roll over their loans (as a means of avoiding a haircut) is intended to induce them to remain "bailed in" to a country after a financial crisis, a response that would help to mitigate the crisis by lessening panic-driven withdrawals of funds. However, while rolling over debts could thus help to reduce volatility, it does not relieve the problem of excessive debt burdens, which calls for other solutions.

To address the problem of excessive debt burdens, several devices are needed in order to reduce them to manageable levels—some of which have been incorporated in the official new architecture proposals discussed above. The first is that debtor countries need to adopt formal bankruptcy codes, which would allow overburdened private companies to force creditors to accept write-downs of part of their asset values while still recuperating a portion that the borrowers can reasonably afford to service. This is an area where the IMF or an alternative institution could provide technical assistance, and even require countries to comply by adopting and enforcing appropriate legislation as a precondition for qualifying for future bailouts. Of course, a move toward more transparent accounting practices, as contemplated in most new architecture proposals, is an essential prerequisite for bankruptcy procedures to be effective and equitable.

Second, debtor countries should be encouraged to engage in debt-for-equity swaps that could reduce cash commitments for debt service while giving foreign creditors more of a stake in the success of domestic enterprises. Debt-equity swaps also result in reductions in the values of foreign-owned assets to more realistic levels determined in the markets for the newly created equity. The IMF could require that creditors accept such swaps as a condition of bailing out debtor nations. Third, banking regulators in creditor countries should require banks to take losses for international loans that effectively cannot be serviced, rather than keeping them on the books and rolling them over indefinitely. While this is not something the IMF can enact on its own, it could help by promoting such policies as a way of reducing the amount of public funds needed for bailout efforts—and other international institutions (such as the BIS or a new international supervisory agency) could help by making such a requirement part of the core principles that countries should adopt for banking regulation. Finally, the unserviceable debts owed by governments of the poorest debtors—the so-called Highly Indebted Poor Countries—should be cancelled outright, as advocated by Sachs (1998a).

On the debtors' side, IMF "conditionality"—the set of policy changes that countries have to agree to in order to receive IMF loans—needs to be reevaluated. A detailed diagnosis of each country's structure and problems should lead to a country-specific, situationally appropriate policy package. This objective cannot be accomplished under the IMF's current modus operandi, in which teams of in-house "experts" fly into a country and concoct a country plan in a few days based on a cookie-cutter model imported from Washington. Countries that are on the receiving end of IMF loans and advice must have more participation and influence in the solutions to their own problems. The IMF should consult with teams of experts from the affected countries on the root causes of their problems and effective approaches for solving them. As Jeffrey Sachs has written,

> it is time to end the IMF's artificial monopoly on policymaking in the
> developing world. The IMF complains frequently that member
> governments don't feel proper "ownership" of the programs that they
> sign with the IMF, and therefore that these governments fail to implement

them adequately. The subtext is clear: "Ownership" is simply a buzzword meaning happier compliance with the directives from Washington. It is time for real ownership in the developing world. This will come when programs are designed by member governments, with the help rather than the command of the IMF, thereby making it far more likely that programs will be tailored to the specific and complex circumstances of the particular countries. (Sachs 1998b, 21)

Of course, the IMF has a responsibility to make sure that its loans are repaid and that the specific conditions that led to the financial problem are corrected. But this does not give the IMF license to dictate a wide range of domestic policies and institutional arrangements unrelated to the immediate crisis as a condition for short-term rescue efforts. If a country is having a short-term liquidity crisis due to a speculative attack or financial panic while its basic policy stance is either fundamentally sound or has only moderate weaknesses, the country needs a rapid infusion of cash in order to restore confidence along with adjustment policies tailored to remedy the immediate payments disequilibrium—not a drawn-out, slow disbursement of small amounts of money conditioned on meeting a laundry list of policy changes and reforms (Feldstein 1998; Taylor 1998a). Worst of all, announcing that a country's whole financial system is weak and needs fundamental reforms in the midst of a crisis (as the IMF did in Korea, for example) is hardly conducive to restoring investors' confidence.

Tying short-term lending to long-term policy reforms, such as improving bank regulation and supervision, is a mistake. By their very nature, such reforms cannot be implemented successfully in the timeframe typically needed for an IMF bailout to work (Calomiris 1998). As a result, the IMF must either disingenuously assert that the targets have been met, or else it must cut off lending that is desperately needed to stave off an immediate balance-of-payments crisis. But the same point applies to broader social criteria, such as labor rights or environmental standards, which also cannot be implemented in the timeframe required for responding to a financial crisis. It makes more sense to focus rescue packages on short-term policy measures that can plausibly help to remedy the immediate crisis, stabilize a country's external payments situation, and revive economic growth. This does not mean that the IMF cannot pursue broader types of reforms; rather, broader social reforms should be made a precondition for qualifying for rescues in advance, as advocated above, with countries given adequate lead time to comply.

The current IMF policy of requiring a commitment to capital account liberalization as a condition for rescuing a country in a balance-of-payments crisis is misguided and counterproductive. Capital controls are permitted under the IMF charter, and the IMF should assist countries in designing them in ways that can enhance their effectiveness for reducing short-term speculative capital movements without undermining the financing of long-term productive investment. Indeed, Article VI of the IMF's charter allows it to *require* countries to *impose* capital controls as a condition of receiving loans (Boughton 1998, 41), and this provision should be utilized in situations like the Asian financial crisis or the Brazilian devaluation. Recent efforts to amend the IMF's charter to make capital account openness one of the Fund's fundamental objectives should be abandoned.

It does make sense for the IMF to require countries to modify their short-run macroeconomic policies as needed to correct their payments imbalances, but the precise policies that are required should be appropriate to each country's situation.[29] Current IMF stabilization programs generally require countries to adopt the three major types of balance-of-payments adjustment policies discussed in Chapter 2: currency devaluation, fiscal austerity, and monetary contraction. While one or more of these policies may be necessary in any given situation, their appropriateness needs to be demonstrated, not assumed. Of course, if a country's currency is markedly overvalued in real terms, a devaluation (or float) may be unavoidable. If a country has a huge structural budget deficit[30] financed by unsustainable foreign borrowing, fiscal austerity may be necessary. And if monetary creation has been demonstrably excessive, for example in a highly inflationary economy, some degree of monetary contraction may be in order, along with other anti-inflationary measures (such as a "heterodox" incomes policy, in which firms and workers agree to restrain their wage and price increases, and possibly a fixed exchange rate or crawling peg).

But the IMF should not assume that all three of these problems are present in every country that has a balance-of-payments problem, and it should stop insisting that this trinity of policies is the right medicine for all countries' ills. Moreover, to prevent undue collapses of domestic demand, any one of these types of adjustment might need to be accompanied by expansionary policies in other areas. For example, in a country without a large budget deficit, a currency devaluation might be accompanied by a fiscal stimulus in order to replace the loss of investment demand due to reduced capital inflows. Alternatively, in a country with highly indebted firms, a devaluation might be combined with a monetary expansion (lower interest rates) in order to allow firms to service their debts and to prevent undue tightening of credit constraints (see Reisen 1998a).

This discussion of IMF conditionality is necessarily open-ended, because there is no unique combination of adjustment policies that will work in every situation. Above all, the IMF needs to determine whether a country in crisis is simply illiquid (i.e., is having a temporary cash flow crunch due to a loss of confidence) or is truly insolvent (i.e., cannot meet its obligations even if it obtains normal inflows of funds). If it is the former, then the IMF should pump funds in with minimal conditionality and try to convince investors to return, while if it is the latter there may be no point in pouring money down a hole until the country makes more fundamental reforms. In intermediate situations, rescue packages with appropriate conditionality may be warranted. In all cases, the Fund needs to work with local experts and officials to design short-term adjustment policies that make sense in terms of the country's macroeconomic situation, financial structure, and social and environmental conditions, while paying due attention to the repercussions for global demand (and the possible need for offsetting stimulus policies).

Stabilizing exchange rates

Many of the problems of the global financial system stem from the instability of exchange rates since the demise of the Bretton Woods system of adjustable pegs in 1973.[31] What has emerged in the quarter century since that time is not a pure system of floating rates, but a hybrid system: several major currencies (such as the dollar, the yen, and the euro) are floating, while many individual countries have adopted various forms of managed exchange rates, ranging from rigidly fixed rates to crawling (frequently adjusted) pegs to dirty floats (floats with occasional intervention) to joint floats (such as the European ERM prior to January 1, 1999).[32] The major countries or currency blocs with floating rates— the United States, Japan, and Europe—have sporadically intervened to keep exchange rates within acceptable ranges since consultation among the G-7 countries (and the earlier G-5) began in the mid-1980s. As Isard (1995, 187) writes, "In practice,...systems of rigidly fixed or perfectly flexible rates are hardly ever observed."

Each kind of exchange rate system that has been tried in the post-Bretton Woods period has shown itself susceptible to some form of instability. Floating rates have exhibited large gyrations, such as the enormous rise in the dollar in 1981-85 followed by the sharp reversal in 1985-87, and the somewhat smaller upward spike in the dollar in 1995-98 (as shown in Figure 2.2 above). As discussed in Chapter 2, much of this volatility can be attributed to herd-like speculative behavior in currency markets, which makes exchange rates depart from levels consistent with the underlying macroeconomic fundamentals for sustained periods of time. But fixed rates have not been any guarantee of stability either. By definition, speculative attacks occur only against currencies whose exchange rates are pegged or managed—and the world has had no shortage of speculative attacks in recent years.

Part of the solution to exchange rate instability lies in taxes on foreign exchange transactions and controls on short-term capital flows, as advocated earlier. These measures would help to reduce the volume of currency transactions and therefore to lessen some of the volatility in exchange rates. But transactions taxes and capital controls cannot do the job alone. If they are too strong, they invite evasion (e.g., black markets for foreign exchange or the moving of financial transactions offshore) and may reduce beneficial capital flows, while, if they are weak, they cannot prevent speculation based on large expected exchange rate changes. Speculative attacks and capital flight did not originate in the era of liberalized financial markets—speculative attacks occurred during the Bretton Woods era, when most countries had capital controls in place—and will not disappear completely if Tobin taxes are adopted or capital controls are reinstituted. Hence, one cannot count on transaction taxes or capital controls alone, and one cannot avoid the issue of how to choose an exchange rate system.

Notwithstanding Isard's point about the exchange rate systems that are observed in practice, it is now frequently asserted that in-between systems such as adjustable pegs, target zones, and crawling bands are all inherently unstable, and that the only viable exchange rate regimes are the polar opposite cases of rigidly fixed rates and freely floating rates (Eichengreen 1999, 105; *Economist* 1999, 15). Either governments should go to one extreme and commit themselves to irrevocable, permanent pegs, it is argued, or they should go to the other extreme and let their exchange rates be purely market-determined with no systematic intervention.[33] This new orthodoxy on exchange rates is profoundly mistaken. To be sure, there are cases of very small, very open countries that can benefit from a rigid fixed exchange rate with a larger trading partner, or even the adoption of the larger country's currency (e.g., Panama using balboas that are worth one U.S. dollar). There are also situations in which a country is hit by so many external shocks that it cannot hope to control its exchange rate and may prefer to use exchange rate flexibility as a shock absorber. But the two systems of rigidly fixed and freely floating rates have their own problems, and hybrid systems of managed rates can be viable—and preferable. In what follows, we review the pros and cons of each major type of exchange rate system and discuss which kind of system makes sense for specific types of countries and situations.

Flexible rates

Many economists claim that countries should give up trying to control exchange rates and instead should simply let them float, i.e., allow exchange rates to be purely market determined. For example, Eichengreen (1999) and Sachs (1998c) both argue that the recent rash of currency crises can be attributed to misguided efforts to peg currency values. Sachs emphasizes that flexible rates would give these countries more monetary policy autonomy. In order for them to set interest rates at levels that can reduce financial fragility and revive economic growth, they have to be freed from the constraints imposed by the necessity of defending a pegged exchange rate. If the countries face unfavorable shocks, they can adjust by letting their currencies depreciate instead of having to raise interest rates in order to ward off speculators and try to sustain a peg.[34]

There are several problems with the argument for flexible rates, however. First, the idea that countries in crisis can revive their growth prospects by letting their currencies float (and, presumably, depreciate) assumes that a large number of countries can simultaneously pull themselves out of depressed conditions by export-led growth. After all, a depreciation stimulates a recovery mainly by making exports more competitive. But while this works well for a single country depreciating its currency in isolation, it cannot be as effective when numerous countries are attempting to depreciate their currencies at the same time, since the competitive gains to each country tend to cancel out. The result is a vicious circle of competitive devaluations in which no nation achieves its intended export gains. In fact, this has already occurred to some extent in the 1990s, as devaluations by some countries (e.g., China or Mexico) have put pressure on others (e.g., Thailand), which in turn put pressure on still others (e.g., Indonesia and Korea). There is no reason to think that even greater exchange rate flexibility would solve this problem.

Second, flexible exchange rates create other problems that can outweigh the intended competitive benefits. For example, depreciation makes it harder for domestic residents to service international debts denominated in foreign currency. Depreciation also makes imports more expensive, which is especially problematic in highly import-dependent, very open economies. In some cases, continuous depreciation feeds into a vicious circle of cost-push inflation and thus ceases to create any real benefit in terms of export competitiveness. And floating rates can collapse too far in a financial panic, as discussed earlier. As noted in Chapter 1, these problems are especially severe in many developing countries, which is exactly why so many of them have not adopted flexible exchange rates in the past. Indeed, Hausmann et al. (1999) conclude that Latin American countries do not obtain the gains from flexible rates that industrialized countries receive: while abandoning a peg usually results in lower interest rates and revives economic growth in the latter, it usually leads to higher interest rates, increased inflation, and reduced output in the former.

Third, much evidence suggests that flexible rates do not in practice give all countries the monetary autonomy that they are supposed to provide in theory. Hausmann et al. (1999) find that, in Latin America, countries with flexible rates have actually had higher real interest rates than countries with fixed rates. The reason, they argue, is that flexible rates lead to greater risks for investors who put their funds into local financial assets (denominated in domestic currency); to compensate for this risk, domestic borrowers must offer higher interest rates. Hausmann et al. also find that countries with flexible rates have not, in fact, used monetary policy more aggressively in a countercyclical direction (i.e., they do not lower interest rates more in recessions) than have countries with fixed rates. In part, these authors attribute the failure of Latin American central banks to take advantage of the potential for greater monetary autonomy with flexible exchange rates to the inflationary dynamics that are set in motion by flexible rates, which encourage more indexation of wages to changes in the price level than is found in countries with fixed rates.

Industrialized countries are also not immune to some of the problems caused by gyrations in flexible exchange rates. As one critic of flexible rates has written,

> In 1986-87, the overvalued yen forced Japanese industrialists to close factories, retire workers, and write off once valuable investments in plant and equipment. This parallels what their American counterparts were forced to do between 1981 and 1985, when the dollar suddenly became overvalued. Similarly, the paring down of the British manufacturing base was precipitated when the pound unexpectedly became a strong petrocurrency in 1979-81. (McKinnon 1988, 83)

It is sometimes argued that governments can't really control exchange rates through foreign exchange market intervention today, because the large volumes of private capital flows can overwhelm the limited resources of central banks and finance ministries. This view is exaggerated. Of course, as discussed in Chapter 2, countries that try to maintain overvalued pegged exchange rates that are inconsistent with their monetary policies and that have inadequate central bank reserves with which to defend their pegs will not be able to prevent successful speculative attacks. But this does not mean that countries with more realistic and consistent exchange rate targets and monetary policies—and with adequate foreign exchange reserves—cannot use exchange market intervention to help stabilize the exchange rate around those targets. There is a widespread consensus that "unsterilized" intervention (which allows the purchases or sales of foreign currencies to affect the domestic monetary base) is effective because it changes the domestic monetary "fundamentals." There is also mounting evidence that "sterilized" intervention (which offsets the purchases or sales of foreign currencies with sales or purchases of government bonds, to prevent any change in the monetary base) can also be effective through both a "portfolio channel" and an "expectations channel" (see, e.g., Catte et al. 1992; Dominguez and Frankel 1993). The key is that intervention is effective only when it is used to support exchange rate targets that are realistic and credible in the first place.

However, it is important to recall the policy "trilemma" discussed earlier, which says that a country cannot simultaneously have a fixed exchange rate, capital market liberalization, and an autonomous monetary policy; only two of these three can be maintained at the same time. Countries that want to have monetary policy autonomy (i.e., to be able to control their own interest rates) must either seal off their capital markets or else adopt a flexible exchange rate. On the other hand, countries that want to manage their exchange rates must either seal off their capital markets or give up on monetary policy autonomy. As long as this trilemma is understood, there is no reason why exchange rates cannot be managed if policy makers are willing to give up one of the other two objectives (open capital markets or autonomous monetary policy).

Fixed nominal rates

A view that might be called "global monetarism"[35] favors the establishment of rigidly fixed nominal exchange rates, which (assuming that capital markets are liberalized) would completely eliminate independent monetary policy at the national level. Under such a system, central banks would be strictly obligated to target their interest rates and money supplies on maintaining the fixed rates. The motivation for putting monetary policy in such a straightjacket lies in a desire to prevent central banks from engaging in inflationary increases in national money supplies—although most major central banks seem to have adopted strong anti-inflationary biases in their monetary policies since the 1980s anyway, even without a commitment to fixed exchange rates. The intention is to foster stable currency values that would guarantee stable domestic price levels (i.e., very low or zero inflation rates).

One scheme along these lines is the proposal by Ronald I. McKinnon (1988, 1990), who advocated a tripartite system of fixed exchange rates among the then-dominant three major currencies, the U.S. dollar, Japanese yen, and West German mark. McKinnon proposed using purchasing-power parity (PPP) estimates[36] to set the nominal parities and then to target the three countries' monetary policies on maintaining those parities for exchange rates. Currency market intervention would be unsterilized so that underlying fundamentals—in this case, money supplies—would be adjusted in a way that would lend credibility to the intervention and deter speculators. This plan would effectively force countries with overvalued currencies (as compared with the PPP targets) to expand their money supplies faster and countries with undervalued currencies to contract their monetary growth. This would force inflation in traded goods prices in all three countries to converge to the same rate. To control this overall inflation rate, the three central banks would have to monitor key indicators of traded goods prices (especially, commodity prices and producer price indexes) and adjust monetary growth rates accordingly.

Currency boards. More recently, Steve H. Hanke has gained prominence for promoting rigidly fixed exchange rates managed by currency boards for developing countries and transition economies (see Hanke et al. 1993; Hanke 1998). Unlike an ordinary central bank, a currency board issues money that is backed 100% by reserves of a hard currency like the U.S. dollar—and the domestic currency is freely convertible into the hard currency. The exchange rate is fixed by law, not just by currency market intervention, and monetary policy is targeted strictly on maintaining balance-of-payments equilibrium with the fixed exchange rate. According to Hanke, countries like Indonesia and Russia need currency boards in order to stabilize their economies. In particular, independent currency boards are supposed to ensure that monetary policy is not influenced by political considerations and does not deviate from these "ultraorthodox rules." A few countries have adopted currency boards already, including Argentina, Hong Kong, and Lithuania (U.S. Council of Economic Advisers 1999, 289).

Like McKinnon's system, Hanke's proposal is intended to make inflation control the chief objective of monetary policy and to eliminate discretionary (autonomous) monetary policy. And, like all proposals for fixed nominal rates, Hanke's system would impose severe constraints on a country's economy: it would have to pursue deflation at all costs in order to maintain the exchange rate parity with the dollar (essentially, it would be forced to maintain inflation at the U.S. rate for tradable goods). But this could severely depress domestic demand, employment, and growth. Also, if the domestic inflation rate remains above the U.S. level, the currency would appreciate in real terms, the country's products would become uncompetitive, and large trade deficits would result. Eventually, this would put pressure on the government to abandon the fixed rate and devalue—or else to tighten monetary policy further. Maintaining a fixed nominal rate could thus require very high interest rates, which can attract large, destabilizing capital inflows while depressing domestic growth. Indeed, there is already evidence that fixed nominal exchange rates have led to chronically higher unemployment in countries such as Argentina and among the European countries in the former ERM (now members of the EMU) (Obstfeld 1998).

Dollarization. An extreme form of a fixed nominal exchange rate is the abandonment of a national currency and the adoption of a foreign currency for domestic use—what in the Latin American context is known as "dollarization." As discussed above, dollarization is an option for regional monetary integration in a region in which there is one hegemonic country with a strong currency and all the other countries have weak currencies that are not accepted in international transactions or used as central bank reserves. Dollarization has some advantages over other forms of fixed exchange rates. In particular, if there is no national currency (or, as in Panama, the national currency unit is legally equivalent to a U.S. dollar), there is no risk of devaluation, and hence the premium for exchange risk disappears from interest rates. Thus, Hausmann et al. find that countries that have moved in the direction of dollarization[37] have lower interest rates and deeper financial markets, especially for long-term lending and borrowing. Although such countries have to accept U.S.-determined interest rates, Hausmann et al. point out that Latin American countries are already subject to interest rate shocks from the U.S. under present conditions (even more so under flexible rates, according to their findings)—and that the costs of being subject to U.S. interest rate policy can be outweighed by the benefits of lower "spreads" between national interest rates and foreign rates (due to reduced risk premiums).

In spite of these potential advantages, one still must be cautious about the current enthusiasm for dollarization. First, there are unique aspects of the Latin American situation that make dollarization attractive there but that are not found in other regions. These features include the proximity to the U.S. and the importance of trade with the U.S., as well as the demonstrated incapacity of many Latin American governments to run independent monetary policies without high inflation. Second, other types of policies, such as capital controls and debt relief, can potentially give developing nations a greater ability to exercise monetary policy autonomy, thus obviating the need to abandon national currencies and dollarize their economies. And third, whether dollarization improves long-term growth prospects (as opposed to short-term macroeconomic stabilization) has yet to be demonstrated.

Fixed rates with real targets

An alternative approach to fixed exchange rates focuses on stabilizing real exchange rates (nominal rates adjusted for inflation) in order to prevent large trade imbalances that can undermine full employment. One such plan comes from Paul Davidson (1991, 1996), who proposes to create an international monetary clearinghouse that would manage the new system of exchange rates. The clearinghouse would issue a reserve asset called the international monetary clearing unit (IMCU). National central banks would hold IMCUs exclusively as international reserves, and individual national currencies would be pegged to the IMCU.[38] The nominal pegs would then be indexed to unit labor costs (money wages adjusted for productivity) in each country, in order to prevent real depreciation or appreciation and the resulting competitive advantages or disadvantages from emerging. Davidson also proposes a series of mechanisms designed to shift the onus of adjustment onto countries with trade surpluses, by requiring them to spend their excess credit balances on either imports, foreign investment, or foreign aid—or else face confiscation of those balances by the international clearinghouse, which would distribute them to debtor nations. These mechanisms are intended to impart an expansionary, rather than a contractionary, bias to the international adjustment process.

Davidson's proposal for fixed exchange rates is preferable to the global monetarist proposals for two reasons. First, Davidson advocates targeting real exchange rates, rather than nominal exchange rates. This avoids the risk that is inherent in any system of rigid nominal pegs, if inflation rates differ between countries, of currencies becoming misaligned in real terms. As a result, his system is much more likely to reduce trade imbalances and, thereby, to limit the build-up of international debt problems. And second, Davidson emphasizes the need to accompany exchange rate management with additional mechanisms designed to shift the burden of adjustment from deficit (debtor) countries to surplus (creditor) countries. Such a shift would tend to foster higher average rates of employment and growth around the world, and would lessen the pressure on deficit countries to contract their economies in times of crisis.

But like all fixed exchange rate proposals, Davidson's has certain inherent problems. There is much uncertainty over the "right" level at which to set exchange rates, and the nominal parities in any system of targeting real exchange rates would have to be subject to frequent revisions if the chosen parities failed to achieve balance-of-payments equilibrium. If the pegs were adjustable, however, they would invite speculative attacks if investors ever perceive the pegs to be unsustainable. Also, any type of fixed exchange rate system ties the hands of monetary policy and eliminates the possibility of using discretionary monetary policy for domestic countercyclical purposes. Finally, Davidson's plan relies heavily on the creation of a new institution with significant enforcement powers, which many countries (especially those surplus countries that might be forced to spend their excess credit balances, such as Japan or China) would be reluctant to join. Thus, his proposal suffers from the same political difficulties as all proposals for major new global institutions.

Target zones and crawling bands

An alternative to both fixed and flexible rates, which combines the best elements of both and does not necessarily require a new global financial institution, is the idea of target zones. All fixed rate systems usually allow some small margin of variation in exchange rates, usually on the order of about ±2% or less around the pegged level. Target zones are much wider bands around the peg, on the order of about ±10% or even more. They thus allow considerable but limited fluctuations in exchange rates, thereby creating more space for autonomous monetary policy than a pure fixed rate system allows. They eliminate the need for central banks to intervene continually in order to offset small "shocks" to exchange rates, as is required under a pure fixed rate system. And target zones require less information about the "right" level at which to peg a currency, since they allow for a much wider margin of error.

Target zones also send a strong message to speculators that the range of variation in the exchange rate is limited and that it is not safe to bet on the rate going outside the bands. To make this message effective, there needs to be a credible commitment of central banks to intervene automatically and massively whenever exchange rates threaten to go outside the target zone. For this purpose, central banks need to have large arsenals of currency reserves on hand in order to dissuade potential speculators. Of course, target zones can potentially be just as vulnerable to speculation as are fixed rates, if the target bands are perceived to be incompatible with underlying fundamentals and therefore the limits to the zones are seen as unsustainable. This problem requires two types of solutions. First, the nominal targets (the pegs around which the bands are set) have to be revised periodically to compensate for international inflation differentials—i.e., currencies from countries with higher (lower) inflation than their trading partners have to be devalued (revalued)—in which case the target zones become "crawling bands." And second, the countries participating in a target zone system have to adopt macroeconomic policies that are consistent with the targets, as discussed in the next section. Under these conditions, a credible set of target zones or crawling bands can influence speculators' expectations in a stabilizing direction, i.e., induce speculators to buy currencies that are near the low end of their range and to sell currencies that are near the top of their range.

One influential plan for target zones comes from John Williamson (1985).[39] He advocates bands of as much as ±10% (possibly reduced to ±5% after the zones have been in effect for some time) around what he calls the "fundamental equilibrium exchange rate" (FEER), which he defines as the rate that "is expected to generate a current account surplus or deficit equal to the underlying [average, net] capital flow over the [business] cycle, given that the country is pursuing 'internal balance' as best as it can and not restricting trade for balance of payments reasons" (Williamson 1985, 14). Internal balance in turn is defined as the highest level and growth rate of output that are sustainable in the sense that they can be achieved without excessively high inflation or large budget deficits.

Williamson has produced much research showing how FEERs can be estimated, most recently in Williamson (1994). However, as Williamson admits, such estimates are inevitably sensitive to "normative" assumptions about targets for internal balance (how much growth is sustainable, how much inflation is excessive, how large a budget deficit should be allowed) and external balance (how large should trade imbalances and net capital flows be, on average). For example, if one thinks that the United States should balance its trade and cease to be a net international borrower, one would estimate a different FEER from what one would estimate if one assumed that the United States should continue to run current account deficits of (say) 2% of GDP indefinitely. Also, Williamson would allow the bands around the target exchange rates to be "soft" in the sense that central banks would not be obligated to defend them in all circumstances. However, critics charge that soft bands would invite speculative attacks when currencies reached the edges of their bands.

John Grieve Smith (1997b, 210-23) has proposed another target zone plan, which combines some of the best elements of Williamson's target zones and

Davidson's fixed but adjustable pegs. Like Williamson, he would set wide bands of ±5% to ±10% around nominal parities that are based on real exchange rate targets, but Grieve Smith would make the bands "hard" in the sense that countries would be obligated to defend them. Grieve Smith would initially set exchange rate targets at levels that would maintain desired levels of current account balances (net capital inflows or outflows), and such levels would have to be internationally agreed upon. This still leaves room for political disagreement over the targets for current account balances, however, and since one would still have to make some assumptions about sustainable growth rates of national income in order to estimate the equilibrium exchange rates, Grieve Smith's initial targets would have to be calculated in a similar manner to Williamson's FEERs.

Once the target zones were initially set, according to Grieve Smith, they would be frequently adjusted to compensate for inflation differentials in order to avoid the build-up of competitive imbalances and speculative pressures—so, in effect, it is also a system of crawling bands.[40] Grieve Smith's indexing plan would, in principle, be simpler to administer than Williamson's, since the latter requires the continual recalculation of FEERs. However, there would still be important issues of which inflation indexes to use, and Grieve Smith's exchange rates could get out of line with the desired current account targets if keeping relative prices constant is not sufficient to maintain those targets—which it would not generally be, if current accounts are also affected by differences in countries' income growth rates and structural changes in their relative competitiveness. At least, there would have to be some flexibility to change real exchange rate targets and deviate from simple indexing if persistent undesired current account imbalances emerged, and FEER calculations would be useful for informing those decisions.

The other key point in Grieve Smith's proposal is to create an International Stabilization Fund, which would have "massive resources under its control and...a clearly defined duty to operate to support agreed exchange rate targets at all times, rather than waiting for a crisis to develop and then discussing under what conditions it will support the country under pressure" (Grieve Smith 1997b, 219). Thus, such a fund would have both the resources and the credibility to deter speculative attacks on currencies when they reached the limits of their target zones. Although Grieve Smith (1997b, 222) recommends that this fund be "set up under the aegis of the IMF," other institutional arrangements are also conceivable, such as having the fund be jointly operated by the major central banks, by the BIS, or by any new global institution that might be created. Importantly, the International Stabilization Fund has a much more limited objective than many of the proposals for new institutions reviewed earlier, such as a world central bank, global supervisory authority, or international clearinghouse, and as a result is less likely to be seen as threatening national sovereignty. For this reason, such a fund is more politically feasible than any of the other proposed new global institutions discussed earlier.[41]

Participation issues

Proposals for international monetary reform vary in regard to how many countries are needed to participate in the new exchange rate system. Some proposals, such as Davidson's international clearinghouse and the various global central banks, envision all or most countries agreeing to a common new exchange rate regime and accompanying set of adjustment policies. Grieve Smith (1997b, 215) also implied that his target zones would be a "world-wide system." Later, he modified his proposal to recommend a "two-tier system," in which exchange rate bands would be set first among currencies within a region (e.g., EU or NAFTA) and then between the regional blocs (Grieve Smith 1998). In contrast, McKinnon's fixed nominal rate system was designed only for the three largest industrial nations in the late 1980s (the United States, Japan, and West Germany). Williamson originally proposed target zones for the major industrialized nations (specified as the G-7 in Williamson and Miller 1987), although he forcefully advocates crawling bands for developing countries as well (in Williamson 1998). Volcker (1996) also endorses target zones for the G-7.

There are three good reasons for confining a new regime to a smaller group of countries or currency blocs.[42] First, it is much easier to reach political agreement on a new system among a smaller group of players than among a larger group. Second, the same exchange rate system may not make sense for countries with different economic structures and levels of development. And third, as long as the included countries account for most of the world's supply of hard currencies, the stabilization of their exchange rates would greatly contribute to stabilizing overall global financial conditions. Especially, stabilizing exchange rates between the dollar, the yen, and the euro would help to avoid exchange rate shocks in countries like Thailand, which (prior to July 1997) had pegged to a single currency (the U.S. dollar) and suffered a rising trade deficit when that currency appreciated in the mid-1990s. The inauguration of the euro in 1999 can be helpful for creating a target zone system, since it reduces the minimum number of key players who have to reach an agreement to three parties: the United States, the EMU, and Japan. Achieving agreement within Europe and then between Europe and the other two parties would not be simple, but would be far easier than trying to reach agreement with a much more diverse group.

Countries that did not initially join the target zone system should be free to choose their own exchange rate regimes, consistent with their internal conditions and objectives. For example, countries that were trying to combat very high inflation might want to adopt fixed nominal rates or slowly crawling pegs, at least temporarily. Countries that were more concerned with maintaining export competitiveness might want to use more rapidly crawling pegs (or wider crawling bands), targeted on a basket of dollars, euros, and yen, and indexed to the difference between their inflation rates and the U.S.-EMU-Japanese average so as to prevent real appreciation.[43] Other countries would be free to try various "national experiments," whether those involved fixed exchange rates and currency boards, Latin American-style dollarization, pure flexible rates, or any other alternatives; time would tell which of these experiments worked well and which didn't, and under what circumstances.

Individual countries outside of the United States, EMU, and Japan should be allowed to join the target zone system, either directly or by affiliating with regional monetary unions that would in turn participate in the new system, provided that suitable exchange rate targets could be agreed upon. Presumably, other major industrialized countries such as the United Kingdom, Canada, and Australia would want to join quickly, and developing countries might choose to affiliate later. As the International Stabilization Fund evolved, it could develop an institutional capacity for estimating equilibrium exchange rates based on politically agreed-upon targets for current account balances for countries that joined the system.

A potential problem with leaving many countries out of a new international monetary system is that it leaves some nations such as China free to engage in beggar-thy-neighbor exchange rate policy by keeping their currencies artificially undervalued through massive accumulation of foreign currency reserves. While this is a genuine problem, an international monetary system that would include all (or almost all) countries seems unlikely to get off the ground since the countries that wanted the freedom to manipulate their currencies to gain competitive advantages would be unwilling to join such a system anyway. This problem thus has to be addressed through other means, such as applying bilateral political pressure or conditioning market access on reasonable exchange rate policies.[44]

In conclusion, a system of target zones or crawling bands among the leading industrial country currencies along the general lines proposed by Williamson and Grieve Smith offers the best prospects for re-stabilizing the international monetary system. An International Stabilization Fund equipped to intervene massively and automatically to defend the target zones would be helpful, but a credible commitment of the leading central banks to do the same would probably be sufficient. Developing countries would benefit from the greater stability this would create in their chief export markets and would be free either to adopt their own currency systems or else to join the multilateral target zone system. Target zones allow a partial escape from the policy "trilemma," because they allow a certain limited amount of monetary policy autonomy. However, they do require some coordination of macro policies, as discussed in the next section.

Coordinating macroeconomic policies

International coordination of macroeconomic policies is an essential pillar of a new financial structure for two reasons. First, macro policy coordination is indispensable for stabilizing exchange rates. No system of fixed or managed rates (including target zones) can succeed without policies that are consistent with the established pegs or bands—and flexible rates are more likely to be stable if policies are coordinated across countries anyway. Indeed, policy inconsistencies are often the fuel that ignites volatile flows of hot money: speculators bet on collapses of currency pegs deemed to be inconsistent with policy differences across countries, while arbitrageurs profit off interest rate differentials that are inconsistent with flexible exchange rates (e.g., in terms of forward premiums or expected rates of depreciation). Thus, policy coordination is vital for cooling down the hot money flows that can destabilize exchange rates.

Second, international coordination can make monetary policy a more powerful force in a world of mostly open capital markets. Coordinated monetary policy offers another way out of the "trilemma"—not for individual countries, but for a group of countries large enough to constitute a major chunk of the global monetary system. Consider, for example, the case of a single country that wants to lower its interest rates in order to stimulate economic activity while keeping its exchange rate within some target range and allowing capital to be mobile. The lower interest rate cannot be sustained because it will induce a net outflow of capital to countries with higher rates, which will put downward pressure on the currency until it falls to the bottom of its target zone—at which point, the central bank has to reverse its policy and raise the interest rate to defend the currency.

Policy coordination can help to solve this problem. A coordinated interest rate cut in all the major countries gives investors no incentive to flee one market for another, and thus nips potential speculative pressures in the bud.[45] Exchange rates need not be affected as long as relative interest rates remain constant and as long as the interest rate cuts do not create a greater fear of increased inflation in some countries than in others (which could stimulate a run on the former's currencies).[46] Thus, policy coordination restores the potency of monetary policy even with managed exchange rates and open capital markets—but only at the international level, not within any single country. The issue, then, is whether countries can gain more by achieving international control over interest rates than they lose by giving up their own autonomy to set interest rates for themselves (or having to either close their capital markets or give up their exchange rate targets instead).

The academic literature is full of theoretical models analyzing the costs and benefits of alternative macroeconomic policy coordination schemes as well as the incentives for governments to cooperate or not to cooperate.[47] What are harder to find are pragmatic proposals for macro policy coordination that have some chance of being adopted in the real world and that would bring clear benefits to the participating countries. In order to be practical, any policy coordination scheme has to be simple enough that real world governments could reasonably be expected to have the information and ability to make the policy decisions required to implement it. Also, given that exchange rate stabilization should be one of the chief objectives of policy coordination, any plan that is to be effective must have some policy instruments targeted on exchange rate objectives.

A modified Williamson-Miller plan

One plan that meets these qualifications is the one proposed by Williamson and Miller (1987), which incorporates the target zones for exchange rates advocated by Williamson (1985) as described earlier. According to this plan, the *average* level of real, short-term interest rates across the participating countries should be set according to targets for demand growth in the group as a whole. Then, international interest rate *differentials* would be set to support the target zones for exchange rates—which, as noted earlier, would themselves be based on ultimate targets for sustainable current account imbalances. Finally, fiscal policies would be used to adjust each national economy to its own targets for aggregate demand growth, taking as given the exchange rate and interest rate targets that the country had agreed to maintain.

In the original Williamson-Miller proposal, the targets for demand growth (in both the individual countries and the group of participating countries as a whole) are set in nominal terms, i.e., the percentage growth rates of total domestic expenditures at current prices.[48] This target is deliberately chosen as a middle ground between a Keynesian policy of targeting real output or employment, which is alleged to create "the danger of inflation creeping up" (Williamson and Miller 1987, 7), and the monetarist approach of targeting the growth of a monetary aggregate in order to stabilize prices, which runs the risk of increasing unemployment.

Williamson and Miller believe that targeting nominal demand essentially forces countries to accept a reasonable trade-off between unemployment and inflation, rather than attacking one problem at the expense of exacerbating the other. However, this approach can be hard to implement, because reliable data on nominal demand growth arrive with considerable lags. More importantly, the effects of nominal demand growth on ultimate targets for real growth, employment, and inflation are hard to predict. And it makes a big difference whether a country achieves (say) 6% nominal demand growth with 2% real growth and 4% price inflation or 4% real growth and 2% price inflation.

Given these difficulties with targeting nominal demand growth, the Williamson-Miller plan should be modified to incorporate more explicit targets for the real objectives of economic policy, such as growth or unemployment rates. Since sustainable real growth rates are hard to estimate reliably, the most sensible alternative is to target the lowest rates of unemployment that can be achieved with acceptable (but not necessarily zero) rates of inflation.[49] This essentially allows the economy to grow at the fastest rate it can, consistent with full employment. Targeting an explicit unemployment–inflation trade-off is also a more practical approach, since data on prices and unemployment are available more frequently and with shorter lags than data on nominal domestic demand or real output growth[50]—thus allowing quicker modifications of policy if it turns out to be either too expansionary or too contractionary.

In setting these targets, policy makers should aim for true full employment and should not be bound by conventional estimates of the so-called "natural rate of unemployment," more precisely known as the "nonaccelerating inflation rate of unemployment," or NAIRU. The most recent estimates even by economists sympathetic to the NAIRU hypothesis (e.g., Gordon 1997) show that the "acceleration" of inflation caused by unemployment rates below the NAIRU is likely to be very slow and gradual at worst. Moreover, the constantly changing estimates of the NAIRU—which seem to largely track trends in actual unemployment rates—raise serious doubts about whether the concept has any meaning at all (see Galbraith 1997b; Baker 1998). Following Galbraith (1997a), policy makers should be willing to experiment and test how far unemployment can be reduced without stimulating excessive inflation. This is exactly what the U.S. Federal Reserve has done since 1996, with the result that unemployment has been brought far below the 6% rate previously believed to be the NAIRU, and growth has been persistently higher than previous estimates of the economy's potential growth rate, without any increase in inflation.

Aside from shifting to a full-employment objective for demand targeting, the Williamson-Miller plan needs to be implemented in a way that best ensures the pursuit of stable, sustainable growth with more balanced trade among the participating nations. In the present global situation, there is a huge drag on economic growth created by the sluggish performance of the two major regions with trade surpluses, Japan and the EU. Most of the world's net capital flows are going to finance the U.S. trade deficit, rather than economic development in the less-developed parts of the world (Blecker 1998a). In order to rectify this imbalanced situation, macroeconomic policy coordination should be guided by the following principles:

- Given the current global growth slowdown and the risk of a serious global deflation (World Bank 1998), *the participating countries should agree to lower average interest rates* by enough to restore the prospects for full employment in the slow-growing regions (primarily, Europe and Asia).

- In order to help reverse the U.S. trade deficits with Europe and Japan, *the U.S. dollar should be targeted to depreciate relative to the euro and the yen.* This would require further reductions in U.S. interest rates *relative* to European and Japanese rates, i.e., the U.S. needs to cut its interest rates by *more* than its major trading partners.

- In order to further help reduce global trade imbalances, as well as to compensate for the contractionary effects of reducing their trade surpluses, *Europe and Japan need to adopt strong domestic demand stimulus policies.* In Europe, this should be achieved through a combination of fiscal and monetary expansion, which would require easing the tight fiscal and monetary targets imposed in the process of creating the EMU. In Japan, monetary policy has run out of room, since short-term nominal interest rates are close to zero, and the primary stimulus has to come from the fiscal side (see Posen 1998) along with structural reforms to encourage private consumer spending and residential investment (see Prestowitz 1997).

Two qualifications

To achieve its objectives, the modified Williamson-Miller plan for policy coordination advocated here would impose considerable constraints on individual countries' ability to control their own interest rates. Because individual countries' domestic situations may vary, it is essential that governments have adequate policy tools in other areas in order to be able to adjust domestic economies that experience either excessive inflation or inadequate growth at the internationally agreed upon interest rates. Such additional policy tools are needed in two primary areas, fiscal policy and monetary policy.

In the fiscal area, the modified Williamson-Miller plan would require governments to commit themselves to a more flexible approach to budgetary policy than many countries have adopted in recent years. In the 1990s, governments in most of the major industrialized countries became fixated with arbitrary deficit reduction targets, such as the move to a budget surplus in the United States and the requirement for budget deficits to be less than 3% of GDP in the countries joining the EMU. Such rigid budgetary targets effectively tie the hands of fiscal policy and preclude it from being used in a discretionary fashion for countercyclical purposes or demand management, as contemplated in the Williamson-Miller plan. If interest rates are to be tied down by targets for exchange rate bands and global demand growth (or global full employment), then it is essential that fiscal policy be freed up to target national goals for demand or employment. To make this possible, governments would have to abandon the ideological obsession with balanced budgets that has gripped fiscal policy in the past decade.[51]

In the monetary area, this plan clearly reduces national policy autonomy by requiring countries to follow internationally determined targets for interest rates—both for average levels (keyed on global demand or full employment) and for international differences (keyed on exchange rates). While the wide bands around the exchange rate targets allow for some degree of monetary autonomy, interest rates still have to be kept within ranges that prevent the exchange rates from going outside the bands. This leaves countries with only limited room to use interest rates for other purposes, such as to control domestic credit creation through the banking system. Therefore, countries concerned with their overall financial stability and the security of their banks and other financial intermediaries need to adopt additional tools for controlling credit creation if they give up most of their ability to manipulate interest rates.

The main tool that could serve this purpose is a renewed use of reserve requirements. As D'Arista (1998) observes, adjusting reserve requirements allows monetary authorities to regulate the supply of credit within the banking system, rather than just operating on the demand for credit via interest rate policy. Palley (1997, 1998c) argues that credit control would be further enhanced if reserve requirements were shifted from the liability side of banks' balance sheets (i.e., their deposit accounts) to the asset side (i.e., their loan portfolios). According to Palley, changes in asset-based reserve requirements would affect interest rates on loans but not on deposits. This would enable central banks to exercise more direct control over credit, since the demand for credit responds mainly to lending rates. It would also enable national monetary authorities to control domestic credit conditions without affecting the key short-term interest rates that affect international capital flows—i.e., money market rates and bank deposit rates.

However, as discussed in Chapter 1, a major reason for the shift away from the active use of reserve requirements since the 1970s has been the competition that domestic banks face from offshore banks and nonbank financial intermediaries (e.g., mutual funds). Therefore, a return to greater reliance on reserve requirements is feasible only if governments in the major financial centers agree to impose similar requirements and if the requirements are applied to all kinds of financial institutions rather than just domestic commercial banks. In particular, in order to rein in offshore currency markets, it is vital that reserve requirements be instituted on loans or deposits denominated in foreign currencies (e.g., Eurodollars), as advocated by Wachtel (1990). Also, as Palley (1998c) notes, delinking reserve requirements from deposit accounts requires reliable systems of deposit insurance and lender-of-last-resort intervention to protect depositors.[52]

Political feasibility

According to Kenen (1989), there are three levels of international cooperation, in ascending order of the strength of the commitment involved: consultation, collaboration, and coordination. Consultation simply means sharing information about conditions and policies. Collaboration means jointly formulating policies to address a specific problem or situation, but without any commitment to longer-term coordination. Coordination requires countries to commit in advance to adopt policies that they might not necessarily adopt otherwise.[53]

Consultation now occurs regularly. The leaders of the major industrialized countries meet annually to discuss their economic policies, while their finance ministers meet more frequently. Central bankers from those countries consult with each other regularly, through monthly meetings at the BIS as well as more informally. But mere consultation usually has limited impact on what countries actually do. Collaboration sometimes occurs when there is a specific problem that needs to be addressed, such as when central banks agree to coordinate intervention in foreign exchange markets. But collaboration is at best an effort to fix a problem that has already occurred, while prior coordination that could prevent problems from occurring is rarely observed.

Examples of failures to coordinate policies, as well as failures to collaborate in solving problems, are not hard to find. U.S. interest rate hikes have helped to trigger major foreign financial crises, as in the cases of the 1982 Mexican debt crisis and the 1994 peso crisis. Germany's decision to raise interest rates in the early 1990s sparked speculative attacks on other currencies in the former ERM, as discussed earlier. And Japan's inability to solve its own banking crisis and to provide an adequate fiscal stimulus for its economy has contributed to worsening the overall Asian crisis as well as to exacerbating Japan's huge trade surpluses. If it is not politically feasible to adopt a more comprehensive scheme for international policy coordination, at least large, influential countries like the United States and Japan and large blocs like the EMU must take responsibility for the global effects of their domestic policies. The potential for the Asian crisis to unleash a global economic collapse forcefully illustrates the dangers of not coordinating policies or at least collaborating in solving problems once they arise.

Yet, international policy coordination is a two-edged sword in regard to policy autonomy and policy effectiveness. Any country agreeing to target its exchange rates and to coordinate its macroeconomic policies with other countries is, of necessity, surrendering some measure of autonomy. It may, for example, have to set its own interest rates higher or lower than it would otherwise, in order to reach agreement with other countries. The hoped-for advantage is that whatever policy results from this type of coordination is more effective and more sustainable than a similar policy carried out by a single country. But from a strictly national viewpoint, there are likely to be situations in which a single country could do better on its own (e.g., because it would adopt a larger interest rate cut, and is willing to either let its currency depreciate or close its capital market) than if it had to coordinate with other countries. One cannot start down the road of policy coordination without recognizing that it may require compromises of some national objectives in the interest of promoting a generally more stable and prosperous global economy, in which all countries are ultimately better off.

Conclusions:
policy autonomy and national objectives

This chapter has reviewed the policy menu for would-be architects of international financial reform. The official proposals emanating from the U.S. government and international summit meetings have been exceptionally cautious. They have emphasized reforming financial institutions and regulations in emerging market countries along with improving transparency and surveillance throughout the international financial system. These measures might help to contain some of the worst excesses of financial crises, but they would not relieve the pressures that financial volatility routinely imposes on policy makers around the world. Overall, these types of policies would do more to make the world safe for short-term investors than they would to restore more balanced and equitable growth.

In order to pursue the larger objective of balanced and equitable economic growth, we have advocated stronger measures to tame global financial flows and stabilize the international economy. In order to reduce the magnitude of currency fluctuations and lessen destabilizing flows of short-term capital, countries need to adopt appropriate packages of capital controls and transactions taxes, as well as prudential regulations of international investments. Target zones for exchange rates and coordination of macroeconomic policies are also needed to stabilize global financial markets and thus to allow capital flows to achieve their intended benefits of enhancing global efficiency and growth. And while it is important to begin thinking about new types of international institutions to regulate global financial markets, a more immediate priority is to reform the IMF in order to make it more responsive to the needs of debtor countries and more concerned with restoring equitable growth rather than bailing out wealthy investors.

This policy agenda is an ambitious one, and while it goes far beyond what the current U.S. administration and its allies (e.g., the IMF leadership) have thus far endorsed, it has been designed with political feasibility in mind. Nevertheless, it is not an agenda that prioritizes the restoration of national policy autonomy for its own sake. Globalization has reached a point where there is no

magical route back to a world of greater policy autonomy for individual nations—and greater national autonomy is not necessarily the best way to achieve
key policy objectives such as more stable exchange rates and higher (sustainable) rates of employment and growth. Countries that wall themselves off to
financial capital flows will undoubtedly gain some autonomy in the process,
but whether they use that autonomy to adopt more expansionary and egalitarian
policies or to impose more restrictive and regressive policies is another question altogether. Much depends on the democratic or authoritarian character of
the state and the nature of the policy objectives that the government adopts.

In the final analysis, the crucial objective is not to maximize national
autonomy for its own sake, but rather to try to gain autonomy for economic
policy (at whatever level) from the dictates of financial interests when these do
not coincide with broader systemic and social interests.[54] In some cases, this
latter goal can best be achieved by enhancing national sovereignty; in other
cases, the solutions lie more in cooperative arrangements (such as exchange
rate target zones and macroeconomic policy coordination) that inevitably involve sacrifices of national autonomy. In many situations, important national
objectives (such as avoiding the painful consequences of overvalued currencies) can better be served by cooperation and sacrifice rather than by trying to
go it alone in an uncoordinated world. Generally, the more developed nations
are better prepared to enter into and benefit from cooperative arrangements,
while the less developed nations probably need to emphasize national autonomy.
Nevertheless, there are possible exceptions—such as the potential for regional
cooperative arrangements among some developing countries (e.g., an Asian
Monetary Fund)—and the larger industrialized countries are relatively more
autonomous to begin with.

Still, international policy coordination is politically difficult to achieve,
and reforming an ossified and unresponsive institution like the IMF that has
been captured by special interests and rigid ideologies is no small task. As a
result, countries need fall-back options in case global systemic reforms of the
type advocated here are not adopted. For a large country like the United States,
or for a major bloc of countries like the EMU, there is much room for maneuver
even under present arrangements. The U.S. and the European countries may be
constrained by global capital flows, but they are far from paralyzed.[55] These
countries could easily lower their interest rates and adopt more expansionary
fiscal policies, if they had both the need and the will, and if they were willing to
let their currencies depreciate if necessary.

Indeed, leadership from the United States and Europe is crucial for moving the world back onto a more expansionary policy track—and for fostering
political support for greater coordination in the future. As Robert Pollin has
written,

the only conditions under which...[international] cooperative relation-ships could form would be through progressive national governments that are attempting to implement egalitarian growth policies within their domestic economies. But such governments are not likely to form if they require an environment of global cooperation as a precondition to attempting a domestic growth agenda. Rather, such governments will need to demonstrate some success with their domestic policy agendas before they acquire the credibility to push for international coopera-tion.... A successful expansionary program in a major OECD country, especially the United States, would be most important in this regard, both because of the rise in world demand that would ensue and the positive model from which other countries could draw. (Pollin 1998, 439-40)

To summarize our conclusions, it is helpful to return to the framework of the policy "trilemma" discussed in Chapter 1 and represented in Figure 1.1. For the developing countries, our main recommendation is that they should be will-ing to close their capital markets to a sufficient degree to restore both monetary policy autonomy and control over their exchange rates. This recommendation is tempered, however, by a recognition that individual developing countries differ greatly in their internal structures and financial capabilities, and that as a result these countries should be free to experiment with different solutions that make sense in terms of their specific needs. For the industrialized countries, our preferred solution of macroeconomic policy coordination involves abandoning autonomous monetary policy at the national level in order to allow for both managed exchange rates (target zones) and largely open capital markets (with some speed bumps, intended to restrain inflows and outflows of hot money and to contain exchange rate volatility). Monetary policy autonomy is not com-pletely lost in this solution, but rather is shifted to the higher plane of an inter-nationally coordinated interest rate policy. If this cooperative solution is not politically feasible, however, the second-best alternative for individual coun-tries (or for a monetary union like the EMU) is to let the exchange rate float in order to restore monetary policy autonomy at the national level, and thus to be able to use interest rate policy to achieve national economic objectives. This ranking of the policy solutions suggests that it is important politically to work on two fronts at the same time: on the one hand, to promote long-term changes in the international financial system that can better foster global growth and widely shared prosperity, and, on the other hand, to push national governments to start moving in a more progressive policy direction as soon as possible with-out waiting for global systemic reforms to be adopted.

Endnotes

Introduction

1.   While gross capital flows (i.e., total amounts of funds crossing national borders) have mushroomed, net capital flows (i.e., differences between inflows and outflows) have remained relatively small for a combination of reasons, including government policies that limit current account imbalances (which are equal to net capital flows in the balance of payments) and "common factors" underlying both national saving and domestic investment (since net capital inflows must also be equal to the difference between a country's domestic saving and investment). See Frankel (1991), Mussa and Goldstein (1993), and Blecker (1997, 1998a) for recent surveys of these issues.

2.   For surveys of the evidence on the degree of international capital mobility see Frankel (1991, 1993), Mussa and Goldstein (1993), Marston (1995), Blecker (1997, 1998a), and Bhaduri (1998).

3.   According to the International Monetary Fund (1998, 63), total world imports of goods and services for 1997 totaled about $5.6 trillion. Note that the daily foreign exchange turnover of $1.5 trillion in 1998 is up from $1.2 billion in 1995, $0.8 trillion in 1992, and $0.6 trillion in 1989 (Bank for International Settlements 1998b; all figures are measured for April of each year).

4.   See Morici (1997), Scott and Rothstein (1998), and Blecker (1998a).

5.   See, among others, Moffitt (1983), Wachtel (1990), Akyüz (1995), D'Arista (1996), Eatwell (1996a, 1996b), Davidson (1997), Greider (1997), Martin and Schumann (1997), Bhaduri (1998), Palley (1998b, 1998c), and UNCTAD (1998).

6.   This term was coined by Williamson (1990), who does not necessarily endorse all of its precepts today. See Taylor (1996) and Stiglitz (1998) for critiques of Washington Consensus policy views.

Chapter 1

1.   The two types of capital mobility are related, for example, because multinational corporations have to worry about foreign exchange risk (the risk that currencies in which they have assets or earn revenue will depreciate) and have therefore been interested in financial innovations such as currency futures and options that allow them to hedge against such risk. Also, there can be a fine line between large international portfolio investments in corporate stock and acquiring significant or controlling interests in foreign companies. More broadly, multinationals want the freedom to move their funds across borders and to obtain credit wherever they want without interference from national governments.

2.   The controversy about multinational corporations concerns the effects of their activities in regard to issues such as technology transfer, national sovereignty, tax incidence, income distribution, and labor conditions (see, e.g., Glickman and Woodward

1989; Graham and Krugman 1991; and Barnet and Cavanagh 1994 for various viewpoints). The fact that these issues are not discussed in the present book should not be taken as an endorsement of any particular view about multinationals, and certainly not of a purely laissez-faire attitude toward direct foreign investment.

3.   Of course, restrictions on short-term flows of financial capital would affect the ability of multinational corporations to move their funds freely around the world or to acquire new companies abroad, as discussed in note 1 above. However, this is a relatively minor concern for companies making long-term investments, compared with financial investors moving money in and out of countries on a daily basis—and would be less of a problem if exchange rates were stabilized, as advocated in Chapter 3.

4.   Of course, domestic and international financial regulations are closely related, insofar as domestic regulations can either block or facilitate international financial flows. Mussa and Goldstein (1993) include numerous domestic financial reforms in their account of the policy changes that have fostered greater international capital mobility. See Dymski et al. (1993) for critical perspectives on domestic financial liberalization in the U.S.

5.   See Cohen et al. (1996, 55-79) for a critical discussion of the insights and limitations of free trade theories.

6.   "Statistically weak" here means that the estimates are not robust in their statistical significance—i.e., they are significant in some specifications of the regression model but not in others.

7.   One reason for the ambiguous results in this literature may be that the effects of removing capital controls are "non-linear": that is, removing excessive controls and regulations that generate large inefficiencies and induce significant rent-seeking can promote growth, while moving toward a completely liberalized regime may fail to stimulate more growth and may even reduce it through higher real interest rates and greater economic instability. One hint of this hypothesis can be found in Grilli and Milesi-Ferretti's result that black market premiums on foreign exchange have negative and significant effects on growth rates, while—after the negative effects of black market premiums are controlled for—capital controls per se have positive effects on growth rates (although these latter effects are not always statistically significant). This suggests that capital controls can potentially stimulate growth, but only where exchange controls are not severe enough to generate large black market premiums for foreign exchange that create highly distorted financial markets.

8.   Ideally, the appropriate ("first-best") response to such distortions is to use domestic taxes or subsidies, e.g., a tax on tree cutting or a subsidy to an alternative industry that doesn't require cutting trees, rather than restricting trade or capital flows. But in practice, such ideal policies are often more difficult to implement than the "second-best" trade or capital restrictions.

9.   Forward contracts allow agents to buy or sell currencies a fixed number of days in advance (e.g., 30 or 90 days), at a price (called the "forward exchange rate") agreed to in advance. The forward exchange rate is distinguished from the "spot" exchange rate, which is for immediate delivery of the purchased currency.

10. Bank balance sheets typically show deposit accounts and certain other items (e.g., borrowing from the central bank or from other banks) as liabilities and loan portfolios plus certain other items (e.g., vault cash, reserve deposits at the central bank, and holdings of government securities) as assets. Off-balance sheet activities do not appear in the balance sheets because the banks themselves do not create the liabilities or hold the assets, but rather function as intermediaries—even though the banks may in fact be instrumental in creating these types of derivatives and profit from the fees for selling them. As a result, banks' official balance sheets do not give a true picture of the riskiness of the financial positions created by their overall activities. See also Neftci (1998).

11. Of course, there can be occasional problems with ordinary merchandise trade, such as unreliable delivery, disappointing quality, or hidden costs. But these problems can be rectified relatively simply and quickly through a variety of standard means, such as withholding payment, suing the suppliers, and—if the problems are not resolved—switching to alternative suppliers.

12. The failure to anticipate such positive correlation of risks across countries is one of the reasons usually cited for the collapse of the Long-Term Capital Management "hedge fund" in September 1998.

13. I am especially indebted to Jane D'Arista and Tom Palley for suggestions that helped me to reformulate this section.

14. In economic terms, these types of needs can be regarded as positive externalities to the extent that private market forces would leave them unfulfilled.

15. If abused, such regulations can provide the government with cheap sources of credit that can fuel inflationary budget deficits and money creation, as emphasized in the concept of "financial repression" discussed by McKinnon (1973). The fact that such abuses often occurred in developing countries in the 1970s and 1980s gave credence to calls for financial deregulation at that time.

16. There is a large literature on "interest rate parity conditions," which are links between interest rates that may be created by the integration of international financial markets. It should be noted that none of these conditions implies that nominal interest rates have to be exactly equal across countries, even when capital markets are completely open, due to such factors as the presence of forward currency premiums, expectations of exchange rate changes, and expectations of different inflation rates. Moreover, the evidence on whether these conditions generally hold in liberalized capital markets is quite mixed, although there is fairly strong evidence for the weakest condition (covered interest parity). See Frankel (1991, 1993), Mussa and Goldstein (1993), Hallwood and MacDonald (1994), Marston (1995), and Blecker (1998a).

17. Note that similar considerations would apply if such a country tried to lower its own interest rate, taking foreign rates as given. In this case, the issue would be whether the new, lower domestic interest rate could be sustained.

18. Generally, the pressure to match a foreign interest rate change is more severe when the foreign interest rates rise than when they decline. In the former case (increased foreign interest rates), the central bank's reserves are likely to be depleted and, as they run out, the central bank eventually becomes incapable of defending its exchange rate target. In the latter case (decreased foreign interest rates), the central bank accumulates

more reserves and the exchange rate peg can be maintained as long as the potential inflationary consequences can be averted by sterilization—albeit at the cost of higher domestic interest rates, which can slow growth.

19. Germany was free to raise its interest rate, even though the mark was pegged to the other old European currencies in the ERM, because the basket of all the major European currencies (the European Currency Unit or ECU, forerunner to the new euro) was floating against the dollar and the yen. Since the mark was the leading currency in the ECU basket, higher interest rates in Germany were feasible as long as the ECU could appreciate—which it did at the time.

20. Italy and Spain also succeeded in lowering their interest rates at that time by allowing their currencies to depreciate. See Hausmann et al. (1999).

21. Although he does not mention it, Epstein's argument would be strengthened by noting that the effectiveness of an expansionary monetary policy can be enhanced by the induced depreciation of the currency if the latter helps to improve the country's balance of trade (although this can be a beggar-thy-neighbor gain, to the extent that it comes at the expense of other countries whose currencies appreciate and whose trade balances worsen).

22. See also Stiglitz (1998), who writes that "The evidence has shown only that high inflation is costly," referring to inflation rates of over 40% as "high," and concludes that "Below that level, *there is little evidence that inflation is costly*" (emphasis in original). Studies that support this conclusion include Fischer and Modigliani (1975), Fischer (1981, 1993), Driffill et al. (1990), and Barro (1997).

23. However, currency depreciation is more likely to be inflationary, contractionary, and ineffective for solving balance-of-payments deficits in developing countries compared with industrialized countries (see Caves et al. 1990; Hausmann et al. 1999). This point is discussed further below.

24. Ironically, in an earlier incarnation, President Cardoso was an advocate of "dependency theory," which claimed that the developing countries were disadvantaged by their "dependency" on the global economy (see Cardoso and Faletto 1979).

25. See Epstein (1993, 70), who cites Huizinga and Mishkin (1986), Mishkin (1988), Fair (1989), Romer and Romer (1989, 1990), Bernanke (1990), and Bernanke and Blinder (1990), on the U.S. Woo and Hirayama (1996) have shown that even smaller, developing countries can have significant monetary policy autonomy in spite of liberalized capital flows, since their risk premiums allow domestic interest rates to diverge from foreign rates.

26. See Palley (1998d) for an especially cogent critique of the notion of a natural equilibrium in economic thought and the policy implications of an alternative view he calls "structural Keynesianism."

27. For example, Friedman and Kuttner (1992, 472; cited in Epstein 1993, 76) conclude that "Including data from the 1980s sharply weakens the post-war time-series evidence indicating significant relationships between money (however defined) and nominal income, or between money and either real income or prices separately. Focusing on data from 1970 onwards destroys this evidence altogether."

28. For alternative views on the idea of a natural rate of unemployment (more technically referred to as the non-accelerating inflation rate of unemployment, or NAIRU) see Stiglitz (1997), Gordon (1997), Staiger et al. (1997), Blanchard and Katz (1997), Rogerson (1997), Galbraith (1997b), and Baker (1998). For conventional estimates that place the "natural rate of growth" (or nonaccelerating inflation output growth rate) around 2.1%, see U.S. Congressional Budget Office (1996).

29. Measured by the chain-type index for gross domestic product, the 1.0% inflation rate recorded in 1998 was the lowest since 1959. Measured by the consumer price index, the 1.6% rate for 1998 was the lowest since 1965. Data are from U.S. Council of Economic Advisers (1999) and U.S. Department of Commerce (1999).

30. In September 1998, the yields on 10-year and 30-year U.S. Treasury securities fell to 4.81% and 5.20%, respectively, compared with a federal funds rate (the rate on overnight interbank loans) of 5.51% maintained by the Fed's open market operations (U.S. Congress, Joint Economic Committee, September 1998).

31. This suggests that financial investors' perceptions of "sound" policies may contain more than a small element of ideology—and need not be completely congruent with their own true self-interests.

32. Of course, it is the intention of orthodox macro policies to "free up resources" from government control in order to permit more private sector growth. But what the orthodoxy did not anticipate was that the private sector growth thus unleashed would be so volatile and unstable.

33. Mexico alone received $63 billion in portfolio investment between 1990 and 1993 (IMF 1997, 71). A total of $119 billion of portfolio investment flowed into the Asian developing countries between 1993 and 1996 (IMF 1997, 70).

34. Wolf (1998) cites data from the Institute for International Finance showing that portfolio capital flows (defined as all private inflows except direct equity) into the hardest-hit Asian economies went from a net inflow of $86.0 billion in 1996 to an estimated net outflow of $19.2 billion in 1997, a negative swing of $105.2 billion in a single year.

35. This point now seems to be conceded even by Milton Friedman (1998a), who once claimed that currency speculation with flexible exchange rates would always be stabilizing (in Friedman 1953).

36. See Greenwald and Stiglitz (1993) for some of the underlying theory of how financial market "imperfections" can lead to business cycle instability through their effects on business firms' behavior. Extending their model to international capital flows is an important area for future research, as discussed in Chapter 2.

37. Neftci's paper contains explicit micro-foundations concerning the behavior of borrowers and lenders that generates highly risky financial positions. See also MacLean et al. (1998) and Kaminsky and Reinhart (1996) for analyses that complement Taylor's.

38. Alternatively, there can be a consumption-led boom, as in the case of Mexico in the early 1990s, when consumers snapped up imported consumption goods at low prices after trade barriers had been reduced and the currency had become overvalued. When there is a high propensity to consume imported goods, as there was in Mexico, a large trade deficit results.

39. Foreign investors' net purchases of U.S. financial assets (excluding direct foreign investment) soared to $624 billion in 1997, more than double the 1995 level of $298 billion. Meanwhile, U.S. investors' net purchases of foreign securities fell from a historical peak of $146 billion in 1993 (just before the Mexican crisis) to only $88 billion in 1997, indicating that more domestic portfolio capital was being kept at home. These figures are taken from DiLullo (1998); foreign investors' net purchases of U.S. financial assets (excluding direct foreign investment) are calculated as "Other foreign assets in the United States, net" (Table 1, line 56) less "Direct investment" (line 57).

40. See the *New York Times*, February 16, 1999, for evidence of U.S. government involvement in the promotion of capital market liberalization without any warning of the risks involved or the need for prior domestic reforms.

Chapter 2

1. See, in ascending order of difficulty, books such as Lindert and Pugel (1995), Caves et al. (1990), Williamson (1983), Rivera-Batiz and Rivera-Batiz (1994), Hallwood and MacDonald (1994), and Frenkel and Razin (1992), or more recent editions of the same books.

2. All dates in this paragraph are approximate. New ideas often have earlier antecedents, while old ideas often reappear in new forms in later models.

3. For the older theories, which are covered in standard international economics textbooks, detailed references will not be given. Interested readers are referred to the textbooks cited in note 1 above, which give references to the main original sources.

4. This model also played a crucial role in Ricardo's (1821) argument for a comparative advantage theory of international trade. Such a theory requires the assumption that trade is balanced, which Ricardo justified using Hume's specie-flow mechanism.

5. Alternatively, if the trade balance is measured in foreign currency terms, the problem is that a devaluation lowers the foreign currency price of exports and therefore decreases the price of any given quantity of exports. In either case, sufficient changes in the quantities of exports and imports are required to offset these unfavorable valuation effects.

6. Elasticity measures the proportional degree of responsiveness of one variable to changes in another variable. For example, if the price elasticity of import demand is 1.2, this means that the quantity of imports demanded by consumers declines by 1.2% when the price of imports rises by 1%.

7. Note that this means that the supply elasticities are infinite—i.e., producers can supply however much of a good that the consumers want, at a constant (non-increasing) cost.

8. Here we follow the convention of defining the exchange rate as the home currency price of foreign exchange, e.g., pesos per dollar in Mexico or yen per dollar in Japan. This convention can be confusing, because the exchange rate thus measured reflects the value of the *foreign* currency (hence, the exchange rate goes up when the home currency depreciates). This convention is helpful for thinking about supply and demand in the foreign exchange market. In this usage, the value of the home currency is the reciprocal of the exchange rate (foreign currency per unit of the home currency).

9. Real wage resistance means that workers are able to win nominal wage increases in order to keep up with rising goods prices and avoid a fall in their real wage. See Dornbusch (1980, 70-74).

10. For theory and evidence on this phenomenon see, among others, Mann (1986), Dornbusch (1987), Hooper and Mann (1989), Marston (1990), Feinberg (1996), and Menon (1996).

11. Since the absorption approach is based on international lending and borrowing, it does allow for international capital flows. However, in this model the capital flows are not autonomous—they simply accommodate the difference between a country's flows of income and expenditures (or domestic saving and investment), with no independent impact on the trade balance. We therefore consider that the absorption approach does not emphasize capital flows in terms of the causal stories it tells about the balance of payments.

12. More formally, start with the national income identity, $Y = C + I + G + X - M$, where Y is national income (GDP), C is consumption, I is investment, G is government spending, X is exports, and M is imports. This equation says that national income must equal aggregate demand for domestically produced goods and services. But national income must also equal the sum of consumption, private saving, and taxes: $Y = C + S + T$. By setting these two equations equal, rearranging terms, and simplifying, it can easily be seen that $X - M = (S + T - G) - I$, where $X - M$ is the trade balance and $T - G$ is the budget balance (both measured as surpluses; a negative surplus is a deficit). "National saving" is defined as $S + T - G$, i.e., private saving plus the budget surplus (public saving).

13. Net income from foreign investments means the difference between the interest, dividends, rents, and other investment income received from investments in other countries and the interest, dividends, rents, and other investment income paid out to foreign investors. Likewise, labor remittances and transfer payments are net concepts, i.e., differences between inflows and outflows of funds. Inflows or outflows of investment income and labor remittances can be thought of as payments for exports or imports of "factor services" (foreign capital and migrant labor, respectively); transfer payments (e.g., gifts, foreign aid) are payments for imports or exports of "goodwill." Note that new foreign investments—i.e., purchases of foreign assets, borrowing from foreign banks, etc.—are counted in the capital account of the balance of payments; only the *flows of income* from these investments are counted in the current account.

14. This effect can be blocked if consumers target their real consumption levels, and therefore increase their nominal spending in order to buy the same quantities of goods, in which case the trade balance will fail to improve. This is known as the Harberger-Laursen-Metzler effect (see Dornbusch 1980).

15. Note that corporate savings (retained earnings) are included in private saving (the variable S in note 12, above) along with the personal saving of wealthy shareholders and bondholders who earn dividends and interest (respectively).

16. This point was originally made by Díaz-Alejandro (1963). Krugman and Taylor (1978) pointed out that this effect could make a devaluation contractionary, since income is redistributed to the class that spends less on consumption. Blecker (1999) points out that a devaluation is more effective for improving the trade balance (and more likely to be contractionary) when a country's domestic expenditures are "wage-led" and less

effective for improving the trade balance (but more likely to be expansionary) if those expenditures are "profit-led."

17. This idea of combining fiscal and exchange rate policies to achieve two targets simultaneously (for output and the trade balance) motivated the model of internal and external balance pioneered by Swan (1955) and Mundell (1962).

18. See Yotopoulos (1996) and Hausmann et al. (1999) for evidence on the contractionary effects of devaluations and for broader perspectives on optimal exchange rate policy in developing countries.

19. One of the earliest statements of the monetary approach is the IMF version by Polak (1957). For other versions and perspectives see Whitman (1975), Frenkel and Johnson (1976), and Johnson (1977).

20. More complex monetary approach models can incorporate other assets and private capital flows (see Williamson 1983).

21. Thus, it is not strictly correct to identify the monetary approach to the balance of payments with monetarism, since the latter assumes the quantity theory of money while the former does not necessarily do so. Nevertheless, many proponents of the monetary approach (e.g., Harry Johnson, Jacob Frenkel) came from the Chicago School, and were generally sympathetic to monetarism. The monetary approach to flexible exchange rates assumes a modified version of the quantity theory in which prices are flexible and real output is exogenous, but the demand for money is sensitive to the interest rate.

22. Advocates of the monetary approach are careful to specify that they do not view excessive money creation as the *only* cause of balance-of-payments problems. See the discussion in Rivera-Batiz and Rivera-Batiz (1994, 578-80) and the citations provided there.

23. The real exchange rate is the theoretical relative price of foreign goods in terms of home goods, i.e., how many home goods one has to sell in order to buy a given quantity of foreign goods. A higher (lower) real exchange rate indicates a lower (higher) real value of the domestic currency, and hence greater (lesser) competitiveness. For example, if Mexico devalues the peso in nominal terms by 25% (say, from 8 pesos per dollar to 10 pesos per dollar), but Mexican prices rise by 30% and U.S. prices stay constant, Mexican goods are actually more expensive (and less competitive) than before. In this example, we say that the peso appreciated in real terms even though it depreciated in nominal terms—Mexicans can buy more U.S. goods with the same quantity of Mexican goods, because the latter have become relatively more expensive.

24. Recall the data on foreign exchange transactions cited in the Introduction.

25. For recent surveys of empirical studies of PPP see Giovannetti (1992), Froot and Rogoff (1995), and Rogoff (1996).

26. Lothian and Taylor (1996) find evidence in support of long-run PPP using 200 years of data for the dollar-sterling and franc-sterling exchange rates. However, their results also imply persistent short-run and medium-run deviations from PPP. For example, they estimate that the "half-life of shocks to the real exchange rate" is about six years for the dollar-sterling rate.

27. For further discussion of fundamental equilibrium exchange rates, see the discussion of John Williamson's proposal for exchange rate target zones in Chapter 3.

28. "IS" stands for investment-saving equilibrium, or equilibrium between the aggregate demand and supply for goods and services. "LM" stands for liquidity preference-money supply equilibrium, or equilibrium between money demand and money supply. This model is explained in most of the international finance textbooks cited in Chapter 2, note 1, as well as in any standard intermediate-level macroeconomics textbook. How well it represents the ideas of Keynes is a controversial issue (see, e.g., Arestis 1992).

29. Country risk is the risk of investing in a particular country, because of the possibility of the country either defaulting on its bonds or else imposing capital controls that would inhibit the repatriation of investment proceeds. Exchange risk is the risk that a currency will depreciate. Both types of risk are very important in reality and thus the basic Mundell-Fleming model is really a very special case.

30. This result does not depend on the assumption of perfect capital mobility, but the latter assumption does make the offsetting monetary flows occur more quickly than they would if capital were immobile.

31. The net capital inflows are attracted by the upward pressure on interest rates on domestic bonds, caused by the government's increased demand for funds, but with perfect capital mobility the inflows are so large that they immediately bring the interest rate back down to the given, world level. In general, a fiscal expansion tends to worsen the current account through its multiplier effects on national income, which raise import demand. Thus, in order for an overall balance-of-payments surplus to result, the capital account must improve by more than the current account worsens, which is exactly what the Mundell-Fleming model predicts in this case.

32. In technical terms, one could say that the endogenous increase in the money supply fully accommodates the fiscal expansion, thus preventing any "crowding out" of either domestic investment or net exports.

33. This is the logic that underlay the notion of the U.S. "twin deficits" in the 1980s. The available evidence indicates that the fiscal deficit explained only part of the rise in the U.S. trade deficit in that decade, and the two deficits have not been correlated at other times. For different perspectives on the twin deficits hypothesis see Blecker (1992) and Bosworth (1993).

34. See the discussion of "interest rate parity conditions" in Chapter 1, note 16, and the sources listed there.

35. The Mundell-Fleming model has been extended to deal with many such complexities as well as with the large-country case. See, for example, Dornbusch (1980), Tobin and Braga de Macedo (1980), and Branson and Buiter (1983).

36. This point has been acknowledged by Branson and Buiter (1983), who cite earlier work by Whitman (1975) and Obstfeld (1980).

37. See Moore (1988), Pollin (1991), and Palley (1996) on the theory of endogenous money. The basic argument for endogenous money is that modern central banks typically operate by setting interest rates (the price of money), thus effectively letting the public and the banks determine the quantity of money (which is mostly bank deposits)

that gets created at that price. Note that the endogeneity of the money supply with fixed exchange rates stems from another type of price setting: fixing the external price of money (the exchange rate), rather than the internal price (the interest rate).

38. This model was originally developed by Branson (1977), among others. The discussion here follows the presentations in Dernburg (1989, 295-319) and Hallwood and MacDonald (1994, 186-98). For a more general model that does not make some of the restrictive assumptions of the basic portfolio balance model see Tobin and Braga de Macedo (1980).

39. One important (and often unstated) implication of the portfolio balance model is that both fiscal and monetary policies are likely to have real effects on national income and employment, even with perfect capital mobility and a flexible exchange rate, at least in the short run. However, simple portfolio balance models often ignore these real effects and their potential feedbacks onto the demand for alternative assets. An exception is Branson and Buiter (1983), who emphasize how the exchange rate effects of fiscal policy can affect real balances (real values of assets), and thereby influence real activity. Their results show that the Mundell-Fleming conclusion that fiscal policy is ineffective with a flexible exchange rate and perfect capital mobility is a special case, which neglects how the exchange rate affects the money market.

40. However, trade in goods and services will *not* generally be balanced in the new long-run equilibrium. This is because the changed international asset position causes a permanent change in net interest flows that has to be compensated by a change in the trade balance in order for the current account as whole to equal zero. In the example in the text, since net foreign assets are reduced, net interest inflows are also reduced in the long run, and hence the trade balance must be higher (to make up for lower net interest inflows) in the new long-run equilibrium than it was ex ante.

41. This lacuna was noted earlier by Tobin and Braga de Macdeo (1980).

42. The same point applies to the one-country version of the model: with a more complete specification of the assets in different types of agents' portfolios, the one-country model can determine only the interest rate or the exchange rate but not both. Taylor also argues that the Mundell-Fleming model is similarly misspecified, because the balance-of-payments equation in the open-economy IS-LM model is not really independent of the goods- and asset-market-clearing equations (the IS and LM curves).

43. The analysis assumes that the home country is "small" and the foreign country is "large," in which case the foreign interest rate can be taken as given. In order to make sense out of the present example, one might think of the "U.K." as representing the entire rest of the world.

44. Note that this assumption provides Dornbusch with the explicit behavioral dynamics of the exchange rate that Taylor (1998c) argues are missing from the standard portfolio balance model.

45. See Isaac (1998) for a model of exchange rate overshooting based on risk premium shocks.

46. Tobin's argument on this point is qualified: he concedes monetary neutrality for a theoretical long run, but argues that such a theoretical construct is irrelevant because price level changes have long-lasting real effects in actual historical time.

47. This point is made by Engel and Hamilton (1990), who quote Dornbusch (1983) as acknowledging this problem. See also Frankel and Rose (1995, 1719).

48. The origins of the intertemporal approach lie in the "Ricardian equivalence hypothesis" (REH), first promulgated by Barro (1974). Barro assumed that far-sighted, rational individuals would adjust their savings so as to offset any increase in the government's budget deficit, in order to set aside enough wealth to be able to pay for the future increased taxes that would inevitably be required (of them or their descendants) at some point in the future to pay off the government's debt. Since total national saving equals the sum of private saving and government saving (the budget balance), if the increase in private saving equals the decrease in public saving (increased fiscal deficit), national saving is unaffected by the deficit financing of government spending. Hence, the fiscal deficit (i.e., government borrowing) has no effect on the current account balance, which equals the difference between national saving and investment. The phrase "Ricardian equivalence" refers to the conclusion that it does not matter if government spending is financed by taxes or by borrowing—a conclusion rather misleadingly attributed to Ricardo (1821).

Barro's REH result ran contrary to standard economic intuition, which suggests that government borrowing is likely to increase domestic spending and therefore to reduce the current account balance. Skeptics quickly pointed out that Barro made a number of special assumptions, even within an intertemporal optimizing framework. For example, the REH result requires the assumption of an infinite time horizon (or an infinite number of generations in a family "dynasty"). By relaxing such special assumptions, many theorists (e.g., Blanchard 1985) have developed intertemporal models in which fiscal deficits do affect current account balances (usually, although not always, lowering them).

49. For example, both Frenkel and Razin's (1992) textbook and Obstfeld and Rogoff's (1995) survey article give rich discussions of the mathematical properties of the intertemporal models and make strident claims about the superiority of these models (some of which are quoted above), but neither provides a clear, comprehensible summary of policy implications that would be of use to (or even comprehensible by) real-world policy makers. The precise effects of fiscal deficits on the current account in the intertemporal models vary greatly, depending on a number of assumptions and parameter values. In particular, these models emphasize the "elasticity of intertemporal substitution," i.e., to what extent consumers are willing to forego current consumption for increased future consumption by saving, as well as the time-horizon over which consumers are assumed to maximize their intertemporal utility.

50. See McCombie and Thirlwall (1994) for a comprehensive overview of this theoretical approach and McCombie (1997) for a recent evaluation of the empirical support for it. See also Alonso and Garcimartín (1998-99) for a novel approach to testing the balance-of-payments-constrained growth model relative to alternative models.

51. Technically speaking, the balance-of-payments-constrained growth rate in an economy without capital mobility is given by $x/\eta = \varepsilon y^*/\eta$, where x is the growth rate of exports, η is the income elasticity of import demand, ε is the income elasticity of export demand, and y^* is the foreign income growth rate (assuming that relative price effects are negligible as discussed in the text).

52. Blecker (1998b) and Alonso and Garcimartín (1998-99) discuss the significance of the distinction between income and price adjustments in this framework. Also see Blecker (1998b) and Pugno (1998) for further analysis of the price assumptions underlying the model.

53. Moreno-Brid (1998-99) does offer an analysis of the stability of his model, i.e., whether an the economy will tend to converge to the growth rate that is consistent with a constant long-run average ratio of net capital inflows to domestic income. For this purpose, he assumes that lower current account deficits improve a country's ability to borrow (because the country is seen as more creditworthy) and thereby allow it to import more, and that domestic investment depends on imports of machinery and equipment (a realistic assumption for most developing countries and smaller industrialized countries). On these assumptions, the balance-of-payments-constrained growth equilibrium is stable under the same condition that makes capital inflows relax the constraint (i.e., an initial trade deficit and a relatively high income elasticity of import demand). But as the quote in the text concedes, this special case falls short of providing a more general stability analysis. See also Pugno (1998) on the dynamics of adjustment in the basic Thirlwall model without capital mobility and the possibility for that model to yield cyclical fluctuations.

54. For an earlier paper that explored the conditions for international borrowing to be stable or unstable in regard to interest rates, saving rates, and import and export propensities see Bhaduri (1987).

55. The original balance-of-payments-constrained growth model of Thirlwall (1979) constitutes an exception to this otherwise rosy picture. As discussed above, this model (which did not allow for capital mobility) implied that balanced trade was likely to be achieved through (painful) limitations on growth rather than (painless) adjustments in prices or exchange rates.

56. For other surveys and discussions of the exchange rate literature that generally reach similar conclusions see Hallwood and MacDonald (1994), Isard (1995), and Obstfeld (1995).

57. It is of course possible that exchange rate movements could be explained by some fundamental determinants that are unobservable by econometricians, but aside from the obvious impossibility of testing such a proposition, most of the candidates for such explanations—such as exogenous changes in technology or tastes—seem implausible based on the evidence that is available (Frankel and Rose 1995, 1708).

58. Rationality, it would seem, is in the eyes of the beholder. It is always possible to consider speculation on an asset that is expected to rise in price as "rational" on the part of the individual investor taking that gamble. However, what may be regarded as rational for a single individual may be irrational for the group of speculators as a whole, if they are continuously investing in something that cannot go up in price indefinitely. Everyone may think that he or she will be smart enough to sell off his or her asset position before the bubble bursts, but not everyone will actually be able to do so. As Kindleberger (1989) argues, a speculative bubble may begin as a rational response to some genuine investment opportunity. As long as the expected capital gains outweigh the expected losses from a fall in price (weighted by the perceived probability of the price falling), continued speculation can be considered individually rational. But if at some point the speculators begin to ignore crucial (and easily available) information that indicates that they are underestimating the risk of the asset price declining, then one

could argue that there is "irrational exuberance" (to use Alan Greenspan's phrase) even at the individual level.

59. Note that this procedure utilizes the uncovered interest parity condition, which was discussed in regard to Dornbusch's overshooting model above.

60. The behavior of the dollar *after* it peaked in March 1985 is entirely consistent with the view that a bubble had burst, since the dollar collapsed at a very rapid rate over the following year—faster than it had previously risen (see Figure 2.2). The puncturing of the bubble was probably stimulated by the announcement in early 1985 of a new policy attitude by incoming U.S. Treasury Secretary James Baker, along with coordinated central bank intervention (primarily by West Germany). While one could argue that monetary policy was also loosened in 1985, thus changing the fundamentals, it would be hard to explain the speed, duration, and extent of the dollar's decline after March 1985 by this factor alone (see Rivera-Batiz and Rivera-Batiz 1994, 442-43). Rather, it seems more plausible that the announcements and interventions in the first few months of 1985 made investors reevaluate the risk of the dollar depreciating, leading to a new set of self-fulfilling expectations—although the subsequent monetary expansion undoubtedly helped to keep the dollar at a permanently lower value thereafter. The famous "Plaza Agreement," in which the G-5 countries agreed to try to stabilize exchange rates, did not occur until September 1985, six months after the dollar began to fall.

61. The empirical literature that analyzes the speculative attacks is enormous and growing rapidly. A few highlights include Blanco and Garber (1986); Cumby and van Wijnbergen (1989); Eichengreen et al. (1994, 1995); Kaminsky and Reinhart (1996); Frankel and Rose (1996); Sachs et al. (1996a); Martínez-Pería (1997); and Tornell (1998).

62. Earlier, Flood and Garber (1984b) showed this possibility for a gold standard.

63. For example, Calvo and Mendoza (1996) cite a model in which the anticipation of a banking system bailout triggers the attack. Sachs et al. (1996b) construct a model focusing on the interaction between the government's credibility in maintaining its peg and investors' expectations of a devaluation. In this model, the crucial variable that determines the probability of a self-fulfilling attack is the level of the country's debt. See also Obstfeld (1994, 1996).

64. According to Morris and Shin (1998), these models assume three possible "regions" a country may find itself in: (1) situations in which the fundamentals are so bad that the government will eventually be forced to devalue or float even if there is no speculation (an "unstable" currency); (2) situations in which the fundamentals are so strong that a speculative attack could not succeed and rational speculators will not launch one (a "stable" currency); and (3) situations with intermediate fundamentals, in which speculation can force abandonment of a peg even though it would be sustainable in the absence of a speculative attack (a currency that is "ripe for attack"). In most such models, region (3) is a zone of indeterminacy, since there are multiple equilibria and the actual timing and extent of the speculative attack cannot be predicted ex ante. Morris and Shin show that, with uncertainty on the part of speculators about the true state of the fundamentals, there can be a unique equilibrium with a determinate level of the fundamentals at which an attack necessarily occurs. Morris and Shin simplify their analysis by assuming that the fundamentals can be represented by a single scalar magnitude, a parameter q that varies between 0 and 1. While this helps to have a tractable model with uncertainty, it remains a heroic oversimplification.

65. The one Asian country that had the highest current account deficit (as a percentage of GDP) before the crisis was, not coincidentally, Thailand. In this respect, the Thai crisis was at least partly driven by a perceived inconsistency between the country's fixed exchange rate and its external macroeconomic equilibrium. However, there is also evidence of a contagion effect from the Mexican crisis, since the attack on the Thai baht did not begin until the Thai current account deficit reached a level similar to what Mexico's deficit had reached before its 1994 crisis (about 8% of GDP). Thailand also had a speculative bubble in its commercial real estate market.

66. Tornell uses a measure of increases in bank lending as a proxy for another variable that is theoretically important—the proportion of "bad" (nonperforming) loans in the banking system—for which reliable data are not available.

67. This is the same variable that was identified by Tornell (1998) as an explanatory factor for contagion effects, as discussed above.

68. This sub-section was inspired by comments by Tom Palley on an earlier draft.

69. Minsky's concepts have been applied to the 1997-98 Asian financial crisis by Kregel (1998b, 1998c).

70. See also Franke and Semmler (1989) and Foley (1987) for other models of financial instability focusing on firms' financing behavior.

71. In the somewhat perverse language of economic theory, the unrealistic models assume "perfect capital markets," while the more realistic models assume "imperfect capital markets."

72. This discussion draws upon and extends remarks by Joseph Stiglitz at the conference on "Globalization in Crisis: An Agenda for Action for the World Economy," American University, Washington, D.C., December 18, 1998.

73. One could argue that the dilemma facing Mexico and Brazil is exacerbated by a special problem in their fundamentals: a history of large budget deficits or private spending sprees financed by excessive monetary expansion and foreign borrowing. But the basic conflict over how to set a country's exchange rate for different objectives exists in all countries.

Chapter 3

1. Some members of the first group claim that their proposed new international institutions would also help to increase domestic policy autonomy. This claim is discussed below.

2. The need for action in all of these areas was foreseen (and many of the specific proposals were discussed) by Wachtel (1990), who advocated reserve requirements for offshore banks, orderly debt restructurings, target zones for exchange rates, and international interest rate coordination, among other things. For more recent discussions of broad ranges of policies for global financial reform see Akyüz (1995), Akyüz and Cornford (1995), Hutton (1996), Palley (1998b, 1998c, 1998d), K. Singh (1998), Soros (1998), UNCTAD (1998), World Bank (1998), U.S. Council of Economic Advisers (1999), Eichengreen (1999), and *Economist* (1999).

3.   The G-7 is the club of major industrialized nations (U.S., U.K., France, Germany, Japan, Italy, and Canada). The G-22 is a newly created extension of the G-7 including 15 developing nations chosen by the G-7 members (and thus does not necessarily represent all Third World perspectives).

4.   The following summary draws upon Griesgraber (1998) and U.S. Council of Economic Advisers (1999, 267-84).

5.   Halifax refers to the location of the June 1995 G-7 summit meeting, where international financial reforms were discussed in the wake of the Mexican peso crisis that occurred during the preceding six months. The label "Halifax II" is intended to signify continuity with the policy approach taken during that summit.

6.   The following summary of Goldstein's analysis and prescriptions paraphrases liberally from various parts of his text. My intention is to present his arguments in as close to his own words as possible, without cluttering up the paragraph with an excessive number of quotation marks and exact page references.

7.   For further discussion of the problems created by uninsured creditors under Soros' plan see Eichengreen (1999, 86-87).

8.   I am indebted to Robin Hahnel for suggesting this point.

9.   The Asian systems were generally designed to channel massive amounts of personal savings into productive investments in directions favored by government development strategies, through intermediation by banks often linked to the borrowing enterprises (hence, the so-called "crony" relationships between borrowers and lenders). These systems worked well for propelling poor, impoverished countries into the ranks of successful, middle-income nations through export-led growth, but do not appear to work as well for making those economies more efficient and for stimulating domestic-led expansion in later stages of the development process.

10.   The one exception is a willingness to tolerate Chilean-style reserve requirements on short-term capital inflows, as expressed by Goldstein (1998), Fischer (1998), and U.S. Council of Economic Advisers (1999, 283-84). Chile's approach to reserve requirements is discussed in detail in the next section.

11.   For other recent discussions of this proposal see Eichengreen, Tobin, and Wyplosz (1995), Felix (1996), Haq, Kaul, and Grunberg (1996), Grieve Smith (1997a), Arestis and Sawyer (1997), Davidson (1997), Wachtel (1997), and Palley (1998c, 1998e).

12.   Mélitz also discusses a number of practical difficulties with his tax, such as the potential for evasion and the inconvenience to ordinary commercial traders.

13.   See the IMF's *Exchange Rate Arrangements and Exchange Restrictions Annual Report* (various years) for comprehensive surveys of capital controls and other restrictions affecting countries' currency markets and balance of payments.

14.   See also Frenkel (1998) and Taylor (1998b), who compare Chile's disastrous experiences with capital market liberalization in the more ideologically free market Pinochet era (late 1970s and early 1980s) with its more pragmatic approach in the 1990s. This history suggests that Chile may actually have learned from its past experiences, unlike many other countries.

15. The package also included a crawling exchange rate band, with sterilized intervention by the central bank to prevent excessive appreciation of the peso without increasing inflation—a policy that resulted in large accumulations of foreign exchange reserves along with large offsetting sales of government bonds by the central bank. Chile also encouraged capital outflows by domestic residents in order to further relieve upward pressures on the value of the peso.

16. This discussion of Malaysia draws heavily upon a presentation by Martin Khor at the conference, "Toward a Progressive International Economy," sponsored by Friends of the Earth and the International Forum on Globalization, Washington, D.C., December 9, 1998, as well as on Ariff (1998) and *Economist* (1998).

17. For broader discussions of the IMF, its relationship to its sister institution, the World Bank, and how its functions and policies have changed since its founding, see (among others) Eichengreen (1996), Feldstein (1998), and Pieper and Taylor (1998).

18. Under the Bretton Woods system, all other currencies were pegged to the U.S. dollar, which in turn was pegged to gold. Thus, the United States could not adjust its own exchange rates with the other currencies, although it could adjust the dollar's value in terms of gold. The "adjustable peg" exchange rates were fixed for long periods of time, but were supposed to be changed as needed to eliminate "fundamental disequilibria" in countries' balance of payments. The fact that the countries that had trade surpluses with the United States (especially West Germany and Japan) did not want to revalue their currencies was an important factor in driving the United States to break up the Bretton Woods system in the early 1970s.

19. Mikesell (1995) notes that this evolution of the IMF calls into question the rationale for maintaining it as a separate institution from the World Bank, which also concentrates its lending efforts in developing countries.

20. For earlier critiques of the IMF see, e.g., Payer (1974) and Wood (1989).

21. Technically, what the IMF does is extend credits that begin with the countries' own reserves at the Fund. These can then be extended through a variety of programs with increasing levels of conditionality and monitoring.

22. I am indebted to Howard Wachtel for suggesting this point.

23. For example, suppose a Chilean firm owed $1 million to a U.S. bank at an initial exchange rate of 450 pesos per dollar, and then the peso was devalued to 500 per dollar before the debt became due. The Chilean firm would now owe 50 million more pesos in order to extinguish this obligation at the ICB, and thus still bears exchange risk—just as it does under the present system. In this sense, exchange risk is not eliminated by having an international clearinghouse accept payment in national currencies, although D'Arista and Schlesinger's intention is that exchange rates would become more stable with the elimination of speculation in private currency markets. D'Arista and Schlesinger also note that (in this example) Chile would not have to earn additional foreign exchange to settle its debt under their scheme, because the Chilean firm could just pay with more pesos (private correspondence from Jane D'Arista, January 25, 1999).

24. Garten (1998) also envisions such an enforcement role for his global central bank, which "would play an oversight role for banks and other financial institutions everywhere, providing some uniform standards for prudent lending in places like China and Mexico."

25. However, Hausmann et al. (1999) cite evidence that Latin American countries with fixed exchange rates or dollarized currencies have actually had lower real interest rates than other Latin American countries with flexible or adjustable exchange rates. The pros and cons of dollarization are discussed further in the section on exchange rates, below.

26. At present, under President James Wolfensohn and Chief Economist Joseph Stiglitz, the World Bank is taking a more independent position by emphasizing the needs of the poorer countries in the global economy as well as those who have been hurt by financial stabilization policies in the crisis countries. But the World Bank has been pressured to support flawed U.S./IMF-sponsored initiatives such as the $41.5 billion rescue package for Brazil that has failed to stabilize its currency and economy. Moreover, only a decade ago, the World Bank was a prime promoter of Washington Consensus policies in all areas of the globe. The Bank's current assertions of limited independence could easily be squelched if the present leadership was removed under pressure from the U.S. government. In other words, the World Bank leadership can only go so far astray as the U.S. administration is willing to tolerate.

27. A related proposal by Mikesell (1995) calls for retaining the IMF as a separate entity for a transition period, but merging it with the World Bank Group and giving it a more restricted role in financial management with long-term objectives set by the World Bank board. Mikesell also calls for transferring authority over capital controls to the World Trade Organization.

28. For some specific ideas on incorporating environmental concerns into the operations of the IMF and World Bank see the platform of the "50 Years Is Enough" group, at website http://www.50years.org/platform.html.

29. For example, Kregel (1998b) argues that Mexico's crisis in 1994-95 was more of a traditional balance-of-payments crisis attributable to excessive spending and an overvalued currency, while Asia's crisis in 1997-98 was more of a pure debt deflation crisis occurring in the context of liberalized financial markets. The implication is that different causes call for different cures.

30. The structural budget deficit is the deficit that would exist if a country was at full employment. The actual budget deficit is generally larger than the structural deficit when a country's economy is depressed, because tax revenue is reduced. Countries should not engage in fiscal belt-tightening to counteract budget deficits caused by business cycle downturns.

31. See Obstfeld (1995) for a retrospective on exchange rate behavior since 1973.

32. In the ERM, individual currencies were pegged to each other but the basket of currencies formerly known as the European Currency Unit (ECU)—the predecessor to the euro—floated against nonmember currencies. The new EMU is similar in this respect, but will eventually (by 2002) eliminate the individual national currencies. Also, while the internal pegs within the ERM were adjustable, the parities in the EMU are irrevocable.

33. Eichengreen (1999, 105-6) allows that countries with flexible rates should be free to intervene occasionally to "dampen temporary fluctuations," and in this sense allows for "dirty floating." But he recommends against any explicit exchange rate targets or bands.

34. While some economists would make an exception for countries attempting to stop a hyperinflation, Eichengreen (1999, 106) opposes using exchange rate pegs even in high inflation situations. He argues that "Smooth exits from currency pegs, whatever the original rationale for the peg, are very much the exception to the rule." Governments that make a fixed exchange rate a cornerstone of their economic strategies will always be loathe to abandon them, argues Eichengreen. As a result, pegs tend to be held in place too long until they are brought down in a speculative attack leading to a severe crisis.

35. I refer to this perspective as "global monetarism" to distinguish it from the more traditional monetarism of Milton Friedman. All monetarists advocate tightly controlled monetary growth in order to suppress inflation—essentially, they view price stability as the chief objective of monetary policy. However, Friedman (1953) advocates a perfectly flexible (freely floating) exchange rate combined with a fixed monetary growth rule at the national level, while the global monetarists advocate rigidly fixed nominal exchange rates and monetary growth restricted by the imperatives of maintaining those rates. Essentially, traditional monetarism favors controlling the quantity of money and letting its external price adjust, while the global variety favors controlling the external price of money and letting the quantity adjust.

36. See Chapter 2 for a discussion of the concept of the PPP theory and the problems with estimates of absolute PPP exchange rates.

37. Even when dollars are not legally accepted as domestic currency, there can be what Hausmann et al. (1999, 14) call "de facto dollarization" when domestic banks accept large amounts of dollar deposits, currencies are rigidly pegged to the dollar, governments and businesses have large dollar-denominated liabilities, or domestic residents think in dollar terms in setting their targets for wage and price increases.

38. Note that D'Arista and Schlesinger's proposed international central bank, discussed earlier, would not issue a new international reserve asset, but would rather utilize existing national currencies to conduct its operations.

39. Williamson and Miller (1987) present a more complete plan for macroeconomic policy coordination incorporating Williamson's target zones for exchange rates, which is discussed in the next subsection.

40. Grieve Smith (1998, 18) emphasizes that the adjustments "should be small and relatively frequent—with an agreed limit on changes in parity of less than half the width of the bands."

41. In contrast, Volcker (1996) calls for the IMF to oversee his system of target zones.

42. Gray (1996) argues that coordination among a small number of leading countries, which he calls a "committee-type hegemonic system," is essential to global monetary stability when no single country can play a leadership role as the U.S. could in the early post-World War II period (or as the U.K. could before World War I).

43. Note that crawling pegs in which the adjustments are set in advance are more useful for restraining inflation, while crawling pegs in which the adjustments are indexed to actual, past inflation are more useful for maintaining external competitiveness.

44. A current example would be to condition most-favored-nation (MFN) trade status for China—or Chinese entry into the WTO—on a higher dollar-yuan exchange rate.

Another solution was advocated by Blecker (1992), who called for a "unit labor cost equalization surcharge" to be placed on U.S. imports from countries that have persistent trade surpluses caused by massive exchange market intervention that keeps their currencies artificially undervalued. Essentially, this would be a tariff that would compensate for the competitive advantage created by the currency undervaluation. The surcharge would be removed if the countries revalued their currencies to levels that roughly equalized their average unit labor costs (wages adjusted for productivity) with U.S. average unit labor costs, for manufacturing industries —which would then permit trade to follow underlying comparative advantages rather than absolute competitive advantages. Indeed, the hope is that the threat of such a surcharge would induce these surplus countries to revalue their currencies and thus to make actual imposition of the surcharge unnecessary.

45. Bergsten (1998, 21) notes this point in regard to reflating the Asian economies when he writes, "If all the countries [in the region] reduced their interest rates together, there would be no risk of destabilising flows from one to another. If they expanded their budget positions in tandem, there would be little fear of unfavourable investor comparisons." But this point also applies globally, not just in Asia.

46. Trade imbalances may either widen or narrow in any given country as a result of lower interest rates, even if exchange rates are unaffected, due to the different degrees to which individual countries' economies expand in response to the interest rate cuts and the different repercussions of such expansion for each country's imports and exports. Furthermore, if trade balances change, this could make some exchange rate realignment necessary in order to maintain balance-of-payments equilibrium. Presumably, such second-order effects would be small compared with the exchange rate changes that can be induced by an uncoordinated interest rate cut.

47. See Hallwood and MacDonald (1994, 100-13) for a survey of models of policy coordination. See also Rogoff (1985), Branson, Frenkel, and Goldstein (1990), and Kenen (1989) for a variety of perspectives.

48. Note that domestic expenditures is the sum of consumption, investment, and government spending, but excludes net exports (the trade balance). Thus, it is not the same as the gross domestic product, which also includes net exports.

49. See Chapter 1, note 22, for citations to studies showing that low-to-moderate inflation rates do not have significant social costs.

50. For example, in the United States data on prices and unemployment are released monthly, while data on domestic demand and real output are released quarterly.

51. This does not imply that budget deficits should be allowed to grow without limits. For example, in cases where there is a history of high inflation often fueled by the monetization of large government deficits (as in many Latin American and African countries), reducing budget deficits can be a rational policy response. Maintaining moderate debt-to-GDP ratios is also a reasonable goal of fiscal policy, but one that does not generally require balanced budgets—only deficits that are limited as percentages of GDP. And these percentages can often be kept low by encouraging GDP growth.

52. See D'Arista (1998) for a proposal to shift deposit insurance away from banks and onto depositors regardless of the type of institution in which they hold their funds.

53. One major example of macro policy coordination is the EMU, which was discussed extensively above.

54. I am indebted to Ilene Grabel for suggesting this point, in her remarks at a meeting at the Political Economy Research Institute (PERI), University of Massachusetts, Amherst, in November 1998.

55. See Galbraith (1989) and Pollin (1998) for ideas on how to reorient U.S. macroeconomic policies in a more progressive direction without necessarily instituting new global arrangements.

Bibliography

Agosin, Manuel, and Ricardo Ffrench-Davis. 1998. "Managing Capital Inflows in Chile." Photocopy, United Nations Economic Commission for Latin America and the Caribbean (July).

Ahmed, Ehsan, Roger Koppl, J. Barkley Rosser Jr., and Mark V. White. 1997. "Complex Bubble Persistence in Closed-End Country Funds." *Journal of Economic Behavior and Organization* 32, pp. 19-37.

Akerlof, George, William Dickens, and George Perry. 1996. "The Macroeconomics of Low Inflation." *Brookings Papers on Economic Activity 1:1996*, pp. 1-76.

Akyüz, Yilmaz. 1995. "Taming International Finance." In J. Michie and J. Grieve Smith, eds., *Managing the Global Economy*. Oxford: Oxford University Press.

Akyüz, Yilmaz, and Andrew Cornford. 1995. "International Capital Movements: Some Proposals for Reform." In J. Michie and J. Grieve Smith, eds., *Managing the Global Economy*. Oxford: Oxford University Press.

Alexander, Sidney S. 1952. "Effects of a Devaluation on a Trade Balance." *IMF Staff Papers* 3, pp. 263-78.

Allsopp, Christopher, and David Vines. 1998. "The Assessment: Macroeconomic Policy After EMU." *Oxford Review of Economic Policy* 14(3), pp. 1-23.

Alonso, José, and Carlos Garcimartín. 1998-99. "A New Approach to the Balance-of-Payments Constraint: Some Empirical Evidence." *Journal of Post Keynesian Economics* 21(2), pp. 259-82.

Amsden, Alice. 1989. *Asia's Next Giant: South Korea and Late Industrialization*. Oxford: Oxford University Press.

Aninat, Eduardo, and Christian Larraín. 1996. "Capital Flows: Lessons From the Chilean Experience." *CEPAL Review* 60 (December), pp. 39-48.

Arestis, Philip. 1992. *The Post-Keynesian Approach to Economics*. Aldershot, U.K.: Edward Elgar.

Arestis, Philip, and Malcolm Sawyer. 1997. "How Many Cheers for the Tobin Financial Transactions Tax?" *Cambridge Journal of Economics* 21(6), pp. 753-68.

Ariff, Mohamed. 1998. "Pros and Cons of Exchange Controls." *New Straits Times Press*, September 19.

Baker, Dean. 1998. "The NAIRU: Is It a Real Constraint?" In Dean Baker, Gerald Epstein, and Robert Pollin, eds., *Globalization and Progressive Economic Policy*. Cambridge, U.K.: Cambridge University Press.

Bank for International Settlements (BIS). 1998a. *Bank for International Settlements, 68th Annual Report*. Basle: BIS.

Bank for International Settlements (BIS). 1998b. "Central Bank Survey of Foreign Exchange and Derivatives Market Activity in April 1998: Preliminary Global Data." Press Release, October 19.

Barnet, Richard J., and John Cavanagh. 1994. *Global Dreams: Imperial Corporations and the New World Order.* New York: Simon & Schuster.

Barro, Robert. 1974. "Are Government Bonds Net Worth?" *Journal of Political Economy* 82 (November-December), pp. 1095-117.

Barro, Robert. 1997. *Determinants of Economic Growth.* Cambridge, Mass.: MIT Press.

Bergsten, C. Fred. 1998. "APEC to the Rescue." *Economist*, November 7, pp. 21-22.

Bernanke, Ben S. 1990. "On the Predictive Power of Interest Rates and Interest Rate Spreads." *New England Economic Review*, Federal Reserve Bank of Boston (November/December), pp. 52-68.

Bernanke, Ben S., and Alan Blinder. 1990. "The Federal Funds Rate and the Channels of Monetary Policy." NBER Working Paper No. 3487. Cambridge, Mass.: National Bureau of Economic Research.

Bhaduri, Amit. 1987. "Dependent and Self-Reliant Growth With Foreign Borrowing." *Cambridge Journal of Economics* 11 (September), pp. 269-73.

Bhaduri, Amit. 1998. "Implications of Globalization for Macroeconomic Theory and Policy in Developing Countries." In Dean Baker, Gerald Epstein, and Robert Pollin, eds., *Globalization and Progressive Economic Policy.* Cambridge, U.K.: Cambridge University Press.

Bhagwati, Jagdish. 1998. "The Capital Myth: The Difference between Trade in Widgets and Dollars." *Foreign Affairs* 77(3), pp. 7-12.

Bhagwati, Jagdish N., and T. N. Srinivasan. 1983. *Lectures on International Trade.* Cambridge, Mass.: MIT Press.

Blanchard, Olivier J. 1985. "Debts, Deficits, and Finite Horizons." *Journal of Political Economy* 93, pp. 223-47.

Blanchard, Olivier J., and Lawrence F. Katz. 1997. "What We Know and Do Not Know About the Natural Rate of Unemployment." *Journal of Economic Perspectives* 11(1), pp. 51-72.

Blanchard, Olivier J., and Mark W. Watson. 1982. "Bubbles, Rational Expectations, and Financial Markets." In P. Wachtel, ed., *Crises in the Economic and Financial Structure.* Lexington, Mass.: Lexington Books.

Blanco, Herminio, and Peter Garber. 1986. "Recurrent Devaluation and Speculative Attacks on the Mexican Peso." *Journal of Political Economy* 94(1), pp. 148-66.

Bleaney, Michael, and Paul Mizen. 1996. "Are Real Exchange Rates Stationary? Evidence From Sterling Bilateral Rates, 1973-93." *Economic Notes* 25(3), pp. 465-82.

Blecker, Robert A. 1992. *Beyond the Twin Deficits: A Trade Strategy for the 1990s.* Economic Policy Institute Series. Armonk, N.Y.: M.E. Sharpe.

Blecker, Robert A. 1997. "Policy Implications of the International Saving-Investment Correlation." In Robert Pollin, ed., *The Macroeconomics of Finance, Saving, and Investment*. Ann Arbor: University of Michigan Press.

Blecker, Robert A. 1998a. "International Capital Mobility, Macroeconomic Imbalances, and the Risk of Global Contraction." Center for Economic Policy Analysis, Working Paper Series III, No. 5 (June). New York: New School for Social Research.

Blecker, Robert A. 1998b. "International Competition, Relative Wages, and the Balance-of-Payments Constraint" *Journal of Post Keynesian Economics* 20(4), pp. 495-526.

Blecker, Robert A. 1999. "Kaleckian Macro Models for Open Economies." In Johan Deprez and John T. Harvey, eds., *Foundations of International Economics: Post Keynesian Perspectives*. London: Routledge, forthcoming.

Bosworth, Barry P. 1993. *Saving and Investment in a Global Economy*. Washington, D.C.: Brookings Institution.

Boughton, James M. 1998. "Harry Dexter White and the International Monetary Fund." *Finance and Development* (September), pp. 39-41.

Branson, William H. 1977. "Asset Markets and Relative Prices in Exchange Rate Determination." *Socialwissenschaftliche Annalen* 1, pp. 67-80.

Branson, William H., and Willem Buiter. 1983. "Monetary and Fiscal Policy With Flexible Exchange Rates." In Jagdeep S. Bhandari and Bluford H. Putnam, eds., *Economic Interdependence and Flexible Exchange Rates*. Cambridge, Mass.: MIT Press.

Branson, William H., Jacob A. Frenkel, and Morris Goldstein, eds. 1990. *International Policy Coordination and Exchange Rate Fluctuations*. Chicago: University of Chicago Press.

Bullard, Nicola, Walden Bello, and Kamal Malhotra. 1998. "Taming the Tigers: The IMF and the Asian Crisis." Bangkok: Focus on the Global South (March).

Calomiris, Charles W. 1998. "The IMF's Imprudent Role as Lender of Last Resort." *Cato Journal* 17(3), pp. 275-94.

Calvo, Guillermo A., and Enrique G. Mendoza. 1996. "Mexico's Balance-of-Payments Crisis: A Chronicle of a Death Foretold." *Journal of International Economics* 41(3/4), pp. 235-64.

Calvo, Sara, and Carmen M. Reinhart. 1996. "Capital Flows to Latin America: Is There Evidence of Contagion Effects?" In Guillermo A. Calvo, Morris Goldstein, and Eduard Hochreiter, eds., *Private Capital Flows to Emerging Markets After the Mexican Crisis*. Washington, D.C.: Institute for International Economics.

Camdessus, Michel. 1998. "Before the Next Crisis Begins." *Washington Post*, September 27.

Cardoso, Fernando Henrique, and Enzo Faletto. 1979. *Dependency and Development in Latin America*, trans. Marjory Mattingly Urquidi. Berkeley: University of California Press.

Carroll, Christopher D., and Lawrence H. Summers. 1991. "Consumption Growth Parallels Income Growth: Some New Evidence." In B. Douglas Bernheim and John B. Shoven, eds., *National Saving and Economic Performance*. Chicago: University of Chicago Press.

Caskey, John, and Steven M. Fazzari. 1987. "Aggregate Demand Contractions With Nominal Debt Commitments: Is Wage Flexibility Stabilizing?" *Economic Inquiry* 25 (October), pp. 583-97.

Cassel, Gustav. 1922. *Money and Foreign Exchange After 1914*. New York: Macmillan.

Cassel, Gustav. 1928. *Post-War Monetary Stabilization*. New York: Columbia University Press.

Catte, Pietro, Giampaolo Galli, and Salvatore Rebecchini. 1992. "Exchange Markets Can Be Managed!" *International Economic Insights* (September/October), pp. 17-21.

Caves, Richard E., Jeffrey A. Frankel, and Ronald W. Jones. 1990. *World Trade and Payments*. Fifth Edition. Chicago: Irwin.

Cline, William R. 1989. *United States External Adjustment and the World Economy*. Washington, D.C.: Institute for International Economics.

Clinton, Bill. 1998. Remarks by the President to the Council on Foreign Relations, New York, September 14, from website http://www.whitehouse.gov.

Cohen, Stephen C., Joel R. Paul, and Robert A. Blecker. 1996. *Fundamentals of U.S. Foreign Trade Policy*. Boulder, Colo.: Westview.

Corbett, Jenny, and David Vines. 1998. "The Asian Crisis: Competing Explanations." Center for Economic Policy Analysis, Working Paper Series III, No. 7. New York: New School for Social Research (July).

Cumby, Robert E., and Sweder van Wijnbergen. 1989. "Financial Policy and Speculative Runs With a Crawling Peg: Argentina 1979-1981." *Journal of International Economics* 27, pp. 111-27.

D'Arista, Jane. 1996. "International Capital Flows and National Macroeconomic Policies." Discussion Paper No. 32, Institute of Economic Research (October). Otaru, Japan: Otaru University of Commerce.

D'Arista, Jane. 1998. "Financial Regulation in a Liberalized Global Environment." Center for Economic Policy Analysis, Working Paper Series III, No. 2. New York: New School for Social Research (May).

D'Arista, Jane, and Stephanie Griffith-Jones. 1998. "The Boom of Portfolio Flows to 'Emerging Markets' and Its Regulatory Implications." In Manuel Montes, ed., *Short-Term Capital Movements and Balance of Payments Crises*. Helsinki: WIDER, forthcoming.

D'Arista, Jane, and Tom Schlesinger. 1998. "Reforming the Privatized International Monetary System." Philomont, Va.: Financial Market Center.

Davidson, Paul. 1991. "What International Payments Scheme Would Keynes Have Suggested for the Twenty-First Century?" In Paul Davidson and J. A. Kregel, eds., *Economic Problems of the 1990s: Europe, the Developing Countries, and the United States*. Aldershot, U.K.: Edward Elgar.

Davidson, Paul. 1996. "Reforming the International Payments System." In Robert A. Blecker, ed., *U.S. Trade Policy and Global Growth*. Economic Policy Institute Series. Armonk, N.Y.: M. E. Sharpe.

Davidson, Paul. 1997. "Are Grains of Sand in the Wheels of International Finance Sufficient to Do the Job When Boulders Are Often Required?" *Economic Journal* 107 (May), pp. 671-86.

Dernburg, Thomas F. 1989. *Global Macroeconomics*. New York: Harper & Row.

Díaz-Alejandro, Carlos F. 1963. "A Note on the Impact of Devaluation and the Redistributive Effect." *Journal of Political Economy* 71, pp. 577-80.

DiLullo, Anthony J. 1998. "U.S. International Transactions, First Quarter 1998." *Survey of Current Business* (July), pp. 59-103.

Dominguez, Kathryn M., and Jeffrey A. Frankel. 1993. "Does Foreign-Exchange Intervention Matter? The Portfolio Effect." *American Economic Review* 83(5), pp. 1356-69.

Dornbusch, Rudiger. 1976. "Expectations and Exchange Rate Dynamics." *Journal of Political Economy* 84(6), pp. 1161-76.

Dornbusch, Rudiger. 1980. *Open Economy Macroeconomics*. New York: Basic Books.

Dornbusch, Rudiger. 1983. "Comment on Shafer and Loopesko." *Brookings Papers on Economic Activity, 1:1983*, pp. 79-85.

Dornbusch, Rudiger. 1987. "Exchange Rates and Prices." *American Economic Review* 77 (March), pp. 93-106.

Dornbusch, Rudiger, Ilan Goldfajn, and Rodrigo O. Valdés. 1995. "Currency Crises and Collapses." *Brookings Papers on Economic Activity, 2:1995*, pp. 219-93.

Dornbusch, Rudiger, and Alejandro Werner. 1994. "Mexico: Stabilization, Reform, and No Growth." *Brookings Papers on Economic Activity, 1:1994*, pp. 253-315.

Driffill, John, Grayham E. Mizon, and Alistair Ulph. 1990. "Costs of Inflation." In Benjamin Friedman and Frank Hahn, eds., *Handbook of Monetary Economics*. Vol. 2. Amsterdam: Elsevier.

Dufey, Gunter, and Ian H. Giddy. 1978. *The International Money Market*. Englewood Cliffs, N.J.: Prentice-Hall.

Gary A. Dymski, Gerald Epstein, and Robert Pollin, eds. 1993. *Transforming the U.S. Financial System: Equity and Efficiency for the 21st Century*. Economic Policy Institute Series. Armonk, N.Y.: M. E. Sharpe.

Eatwell, John. 1996a. "International Capital Liberalisation: The Record." Center for Economic Policy Analysis, Working Paper Series I, No. 1 (August). New York: New School for Social Research.

Eatwell, John. 1996b. "International Financial Liberalization: The Impact on World Development." Office of Development Studies, Discussion Paper Series (September). New York: United Nations Development Programme.

Eatwell, John, and Lance Taylor. 1998a. "International Capital Markets and the Future of Economic Policy." Center for Economic Policy Analysis, Working Paper Series III, No. 9 (August). New York: New School for Social Research.

Eatwell, John, and Lance Taylor. 1998b. "The Performance of Liberalized Capital Markets." Center for Economic Policy Analysis, Working Paper Series III, No. 8 (August). New York: New School for Social Research.

Eatwell, John, and Lance Taylor. 1998c. "A World Financial Authority." *Journal of Commerce*, November 3.

Economist. 1998. "Malaysia: Under Control?" November 21.

Economist. 1999. "Global Finance: Time for a Redesign?" January 30.

Eichengreen, Barry. 1996. *Globalizing Capital: A History of the International Monetary System*. Princeton, N.J.: Princeton University Press.

Eichengreen, Barry. 1999. *Toward a New International Financial Architecture: A Practical Post-Asia Agenda*. Washington, D.C.: Institute for International Economics.

Eichengreen, Barry, and Michael Mussa. 1998. "Capital Account Liberalization and the IMF." *Finance and Development* (December), pp. 16-19.

Eichengreen, Barry, Andrew K. Rose, and Charles Wyplosz. 1994. "Speculative Attacks on Pegged Exchange Rates: An Empirical Exploration With Special Reference to the European Monetary System." NBER Working Paper No. 4898. Cambridge, Mass.: National Bureau of Economic Research.

Eichengreen, Barry, Andrew K. Rose, and Charles Wyplosz. 1995. "Exchange Market Mayhem: The Antecedents and Aftermaths of Speculative Attacks." *Economic Policy* 21 (October), pp. 249-312.

Eichengreen, Barry, James Tobin, and Charles Wyplosz. 1995. "The Case for Sand in the Wheels of International Finance." *Economic Journal* 105, pp. 162-72.

Eichengreen, Barry, and Charles Wyplosz. 1993. "The Unstable EMS." *Brookings Papers on Economic Activity, 1:1993*, pp. 51-143.

Engel, Charles M. 1992. "Can the Markov Switching Model Forecast Exchange Rates." NBER Working Paper No. 4210. Cambridge, Mass.: National Bureau of Economic Research.

Engel, Charles M., and James D. Hamilton. 1990. "Long Swings in the Dollar: Are They in the Data and Do Markets Know It?" *American Economic Review* 80(4), pp. 689-713.

Epstein, Gerald A. 1993. "Monetary Policy in the 1990s: Overcoming the Barriers to Equity and Growth." In Gary A. Dymski et al., eds., *Transforming the U.S. Financial System: Equity and Efficiency for the 21st Century*. Economic Policy Institute Series. Armonk, N.Y.: M. E. Sharpe.

Fair, Ray. 1989. "Does Monetary Policy Matter: Narrative vs. Structural Approaches." NBER Working Paper No. 3045. Cambridge, Mass.: National Bureau of Economic Research.

Federal Reserve Bank of Kansas City. 1993. *Changing Capital Markets: Implications for Monetary Policy.* Kansas City, Mo.: Federal Reserve Bank of Kansas City.

Feinberg, Robert M. 1996. "A Simultaneous Analysis of Exchange-Rate Passthrough Into Prices of Imperfectly Substitutable Domestic and Import Goods." *International Review of Economics and Finance* 5(4), pp. 407-16.

Feldstein, Martin. 1998. "Refocusing the IMF." *Foreign Affairs* 77(2), pp. 20-33.

Felix, David. 1996. "Financial Globalization Versus Free Trade: The Case for the Tobin Tax." *UNCTAD Review 1996*, pp. 63-103.

Fischer, Bernhard, and Helmut Reisen. 1992. *Towards Capital Account Convertibility.* OECD Development Centre, Policy Brief No. 4. Paris: OECD.

Fischer, Stanley. 1981. "Toward an Understanding of the Costs of Inflation, II." In K. Brunner and A. Meltzer, eds., *The Costs and Consequences of Inflation.* Vol. 15. Carnegie-Rochester Conference Series on Public Policy. Amsterdam: North-Holland, pp. 5-41.

Fischer, Stanley. 1993. "The Role of Macroeconomic Factors in Growth." *Journal of Monetary Economics* 32, pp. 485-512.

Fischer, Stanley. 1998. "Reforming World Finance: Lessons From a Crisis." *Economist*, October 3-9.

Fischer, Stanley, and Franco Modigliani. 1975. "Toward an Understanding of the Real Effects and Costs of Inflation." *Weltwirtschaftliches Archiv* 114, pp. 810-33.

Fisher, Irving. 1933. "The Debt-Deflation Theory of Great Depressions." *Econometrica* 1 (October), pp. 337-57.

Fleming, J.M. 1962. "Domestic Financial Policies Under Fixed and Floating Exchange Rates." *IMF Staff Papers* 3, pp. 369-79.

Flood, Robert, and Peter Garber. 1984a. "Collapsing Exchange-Rate Regimes: Some Linear Examples." *Journal of International Economics* 17 (August), pp. 1-14.

Flood, Robert, and Peter Garber. 1984b. "Gold Monetization and Gold Discipline." *Journal of Political Economy* 92 (February), pp. 90-107.

Foley, Duncan K. 1987. "Liquidity-Profit Rate Cycles in a Capitalist Economy." *Journal of Economic Behavior* 8, pp. 363-76.

Franke, R., and Willi Semmler. 1989. "Debt Financing of Firms, Stability, and Cycles in a Macroeconomic Growth Model." In Willi Semmler, ed., *Financial Dynamics and Business Cycles: New Perspectives.* Armonk, N.Y.: M. E. Sharpe.

Frankel, Jeffrey A. 1991. "Quantifying International Capital Mobility in the 1980s." In B. Douglas Bernheim and John B. Shoven, eds., *National Saving and Economic Performance.* Chicago: University of Chicago Press.

Frankel, Jeffrey A. 1993. "International Financial Integration: Relations Between Interest Rates and Exchange Rates." In Dilip K. Das, ed., *International Finance: Contemporary Issues.* London: Routledge.

Frankel, Jeffrey A., and Kenneth Froot. 1990. "Chartists, Fundamentalists, and the Demand for Dollars." In A. S. Courakis and M. P. Taylor, eds., *Policy Issues for Interdependent Economies*. Oxford: Oxford University Press.

Frankel, Jeffrey A., and Andrew K. Rose. 1995. "Empirical Research on Nominal Exchange Rates." In Gene M. Grossman and Kenneth Rogoff, eds., *Handbook of International Economics*. Vol. III. Amsterdam: Elsevier.

Frankel, Jeffrey A., and Andrew K. Rose. 1996. "Currency Crashes in Emerging Markets: An Empirical Treatment." International Finance Discussion Papers, No. 534 (January). Washington, D.C.: Board of Governors of the Federal Reserve System.

Frenkel, Jacob A., and Harry G. Johnson, eds. 1976. *The Monetary Approach to the Balance of Payments*. Toronto: University of Toronto Press.

Frenkel, Jacob A., and Assaf Razin. 1992. *Fiscal Policies and the World Economy*. Second Edition. Cambridge, Mass.: MIT Press.

Frenkel, Roberto. 1998. "Capital Market Liberalization and Economic Performance in Latin America." Center for Economic Policy Analysis, Working Paper Series III, No. 1. New York: New School for Social Research.

Friedman, Benjamin M., and Kenneth N. Kuttner. 1992. "Money, Income, Prices and Interest Rates." *American Economic Review* 82(3), pp. 472-92.

Friedman, Milton. 1953. "The Case for Flexible Exchange Rates." In Milton Friedman, *Essays in Positive Economics*. Chicago: University of Chicago Press.

Friedman, Milton. 1998a. "Bubble Trouble." *National Review*, September 28, p. 16.

Friedman, Milton. 1998b. "Markets to the Rescue." *Wall Street Journal*, October 13.

Froot, Kenneth A., and Kenneth Rogoff. 1995. "Perspectives on PPP and Long-Run Real Exchange Rates." In Gene M. Grossman and Kenneth Rogoff, eds., *Handbook of International Economics*. Vol. III. Amsterdam: Elsevier.

Galbraith, James K. 1989. *Balancing Acts: Technology, Finance, and the American Future*. New York: Basic Books.

Galbraith, James K. 1997a. "Test the Limit." *The American Prospect* (September-October), pp. 66-67.

Galbraith, James K. 1997b. "Time to Ditch the NAIRU." *Journal of Economic Perspectives* 11(1), pp. 93-108.

Garten, Jeffrey. 1998. "Needed: A Fed for the World." *New York Times*, September 23.

Giovannetti, Giorgia. 1992. "A Survey of Recent Empirical Tests of the Purchasing Power Parity Hypothesis." *Banca Nazionale del Lavoro Quarterly Review*, No. 180 (March), pp. 82-97.

Glickman, Norman, and Douglas Woodward. 1989. *The New Competitors: How Foreign Investors Are Changing the U.S. Economy*. New York: Basic Books.

Glyn, Andrew. 1998. "Internal and External Constraints on Egalitarian Policies." In Dean Baker, Gerald Epstein, and Robert Pollin, eds., *Globalization and Progressive Economic Policy*. Cambridge, U.K.: Cambridge University Press.

Godley, Wynne A. 1996. "A Simple Model of the Whole World With Free Trade, Free Capital Movements, and Floating Exchange Rates." Photocopy, Jerome Levy Institute, Bard College.

Goldstein, Morris. 1998. *The Asian Financial Crisis: Causes, Cures, and Systemic Implications*. Washington, D.C.: Institute for International Economics.

Goldstein, Morris, and Guillermo A. Calvo. 1996. "What Role for the Official Sector?" In Guillermo A. Calvo, Morris Goldstein, and Eduard Hochreiter, eds., *Private Capital Flows to Emerging Markets After the Mexican Crisis*. Washington, D.C.: Institute for International Economics.

Gordon, Robert J. 1997. "The Time-Varying NAIRU and Its Implications for Economic Policy." *Journal of Economic Perspectives* 11(1), pp. 11-32.

Graham, Edward M., and Paul R. Krugman. 1991. *Foreign Direct Investment in the United States*. Second Edition. Washington, D.C.: Institute for International Economics.

Gray, H. Peter. 1996. "The Ongoing Weakening of the International Financial System." *Banca Nazionale del Lavoro Quarterly Review*, No. 197 (June), pp. 165-86.

Greenwald, Bruce C., and Joseph E. Stiglitz. 1993. "Financial Market Imperfections and Business Cycles." *Quarterly Journal of Economics* 108(1), pp. 73-114.

Greider, William. 1997. *One World, Ready or Not: The Manic Logic of Global Capitalism*. New York: Simon & Schuster.

Griesgraber, Jo Marie. 1998. "An Overview of Official Proposals for the New Global Architecture." Discussion paper for the Center for Concern conference, "Toward a Progressive International Economy," Washington, D.C., November.

Grieve Smith, John. 1997a. "Exchange Rate Instability and the Tobin Tax." *Cambridge Journal of Economics* 21(6), pp. 753-68.

Grieve Smith, John. 1997b. *Full Employment: A Pledge Betrayed*. London: Macmillan.

Grieve Smith, John. 1998. "A New Bretton Woods: Reforming the Global Financial System." Paper presented at Robinson College, Cambridge University (U.K.), May.

Grilli, Vittorio, and Gian Maria Milesi-Ferretti. 1995. "Economic Effects and Structural Determinants of Capital Controls." *IMF Staff Papers* 42(3), pp. 517-51.

Gurley, John G., and Edward S. Shaw. 1967. "Financial Development and Economic Development." *Economic Development and Cultural Change* 15(3), pp. 257-68.

Haass, Richard N., and Robert E. Litan. 1998. "Globalization and Its Discontents: Navigating the Dangers of a Tangled World." *Foreign Affairs* 77(3), pp. 2-6.

Hallwood, C. Paul, and Ronald MacDonald. 1994. *International Money and Finance*. Second Edition. Oxford: Blackwell.

Hanke, Steve H. 1998. "How to Establish Monetary Stability in Asia." *Cato Journal* 17(3), pp. 295-301.

Hanke, Steve H., Lars Jonung, and Kurt Schuler. 1993. *Russian Currency and Finance: A Currency Board Approach to Reform*. London: Routledge.

Haq, Mahbub ul, Inge Kaul, and Isabelle Grunberg, eds. 1996. *The Tobin Tax: Coping With Financial Volatility.* New York: Oxford University Press.

Hausmann, Ricardo, Michael Gavin, Carmen Pages-Serra, and Ernesto Stein. 1999. "Financial Turmoil and the Choice of Exchange Rate Regime." Photocopy, Inter-American Development Bank (March).

Helfer, Ricki Tigert. 1998. "Rethinking IMF Rescues." Brookings Conference Report, No. 1 (August).

Hooper, Peter, and Catherine L. Mann. 1989. "Exchange Rate Pass-Through in the 1980s: The Case of U.S. Imports of Manufactures." *Brookings Papers on Economic Activity, 1:1989*, pp. 297-337.

Houthakker, Hendrik S., and Stephen P. Magee. 1969. "Income and Price Elasticities in World Trade." *Review of Economics and Statistics* 51(2), pp. 111-25.

Huizinga, John, and Frederic S. Mishkin. 1986. "Monetary Policy Regime Shifts and the Unusual Behavior of Real Interest Rates." *Carnegie-Rochester Conference Series on Public Policy* (Spring), pp. 231-74.

Hume, David. 1752. "Of the Balance of Trade." In David Hume, *Political Discourses*, extracted in Ronald L. Meek, ed., *Precursors of Adam Smith, 1750-1775*. London: Dent, 1973.

Hutton, Will. 1996. "Relaunching Western Economies: The Case for Regulating Financial Markets." *Foreign Affairs* 75(6), pp. 8-12.

International Monetary Fund. 1997. *Balance of Payments Statistics Yearbook*. Washington, D.C.: IMF.

International Monetary Fund. 1998. *Balance of Payments Statistics Yearbook*. Washington, D.C.: IMF.

International Monetary Fund. Various years. *Exchange Rate Arrangements and Exchange Restrictions Annual Report*. Washington, D.C.: IMF.

Isaac, Alan G. 1998. "Risk Premia and Overshooting." Photocopy, American University (June).

Isard, Peter. 1995. *Exchange Rate Economics*. Cambridge, U.K.: Cambridge University Press.

Johnson, Harry G. 1977. "The Monetary Approach to the Balance of Payments: A Non-Technical Guide." *Journal of International Economics* 7, pp. 251-68.

Kalecki, Mikhal. 1937. "The Principle of Increasing Risk." *Economica* 4 (November), pp. 440-47.

Kaminsky, Graciela L., Saul Lizondo, and Carmen M. Reinhart. 1997. "Leading Indicators of Currency Crises." International Monetary Fund, Working Paper No. WP/97/79 (July). Washington, D.C.: IMF.

Kaminsky, Graciela L., and Carmen M. Reinhart. 1996. "The Twin Crises: The Causes of Banking and Balance-of-Payments Problems." International Finance Discussion Papers, No. 544 (March). Washington, D.C.: Board of Governors of the Federal Reserve System.

Kaufman, Henry. 1998. "Preventing the Next Global Financial Crisis." *Washington Post*, January 28.

Kenen, Peter B. 1989. *Exchange Rates and Policy Coordination*. Ann Arbor: University of Michigan Press.

Keynes, John Maynard. 1933. "National Self-Sufficiency." Reprinted in Donald Moggridge, ed., *Collected Writings of John Maynard Keynes*. Vol. 21. London: Macmillan and Cambridge University Press, 1982.

Keynes, John Maynard. 1936. *The General Theory of Employment, Interest, and Money*. London: Harcourt, Brace.

Kindleberger, Charles P. 1967. "The Pros and Cons of an International Capital Market." *Zeitschrift für die gesamte Staatswissenschaft* (October), pp. 600-617.

Kindleberger, Charles P. 1989. *Manias, Panics, and Crashes: A History of Financial Crises*, Revised Edition. New York: Basic Books.

Kissinger, Henry. 1998. "Perils of Globalism." *Washington Post*, October 5.

Kregel, J. A. 1998a. "Derivatives and Global Capital Flows: Applications to Asia." *Cambridge Journal of Economics* 22(6), pp. 677-92.

Kregel, J. A. 1998b. "East Asia Is Not Mexico: The Difference Between Balance of Payments Crises and Debt Deflations." Jerome Levy Economics Institute, Bard College, Working Paper No. 235 (May).

Kregel, J. A. 1998c. "Yes, 'It' Did Happen Again—A Minsky Crisis Happened in Asia." Jerome Levy Economics Institute, Bard College, Working Paper No. 234 (April).

Krugman, Paul R. 1979. "A Model of Balance-of-Payments Crises." *Journal of Money, Credit, and Banking* 11(3), pp. 311-25.

Krugman, Paul R. 1985. "Is the Strong Dollar Sustainable?" In Federal Reserve Bank of Kansas City, ed., *The U.S. Dollar: Prospects and Policy Options*. Kansas City, Mo.: Federal Reserve Bank of Kansas City.

Krugman, Paul R. 1987. "Sustainability and the Decline of the Dollar." In R. Bryant et al., eds., *External Deficits and the Dollar*. Washington, D.C.: Brookings Institution.

Krugman, Paul R. 1989. *Exchange-Rate Instability*. Cambridge, Mass.: MIT Press.

Krugman, Paul R. 1998a. "The Confidence Game." *New Republic*, October 5.

Krugman, Paul R. 1998b. "Saving Asia: It's Time to Get Radical." *Fortune*, September 7.

Krugman, Paul R., and Lance Taylor. 1978. "Contractionary Effects of Devaluation." *Journal of International Economics* 8, pp. 445-56.

Lindert, Peter H., and Thomas A. Pugel. 1996. *International Economics*, 10th Edition. Chicago: Irwin.

Litan, Robert E. 1998. "A Three-Step Remedy for Asia's Financial Flu." Brookings Policy Brief No. 30 (February).

Lothian, James R., and Mark P. Taylor. 1996. "Real Exchange Rate Behavior: The Recent Float From the Perspective of the Past Two Centuries." *Journal of Political Economy* 104(3), pp. 488-509.

MacLean, Brian K., Paul Bowles, and Osvaldo Croci. 1998. "Understanding the Asian Crisis and Its Implications for Regional Economic Integration." In Gavin Boyd and Alan Rugman, eds., *Deepening Integration in the Pacific*. London: Edward Elgar, forthcoming.

Mann, Catherine L. 1986. "Prices, Profit Margins, and Exchange Rates." *Federal Reserve Bulletin* 72 (June), pp. 366-79.

Mann, Catherine L. 1999. "Market Mechanisms to Reduce the Need for IMF Bailouts." International Economics Policy Brief No. 99-4 (February). Washington, D.C.: Institute for International Economics.

Marston, Richard C. 1990. "Pricing to Market in Japanese Manufacturing." *Journal of International Economics* 29, pp. 217-36.

Marston, Richard C. 1995. *International Financial Integration: A Study of Interest Differentials Between the Major Industrial Countries*. Cambridge, U.K.: Cambridge University Press.

Martin, Hans-Peter, and Harald Schumann. 1997. *The Global Trap: Globalization and the Assault on Prosperity and Democracy*, trans. Patrick Camiller. London: Zed Books.

Martínez-Pería, María Soledad. 1997. "A Regime Switching Approach to the Study of Speculative Attacks: A Focus on EMS Crises." Photocopy, University of California at Berkeley (November).

McCombie, John S. L. 1997. "Empirics of Balance-of-Payments-Constrained Growth." *Journal of Post Keynesian Economics* 19(3), pp. 345-75.

McCombie, John S. L., and A. P. Thirlwall. 1994. *Economic Growth and the Balance-of-Payments Constraint*. New York: St. Martin's.

McKinnon, Ronald I. 1973. *Money and Capital in Economic Development*. Washington, D.C.: Brookings Institution.

McKinnon, Ronald I. 1988. "Monetary and Exchange Rate Policies for International Financial Stability: A Proposal." *Journal of Economic Perspectives* 2 (Winter), pp. 83-103.

McKinnon, Ronald I. 1990. "Interest Rate Volatility and Exchange Risk: New Rules for a Common Monetary Standard." *Contemporary Policy Issues* 8(2), pp. 1-17.

McKinnon, Ronald I. 1993. *The Order of Economic Liberalization: Financial Control in the Transition to a Market Economy*. Second Edition. Baltimore: Johns Hopkins University Press.

McKinnon, Ronald I., and Huw Pill. 1996. "Credible Liberalization and International Capital Flows: The Overborrowing Syndrome." In T. Ito and A. Krueger, eds. *Financial Deregulation and Integration in East Asia*. Chicago: University of Chicago Press.

Meese, Richard A. 1986. "Testing for Bubbles in Exchange Markets: A Case of Sparkling Rates?" *Journal of Political Economy* 94(2), pp. 345-73.

Meese, Richard A., and Kenneth Rogoff. 1983a. "Empirical Exchange Rate Models of the Seventies." *Journal of International Economics* 14, pp. 3-24.

Meese, Richard A., and Kenneth Rogoff. 1983b. "The Out-of-Sample Failure of Empirical Exchange Rate Models." In Jacob Frenkel, ed., *Exchange Rates and International Macroeconomics.* Chicago: University of Chicago Press.

Mélitz, Jacques. 1994. "Comment on the Tobin Tax." Paper presented at Conference on Globalization of Markets, CIDEI, Università di Roma "La Sapienza," October 27-28. (forthcoming, *Journal of International and Comparative Economics*).

Menon, Jayant. 1996. *Exchange Rates and Prices: The Case of Australian Manufactured Imports.* Berlin: Springer-Verlag.

Mikesell, Raymond F. 1995. "Proposals for Changing the Functions of the International Monetary Fund (IMF)." Jerome Levy Economics Institute, Bard College, Working Paper No. 150 (December).

Minsky, Hyman P. 1982. *Can "It" Happen Again? Essays on Instability and Finance.* Armonk, N.Y.: M. E. Sharpe.

Minsky, Hyman P. 1986. *Stabilizing an Unstable Economy.* New Haven: Yale University Press.

Mishkin, Frederic S. 1988. "Understanding Real Interest Rates." NBER Working Paper No. 2691 (August). Cambridge, Mass.: National Bureau of Economic Research.

Moffitt, Michael. 1983. *The World's Money: International Banking From Bretton Woods to the Brink of Insolvency.* New York: Simon & Schuster.

Moore, Basil J. 1988. *Horizontalists and Verticalists: The Macroeconomics of Credit Money.* Cambridge, U.K.: Cambridge University Press.

Moreno-Brid, Juan Carlos. 1998-99. "On Capital Flows and the Balance-of-Payments-Constrained Growth Model." *Journal of Post Keynesian Economics* 21(2), pp. 283-98.

Morici, Peter. 1997. *The Trade Deficit: Where Does It Come from and What Does It Do?* Washington: Economic Strategy Institute, October.

Morris, Stephen, and Hyun Song Shin. 1998. "Unique Equilibrium in a Model of Self-Fulfilling Currency Attacks." *American Economic Review* 88(3), pp. 587-97.

Mundell, Robert. 1962. "The Appropriate Use of Monetary and Fiscal Policy for Internal and External Balance." *IMF Staff Papers* 9, pp. 70-79.

Mundell, Robert. 1963. "Capital Mobility and Stabilization Policy Under Fixed and Flexible Exchange Rates." *Canadian Journal of Economics and Political Science*, pp. 475-85.

Mussa, Michael, and Morris Goldstein. 1993. "The Integration of World Capital Markets." In Federal Reserve Bank of Kansas City, *Changing Capital Markets: Implications for Monetary Policy.* Kansas City, Mo.: Federal Reserve Bank of Kansas City.

Neftci, Salih N. 1998. "FX Short Positions, Balance Sheets, and Financial Turbulence: An Interpretation of the Asian Financial Crisis." Paper presented at Conference on International Capital Markets and the Future of Economic Policy, Queens' College, University of Cambridge (U.K.), April.

Noland, Marcus, Li-Gang Liu, Sherman Robinson, and Zhi Wang.1998. *Global Economic Effects of the Asian Currency Devaluations.* Washington, D.C.: Institute for International Economics.

Obstfeld, Maurice. 1980. "Imperfect Asset Substitutability and Monetary Policy Under Fixed Exchange Rates." *Journal of International Economics* 10(2).

Obstfeld, Maurice. 1984. "Balance-of-Payments Crises and Devaluation." *Journal of Money, Credit, and Banking* 16 (May), pp. 208-17.

Obstfeld, Maurice. 1986. "Rational and Self-Fulfilling Balance-of-Payments Crises." *American Economic Review* 76(1), pp. 72-81.

Obstfeld, Maurice. 1994. "The Logic of Currency Crises." *Cahiers Economiques et Monetaires (Banque de France)* 43, pp. 189-213.

Obstfeld, Maurice. 1995. "International Currency Experience: New Lessons and Lessons Relearned." *Brookings Papers on Economic Activity, 1:1995*, pp. 119-220.

Obstfeld, Maurice. 1996. "Models of Currency Crises with Self-Fulfilling Features." *European Economic Review* 40 (April), pp. 1037-47.

Obstfeld, Maurice. 1998. "The Global Capital Market: Benefactor or Menace?" *Journal of Economic Perspectives* 12(4), pp. 9-30.

Obstfeld, Maurice, and Kenneth Rogoff. 1995. "The Intertemporal Approach to the Current Account." In Gene M. Grossman and Kenneth Rogoff, eds., *Handbook of International Economics.* Vol. III. Amsterdam: Elsevier.

Organization for Economic Cooperation and Development (OECD). 1998. *OECD Economic Outlook*, No. 63. Paris: OECD (June).

Palley, Thomas I. 1994. "Debt, Aggregate Demand and the Business Cycle: A Model in the Spirit of Kaldor and Minsky." *Journal of Post Keynesian Economics* 16(3), pp. 371-90.

Palley, Thomas I. 1996. *Post-Keynesian Economics: Debt, Distribution, and the Macro Economy.* New York: St. Martin's.

Palley, Thomas I. 1997. "Asset Based Reserve Requirements: An Unappreciated Instrument of Monetary Policy." Public Policy Department, Technical Working Paper T007. Washington, D.C.: AFL-CIO.

Palley, Thomas I. 1998a. "The Beneficial Effect of Core Labor Standards on Economic Growth." Public Policy Department, Technical Working Paper T010. Washington, D.C.: AFL-CIO.

Palley, Thomas I. 1998b. "International Finance and Global Deflation: There Is an Alternative." In J. Grieve Smith and J. Michie, eds., *Global Instability and World Economic Governance.* Cambridge, U.K.: Cambridge University Press, forthcoming.

Palley, Thomas I. 1998c. "International Finance and the Problem of Capital Account Governance: A Blue Print for Reform." Public Policy Department, Economic Policy Paper E017. Washington, D.C.: AFL-CIO.

Palley, Thomas I. 1998d. *Plenty of Nothing: The Downsizing of the American Dream and the Case for Structural Keynesianism*. Princeton, N.J.: Princeton University Press.

Palley, Thomas I. 1998e. "Speculation and Tobin Taxes: Why Sand in the Wheels Can Increase Economic Efficiency." Public Policy Department, Working Paper. Washington, D.C.: AFL-CIO.

Pastor, Manuel. 1989. *Capital Flight and the Latin American Debt Crisis*. Washington, D.C.: Economic Policy Institute.

Pastor, Manuel. 1990. "Capital Flight From Latin America." *World Development* 18(1).

Payer, Cheryl. 1974. *The Debt Trap: The IMF and the Third World*. New York: Monthly Review Press.

Pieper, Ute, and Lance Taylor. 1998. "The Revival of the Liberal Creed: The IMF, the World Bank, and Inequality in a Globalized Economy." In Dean Baker, Gerald Epstein, and Robert Pollin, eds., *Globalization and Progressive Economic Policy*. Cambridge, U.K.: Cambridge University Press.

Polak, J. J. 1957. "Monetary Analysis of Income Formation and Payments Problems." *IMF Staff Papers* 4 (November), pp. 1-50.

Polanyi, Karl. 1944. *The Great Transformation*. New York: Rinehart.

Pollin, Robert. 1991. "Two Theories of Money Supply Endogeneity." *Journal of Post Keynesian Economics* 13(3), pp. 366-96.

Pollin, Robert. 1998. "Can Domestic Expansionary Policy Succeed in a Globally Integrated Environment? An Examination of Alternatives." In Dean Baker, Gerald Epstein, and Robert Pollin, eds., *Globalization and Progressive Economic Policy*. Cambridge, U.K.: Cambridge University Press.

Posen, Adam S. 1998. *Restoring Japan's Economic Growth*. Washington, D.C.: Institute for International Economics.

Prestowitz, Clyde. 1997. "Retooling Japan Is the Only Way to Rescue Asia Now." *Washington Post*, December 14.

Pugno, Maurizio. 1998. "The Stability of Thirlwall's Model of Economic Growth and the Balance-of-Payments Constraint." *Journal of Post Keynesian Economics* 20(4), pp. 559-81.

Radelet, Steven, and Jeffrey D. Sachs. 1998a. "The East Asian Financial Crisis: Diagnosis, Remedies, Prospects." Photocopy, Harvard Institute for International Development (April).

Radelet, Steven, and Jeffrey D. Sachs. 1998b. "The Onset of the East Asian Financial Crisis." Photocopy, Harvard Institute for International Development (March).

Reisen, Helmut. 1998a. "After the Great Asian Slump: Toward a Coherent Approach to Global Capital Flows." OECD Development Centre, Policy Brief No. 16. Paris: OECD (January).

Reisen, Helmut. 1998b. "Domestic Causes of Currency Crises: Policy Lessons for Crisis Avoidance." OECD Development Centre, Technical Paper No. 136. Paris: OECD (June).

Ricardo, David. 1821. *Principles of Political Economy and Taxation.* Third Edition. Cambridge, U.K.: Cambridge University Press, 1951.

Rivera-Batiz, Francisco L., and Luis A. Rivera-Batiz. 1994. *International Finance and Open Economy Macroeconomics.* Second Edition. New York: Macmillan.

Rodrik, Dani. 1998. "Who Needs Capital-Account Convertibility?" Forthcoming in Peter Kenen, ed., *Princeton Essays in International Finance.*

Rogerson, Richard. 1997. "Theory Ahead of Language in the Economics of Unemployment." *Journal of Economic Perspectives* 11(1), pp. 73-92.

Rogoff, Kenneth. 1985. "Can International Monetary Policy Coordination Be Counterproductive?" *Journal of International Economics* 18 (May), pp. 199-217.

Rogoff, Kenneth. 1996. "The Purchasing Power Parity Puzzle." *Journal of Economic Literature* 34(2), pp. 647-68.

Romer, Christina, and David Romer. 1989. "Does Monetary Policy Matter? A New Test in the Spirit of Friedman and Schwartz." NBER Working Paper No. 2966. Cambridge, Mass.: National Bureau of Economic Research.

Romer, Christina, and David Romer. 1990. "New Evidence on the Monetary Transmission Mechanism." *Brookings Papers on Economic Activity 1:1990*, pp. 149-214.

Rosser, J. Barkley Jr. 1996. "On the Possibility of Rational Deflationary Bubbles." *Rivista Internazionale di Scienze Economiche e Commerciale* 43(4), pp. 729-40.

Rosser, J. Barkley Jr. 1997. "Speculations on Nonlinear Speculative Bubbles." *Nonlinear Dynamics, Psychology, and Life Sciences* 1(4), pp. 275-300.

Rubin, Robert. 1998. "Strengthening the Architecture of the International Financial System." Speech delivered at the Brookings Institution, Washington, D.C., April 14.

Sachs, Jeffrey D. 1998a. "Global Capitalism: Making It Work." *The Economist*, September 12, pp. 23-25.

Sachs, Jeffrey D. 1998b. "The IMF and the Asian Flu." *The American Prospect* (March-April), pp. 16-21.

Sachs, Jeffrey D. 1998c. "Rule of the Ruble." *New York Times*, June 4.

Sachs, Jeffrey D., Aaron Tornell, and Andrés Velasco. 1996a. "Financial Crises in Emerging Markets: The Lessons From 1995." *Brookings Papers on Economic Activity, 1:1996*, pp. 147-215.

Sachs, Jeffrey D., Aaron Tornell, and Andrés Velasco. 1996b. "The Mexican Peso Crisis: Sudden Death or Crisis Foretold?" *Journal of International Economics* 41(3/4), pp. 265-83.

Schwartz, Anna J. 1998. "Time to Terminate the ESF and the IMF." Foreign Policy Briefing No. 48. Washington, D.C.: Cato Institute (August 26).

Scott, Robert E., and Jesse Rothstein. 1998. "American Jobs and the Asian Crisis: The Employment Impact of the Coming Rise in the U.S. Trade Deficit." Briefing Paper. Washington, D.C.: Economic Policy Institute.

Shadow Financial Regulatory Committee. 1998. Statement on "Principles for Reforming the 'Global Financial Architecture,'" September 28.

Singh, Ajit. 1998. "'Asian Capitalism' and the Financial Crisis." Photocopy, Cambridge University (U.K.), April.

Singh, Kavaljit. 1998. *Capital Controls, State Intervention and Public Action in the Era of Financial Globalization.* Delhi: Public Interest Research Group.

Soros, George. 1997. "Avoiding a Breakdown." *Financial Times*, December 31.

Soros, George. 1998. *The Crisis of Global Capitalism.* New York: Public Affairs.

Staiger, Douglas, James H. Stock, and Mark W. Watson. 1997. "The NAIRU, Unemployment and Monetary Policy." *Journal of Economic Perspectives* 11(1), pp. 33-49.

Stiglitz, Joseph E. 1997. "Reflections on the Natural Rate Hypothesis." *Journal of Economic Perspectives* 11(1), pp. 3-10.

Stiglitz, Joseph E. 1998. "More Instruments and Broader Goals: Moving Toward the Post-Washington Consensus." United Nations University, World Institute for Development Economics Research, WIDER Annual Lectures 2 (January), website http://www.wider.unu.edu/stiglitx.htm.

Summers, Lawrence H. 1999. "Reflections on Managing Global Integration." Speech delivered at the Association of Government Economists, Annual Meeting, New York, January 4.

Summers, Lawrence H., and Victoria P. Summers. 1989. "When Financial Markets Work Too Well: A Cautious Case for a Securities Transactions Tax." *Journal of Financial Services Research* 3, pp. 163-88.

Swan, Trevor. 1955. "Longer-Run Problems of the Balance of Payments." In H. W. Arndt and W. M. Corden, eds., *The Australian Economy: A Volume of Readings.* Melbourne: Cheshire Press.

Taylor, Lance. 1991. *Income Distribution, Inflation, and Growth.* Cambridge, Mass.: MIT Press.

Taylor, Lance. 1996. "Income Distribution, Trade, and Growth." In Robert A. Blecker, ed., *U.S. Trade Policy and Global Growth.* Economic Policy Institute series. Armonk, N.Y.: M. E. Sharpe.

Taylor, Lance. 1997. "Growth in Two Countries With International Debt." Photocopy, New School for Social Research (April).

Taylor, Lance. 1998a. "Capital Market Crises: Liberalisation, Fixed Exchange Rates and Market-Driven Destabilisation." *Cambridge Journal of Economics* 22(6), pp. 663-76.

Taylor, Lance. 1998b. "Lax Public Sector, Destabilizing Private Sector: Origins of Capital Market Crises." Photocopy, New School for Social Research (June).

Taylor, Lance. 1998c. "Neither the Portfolio Balance Model nor the Mundell-Fleming Model Can Determine the Exchange Rate: Each Has One Fewer Independent Equation Than People Usually Think." Photocopy, New School for Social Research (December).

Taylor, Lance, and Stephen O'Connell. 1985. "A Minsky Crisis." *Quarterly Journal of Economics* 100, pp. 383-403.

Thirlwall, A. P. 1979. "The Balance of Payments Constraint as an Explanation of International Growth Rate Differences." *Banca Nazionale del Lavoro Quarterly Review*, No. 128 (March), pp. 45-53.

Thirlwall, A. P., and M. Nureldin Hussain. 1982. The Balance of Payments Constraint, Capital Flows and Growth Rate Differences Between Developing Countries." *Oxford Economic Papers* 34(3), pp. 498-510.

Thurow, Lester. 1998. "Asia: The Collapse and the Cure." *New York Review of Books*, February 5, website version http://www.nybooks.com/nyrev/WWWarchdisplay.cgi.

Tobin, James. 1958. "Liquidity Preference as Behaviour Towards Risk." *Review of Economic Studies* 25(1), pp. 65-86.

Tobin, James. 1974. *The New Economics One Decade Older*. The Elliot Janeway Lectures on Historical Economics in Honour of Joseph Schumpeter, 1972. Princeton: Princeton University Press.

Tobin, James. 1978. "A Proposal for International Monetary Reform." *Eastern Economic Journal* 4 (July-October), pp. 153-59.

Tobin, James. 1980. *Asset Accumulation and Economic Activity*. Chicago: University of Chicago Press.

Tobin, James, and Jorge Braga de Macedo. 1980. "The Short-Run Macroeconomics of Floating Exchange Rates: An Exposition." In John S. Chipman and Charles P. Kindleberger, eds., *Flexible Exchange Rates and the Balance of Payments*. Amsterdam: North-Holland.

Tornell, Aaron. 1998. "Common Fundamentals in the Tequila and Asian Crises." Photocopy, Harvard University and NBER (July).

United Nations Conference on Trade and Development (UNCTAD). 1998. *Trade and Development Report, 1998*. New York and Geneva: United Nations.

U.S. Congress, Joint Economic Committee. 1998. *Economic Indicators*. Washington, D.C.: U.S. Government Printing Office (September).

U.S. Congressional Budget Office. 1996. *The Economic and Budget Outlook: Fiscal Years 1997-2006*. Washington, D.C.: U.S. Government Printing Office (May).

U.S. Council of Economic Advisers. 1999. *Economic Report of the President*. Washington, D.C.: U.S. Government Printing Office.

U.S. Department of Commerce. 1999. "Gross Domestic Product: Fourth Quarter 1998 (Advance)." Press Release, January 29.

Valdés-Prieto, Salvador, and Marcelo Soto. 1998. "The Effectiveness of Capital Controls: Theory and Evidence From Chile." *Empirica* 25(2) (forthcoming).

Volcker, Paul. 1996. "Toward Monetary Stability." *Wall Street Journal*, January 24.

Wachtel, Howard M. 1990. *The Money Mandarins: The Making of a Supranational Economic Order*. Second Edition. Armonk, N.Y.: M. E. Sharpe.

Wachtel, Howard M. 1997. "The Mosaic of Global Taxes." Paper presented at conference on Global Futures, Institute for Social Studies, The Hague, October.

Wade, Robert. 1990. *Governing the Market: Economic Theory and the Role of Government in East Asian Industrialization*. Princeton, N.J.: Princeton University Press.

Wade, Robert. 1998a. "The Asian Debt-and-Development Crisis of 1997? Causes and Consequences." *World Development* (August).

Wade, Robert. 1998b. "From 'Miracle' to 'Cronyism': Explaining the Great Asian Slump." *Cambridge Journal of Economics* 22(6), pp. 693-706.

Wade, Robert, and Frank Veneroso. 1998a. "The Asian Crisis: The High Debt Model vs. the Wall Street-Treasury-IMF Complex." *New Left Review*, No. 228 (March/April).

Wade, Robert, and Frank Veneroso. 1998b. "The Resources Lie Within." *Economist*, November 7, pp. 19-21.

White, Eugene N., ed. 1990. *Crashes and Panics: The Lessons from History*. Homewood, Ill.: Business One Irwin.

Whitman, Marina V. N. 1975. "Global Monetarism and the Monetary Approach to the Balance of Payments." *Brookings Papers on Economic Activity, 3:1975*, pp. 491-536.

Williamson, John. 1983. *The Open Economy and the World Economy: A Textbook in International Economics*. New York: Basic Books.

Williamson, John. 1985. *The Exchange Rate System*. Revised Edition. Washington, D.C.: Institute for International Economics.

Williamson, John. 1987. "Exchange Rate Management: The Role of Target Zones." *American Economic Review, Papers and Proceedings* 77 (May), pp. 200-4.

Williamson, John. 1990. "What Washington Means by Policy Reform." In John Williamson, ed., *Latin American Adjustment: How Much Has Happened?* Washington, D.C.: Institute for International Economics.

Williamson, John. 1994. "Estimates of FEERs." In John Williamson, ed., *Estimating Equilibrium Exchange Rates*. Washington, D.C.: Institute for International Economics.

Williamson, John. 1998. "Crawling Bands or Monitoring Bands: How to Manage Exchange Rates in a World of Capital Mobility." Paper presented at conference at American University, December (forthcoming, *International Finance*).

Williamson, John, and Marcus H. Miller. 1987. *Targets and Indicators: A Blueprint for the International Coordination of Economic Policy.* Washington, D.C.: Institute for International Economics.

Wolf, Martin. 1998. "Flows and Blows: After the Asian Crisis, the Question Is Not Whether Capital Flows Should Be Regulated, but How?" *Financial Times*, March 3, p. 16.

Woo, Wing Thye, and Kenjiro Hirayama. 1996. "Monetary Autonomy in the Presence of Capital Flows: And Never the Twain Shall Meet, Except in East Asia?" In T. Ito and A. Krueger, eds. *Financial Deregulation and Integration in East Asia.* Chicago: University of Chicago Press.

Wood, Robert E. 1989. "The International Monetary Fund and the World Bank in a Changing World Economy." In Arthur MacEwan and William K. Tabb, eds., *Instability and Change in the World Economy.* New York: Monthly Review Press.

Woodward, Bob. 1994. *The Agenda: Inside the Clinton White House.* New York: Simon & Schuster.

World Bank. 1998. *Global Economic Prospects and the Developing Countries 1989/99: Beyond Financial Crises.* Washington, D.C.: World Bank.

Wren-Lewis, Simon. 1998. "Exchange Rates for the Dollar, Yen, and Euro." International Economics Policy Brief No. 98-3 (July). Washington, D.C.: Institute for International Economics.

Wren-Lewis, Simon, and Rebecca Driver. 1998. *Real Exchange Rates for the Year 2000.* Washington, D.C.: Institute for International Economics.

Yotopoulos, Pan A. 1996. *Exchange Rate Parity for Trade and Development: Theory, Tests, and Case Studies.* Cambridge, U.K.: Cambridge University Press.

Zysman, John. 1983. *Governments, Markets, and Growth: Financial Systems and the Politics of Industrial Change.* Ithaca, N.Y.: Cornell University Press.

Glossary

Arbitrage. In general, buying cheap and selling dear, i.e., profiting from differences in prices between two different markets or locations. In international finance, arbitrage can occur in various situations in which investors take advantage of actual or perceived discrepancies between exchange rates and interest rates in different countries and at different time horizons in order to reap a profit. For example, "covered interest arbitrage" involves buying foreign exchange in the spot market and then using the foreign currency to buy a foreign treasury bill (short-term government bond), while selling the future foreign currency proceeds of the bond (principal plus interest) in the *forward exchange market* in advance for domestic currency. The arbitrageur would take this route if it yields higher returns than simply investing in a domestic treasury bill of the same maturity.

Balance of payments. A double-entry bookkeeping record of a country's international transactions. Sales of goods, services, or assets to foreigners are recorded as credits (+), while purchases of goods, services, or assets from foreigners are recorded as debits (–). The balance of payments is divided into various "accounts" or "balances," each of which may be in surplus (credits exceed debits) or deficit (debits exceed credits)—see *current account, capital account,* and *official reserve transactions*. A current account deficit must be offset by a surplus in the capital account and official reserve transactions combined, while a current account surplus must be offset by a combined capital account and official reserve deficit. In principle, total credits and debits should be equal in value, although in practice there may be statistical discrepancies. What is (somewhat misleadingly) referred to as the "overall balance of payments" (the current and capital accounts summed together) can be in surplus or deficit, because it excludes official reserve transactions.

Capital account. The part of the *balance of payments* that covers international purchases and sales of assets, including direct foreign investment in productive enterprises, portfolio investment in equities (stock markets), bank loans and deposits, various kinds of securities (such as government or corporate bonds), and foreign currency holdings. International borrowing and sales of assets to foreigners are recorded as credits (+), while international lending and purchases of assets abroad are recorded as debits (–). Note that the returns to international investment (e.g., interest payments) are recorded on the *current account*, while the investments that generate these returns are recorded in the capital account. Usually the capital account is defined to include both private and government transactions but to exclude official reserve transactions by central banks (see *balance of payments*).

Country risk. The potential hazards of investing in a particular country, such as a government defaulting on its bonds or imposing controls on taking funds out of the country. It does not include the risk of the currency value changing (see *exchange risk*).

Current account. The part of the *balance of payments* that includes trade in goods and services plus net income from foreign investment (e.g., interest payments), migrant labor remittances, and transfer payments. Exports of goods and services and inflows of interest, salaries, and transfers are recorded as credits (+), while imports of goods and services and outflows of interest, salaries, and transfers are recorded as debits (–). The current account is a broader measure of a nation's trade balance than the merchandise trade balance, which includes only trade in goods. A current account surplus implies that a country is a net lender to other nations, while a current account deficit implies that a country is a net borrower.

Dirty float. A *flexible exchange rate* that is actively influenced by government intervention in the *foreign exchange* market. For example, the government may (usually through the central bank) buy foreign exchange to push up the value of the foreign currency and depreciate the home currency, or sell foreign exchange to push down its value and appreciate the home currency. Such intervention can be observed in the *official reserve transactions* balance in a country's *balance of payments*. A dirty float differs from a *fixed* or *pegged exchange rate* because there is no official target or "par value," and the government intervention is only sporadic. Also known as a "managed float."

Dollarization. In the direct sense, a policy of accepting the U.S. dollar as legal tender, or issuing a domestic currency unit (such as the Panamanian balboa) that is legally equal in value to the U.S. dollar. More broadly, the term is sometimes used to refer to less extreme uses of dollars outside the U.S., such as: domestic residents hold large amounts of dollars in cash or bank deposits; the domestic currency is rigidly pegged to the dollar; the government and business firms have large dollar-denominated liabilities; or domestic residents think in dollar terms in setting their targets for wage and price increases.

Exchange rate. The price of one currency in terms of another, e.g., U.S. dollars per U.K. pound. While an exchange rate can be expressed either way (i.e., dollars per pound or pounds per dollar), a common convention is to express it as the amount of domestic currency per unit of *foreign exchange*; this is useful for thinking of the exchange rate as the price that prevails in the foreign exchange market. In this convention, a rise in the exchange rate indicates an increase in the value of the foreign currency and a depreciation of the home currency, while a fall in the exchange rate implies a decrease in the value of the foreign currency and an appreciation of the home currency. The "nominal" exchange rate refers to the exchange rate in standard currency units (e.g., nine Mexican pesos per U.S. dollar); the "real" exchange rate refers to the value of the currency adjusted for inflation at home and abroad (e.g., if the Mexican currency has depreciated from three pesos per dollar to nine, but Mexican prices have increased three times as much as U.S. prices, then the real value of the peso is unchanged).

Exchange risk. The danger that a currency held by an investor will depreciate (if the *exchange rate* is flexible or floating) or be devalued (if the exchange rate is fixed or pegged).

Fixed exchange rate. An *exchange rate* that is officially set by government policy. Governments that are committed to a fixed rate are obligated to intervene in foreign exchange markets by buying or selling currencies as needed in order to keep the exchange rate within the target range (usually, a small band of plus or minus a few percentage points or less around a central target called the "par value" or "parity"). Governments can also be forced to adjust domestic policies (such as interest rates) to levels that are consistent with a fixed exchange rate target. When a fixed exchange rate is changed, the home currency is said to be "devalued" if the exchange rate is increased (i.e., it takes more domestic currency to buy one unit of foreign exchange) and to be "revalued" if the exchange rate is decreased (i.e., it takes less domestic currency to buy one unit of foreign exchange). See also *pegged exchange rate*.

Flexible exchange rate. An *exchange rate* that is not officially set by government policy and is allowed to be determined by supply and demand in the *foreign exchange* market. Even when the exchange rate is flexible in this sense, the government may choose to intervene in the foreign exchange market occasionally by buying or sell currencies (see *dirty float*). Also referred to as a "floating" exchange rate.

Foreign exchange. The act of trading national currencies; the term also refers to holdings of foreign currency (e.g., U.S. dollars owned by Brazilians). Most foreign exchange takes place between large international banks; actual exchanges of cash are only a small part of total currency trading. The so-called "foreign exchange market" is actually an interconnected network of large international banks and specialized currency traders; this market does not exist in any specific location, but most currency trading is concentrated in a few major financial centers such as New York, London, Frankfurt, Hong Kong, and Singapore.

Forward exchange market. The market for currency that will be delivered a fixed number of days in the future, e.g., 60 or 90 days, as distinguished from the "spot" market, where currencies are traded for immediate delivery. The forward exchange rate is the price of *foreign exchange* bought or sold in the forward market; this price is agreed to in advance based on market conditions and expectations at the time the forward contract is made. The forward rate is locked in for the duration of the contract, but the actual purchase or sale takes place at the end of the time period. Forward exchanges are useful for activities such as *arbitrage*, *hedging*, and *speculation*. The forward exchange rate need not be the same as (and is usually different from) the future spot rate, i.e., the spot rate that actually prevails at the time when the forward contract matures.

Hedging. A transaction engaged in by a business or investor to acquire equal amounts of assets and liabilities in any given foreign currency, in order to avoid exposure to *exchange risk*. For example, if a European firm owes a payment of $1 million in 30 days, it can hedge by buying a 30-day forward contract for dollars (see *forward exchange market*). In this way, the firm covers itself against the risk of the euro falling in value relative to the dollar before the payment comes due. Note that what are commonly (and misleadingly) referred to as "hedge funds" are pooled funds that usually take speculative positions; they are not generally engaged in hedging activities (see *speculation*).

Joint float. An arrangement in which several nations peg their currencies with each other but adopt a *flexible exchange rate* vis-à-vis other currencies. A prominent example is the former European Exchange Rate Mechanism (ERM), in which a number of European currencies were pegged to each other but floated against the U.S. dollar and other nonmember currencies.

Lender of last resort. An institution (usually, a central bank) that can step in and lend funds to a bank facing a panic (i.e., when depositors are trying to take their funds out of the bank at the same time, and the bank cannot obtain the needed reserves through private market channels). The purpose of lender-of-last-resort intervention is to stop the run on the bank and reassure depositors. In the international arena, a lender of last resort is an agency (such as the International Monetary Fund) that can lend money to a country when its central bank is running out of foreign currency reserves—usually, when the government is trying to defend a *pegged exchange rate* by selling off its existing holdings of *foreign exchange*—and when private lenders refuse to lend any more to the country. A domestic lender of last resort usually has regulatory authority over the commercial banks to which it lends and can actually increase the supply of domestic money through its operations (e.g., by emitting additional currency to buy government securities). In this sense, the IMF is not a true lender of last resort because it lacks these powers.

Monetary union. A group of countries that share a common currency. An important example is the new European Monetary Union (EMU), which replaced the ERM (see *joint float*) and issues the new euro currency. Note that a true monetary union has a common central bank, such as the new European Central Bank (ECB), in which all members have a voice in setting monetary policy. By contrast, under *dollarization,* a country using the dollar as domestic legal tender has to accept the monetary policies (e.g., interest rates) set by a foreign central bank (the U.S. Federal Reserve).

Moral hazard. The problem that insurance against some contingency (e.g., a fire) may create incentives to take greater risks on the expectation that the insurance will cover any losses. In financial economics, moral hazard problems can result when a promise (either explicit or implicit) of *lender-of-last-resort* intervention or a "bailout," either by a domestic regulatory agency or an international institution such as the IMF, induces private investors and lenders to take extra risks (e.g., by buying bonds issued by a government in danger of defaulting on its obligations).

Off-balance-sheet transactions. Certain innovative types of financial transactions, such as derivatives sales, that do not appear on banks' balance sheets. Most bank activities are entered on a balance sheet, which is an accounting statement that lists assets (such as vault cash, reserve deposits, loans, and securities) and liabilities (such as deposits and borrowed funds) plus the bank's net worth (i.e., the difference between assets and liabilities). Off-balance-sheet transactions create problems for financial management because they tend to hide some of the risks created by the full range of banking activities.

Official reserve transactions (ORT). The part of the *balance of payments* that records purchases and sales of monetary reserve assets (gold, *foreign exchange*) conducted by national central banks, such as the U.S. Federal Reserve. A sale of an official asset reduces the central bank's monetary reserves and is counted as a credit item. Conversely, a purchase of an official asset increases the central bank's monetary reserves and is recorded as a debit. In addition, for countries such as the United States whose currencies are accepted as reserve assets abroad, the purchase of domestic currency by foreign central banks counts as a credit, and a sale counts as a debit (for the home country). The ORT balance must offset the so-called "overall balance of payments," which is the sum of the *current account* and the *capital account*, i.e., ORT must be in surplus when the overall balance is in deficit and in deficit when the overall balance is in surplus. The ORT balance is significant because it indicates central bank intervention to maintain a *fixed exchange rate* or to operate a *dirty float*: an ORT surplus implies an effort to raise the value of the home currency, while an ORT deficit implies an effort to depreciate the home currency, compared with the value the currency would have if it were floating (see *flexible exchange rate*).

Pegged exchange rate. A *fixed exchange rate* that can be adjusted or changed, in contrast to a pure fixed rate, which is intended to be permanent. An "adjustable peg" is an exchange rate that may be changed occasionally or irregularly, while a "crawling peg" is a rate that is changed regularly or frequently. The terms "fixed exchange rate" and "pegged exchange rate" are often used interchangeably in the literature, but advocates of pure fixed rates tend to stress the difference.

Speculation. In international currency markets, the act of betting on changes in exchange rates by deliberately exposing oneself to *exchange risk*. For example, a European investor who expects that the euro will depreciate and the dollar will appreciate can sell euros and buy dollars. If the investor holds net assets in dollars (i.e., dollar holdings not fully offset by dollar liabilities), he or she is taking a risk in case the dollar falls instead of rises. If the investor is right, however, then he or she will be able to sell dollars back for more euros in the future and make a profit. A "speculative attack" occurs when investors sell off a currency with a fixed (or pegged) exchange rate in the anticipation that the government will be forced to devalue. However, investors can also speculate based on expectations of changes in flexible exchange rates, such as the euro/dollar rate.

Index

About the author

ROBERT A. BLECKER is a professor of economics at American University and a research associate of the Economic Policy Institute (EPI), both in Washington, D.C. Professor Blecker has published several reports and books for EPI, including *Are Americans on a Consumption Binge?* (1990), *Beyond the Twin Deficits* (1992), and an edited volume on *U.S. Trade Policy and Global Growth* (1996). His articles have been published in a variety of scholarly journals and edited books. He is also a co-author of the college text, *Fundamentals of U.S. Foreign Trade Policy* (with Stephen D. Cohen and Joel R. Paul, 1996). Dr. Blecker's research interests include international capital mobility, growth and distribution in open economies, North-South trade and economic development, U.S.-Latin American economic integration, and U.S. trade policy. He holds a B.A. in economics from Yale University and a Ph.D. in economics from Stanford University.

About EPI

The Economic Policy Institute was founded in 1986 to widen the debate about policies to achieve healthy economic growth, prosperity, and opportunity.

Today, America's economy is threatened by slow growth and increasing inequality. Expanding global competition, changes in the nature of work, and rapid technological advances are altering economic reality. Yet many of our policies, attitudes, and institutions are based on assumptions that no longer reflect real world conditions.

With the support of leaders from labor, business, and the foundation world, the Institute has sponsored research and public discussion of a wide variety of topics: trade and fiscal policies; trends in wages, incomes, and prices; the causes of the productivity slowdown; labor-market problems; rural and urban policies; inflation; state-level economic development strategies; comparative international economic performance; and studies of the overall health of the U.S. manufacturing sector and of specific key industries.

The Institute works with a growing network of innovative economists and other social science researchers in universities and research centers all over the country who are willing to go beyond the conventional wisdom in considering strategies for public policy.

Founding scholars of the Institute include Jeff Faux, EPI president; Lester Thurow, Sloan School of Management, MIT; Ray Marshall, former U.S. secretary of labor, professor at the LBJ School of Public Affairs, University of Texas; Barry Bluestone, University of Massachusetts-Boston; Robert Reich, former U.S. secretary of labor; and Robert Kuttner, author, editor of *The American Prospect,* and columnist for *Business Week* and the Washington Post Writers Group.

For additional information about the Institute, contact EPI at 1660 L Street, NW, Suite 1200, Washington, DC 20036, (202) 775-8810, or visit www.epinet.org.